False Expectations

False Expectations

POLITICS AND THE PURSUIT
OF THE SASKATCHEWAN MYTH

Dale Eisler

2006

UNIVERSITY OF
REGINA

CANADIAN PLAINS
RESEARCH CENTER

971.24
E365f
2006

Canadian Plains Research Center
University of Regina
Regina, Saskatchewan S4S 0A2
Canada
Tel: (306) 585-4758
Fax: (306) 585-4699
e-mail: canadian.plains@uregina.ca
http://www.cprc.uregina.ca

Library and Archives Canada Cataloguing in Publication
Eisler, Dale
False expectations : politics and the pursuit of the Saskatchewan myth / Dale Eisler.

(Canadian plains studies, 0317-6290 48)
Includes index.
ISBN 0-88977-194-4

1. Saskatchewan—History. 2. Saskatchewan—Politics and government. 3. Saskatchewan--Social policy. 4. Saskatchewan—Economic policy. I. University of Regina. Canadian Plains Research Center II. Title III. Series.

FC3511.E37 2006   971.24   C2006-901184-2

We acknowledge the financial support of the Government of Canada through the Book Publishing Industry Development Program (BPDIP) for our publishing activities.

Cover design: Brian Danchuk Design, Regina, Saskatchewan
Index: Patricia Furdek (www.userfriendlyindexes.com)

This work was prepared separately from the author's employment responsibilities with the government of Canada. The views, opinions and conclusions expressed herein are personal to the author and should not be construed as those of the Privy Council Office or the federal Crown.

Contents

To Madeline

Acknowledgements

This book is a product of many sources, people, places and events. So, even though writing is by its nature a personal effort, inevitably any book is an endeavour that draws on countless relationships, experiences and inspirations. This one is no different.

Many people have provided me with insights, perspectives and motivation. But no one more than my friend Henry Kloppenburg. Few people have the commitment to Saskatchewan and Canada, coupled with a passion for public policy and the dialogue that results, than Henry. He encouraged me from the beginning and has provided his ever-keen comments along the way.

There are others who have also helped by simply urging its completion. They include Caroline Andrew, Greg Marchildon, Tom Townsend, and Kirsten Grimstad. I also want to acknowledge Michael Wernick, Kevin Lynch, Alex Himelfarb, Jodi Redmond, Luc Gauthier, John Barrett, and Jeremy Rudin, who either took the time to review all, or parts, of the manuscript or offered their encouragement. But, at the same time, it's important to know none of the people I have mentioned bears any responsibility for the final product, nor will they necessarily agree with the perspective on Saskatchewan that this book sets out. In fact, I would assume many will disagree, in whole or in part. So, in defence of their integrity, any inconsistencies, errors, or lapses in logic are entirely my own.

I also want to thank the staff at the Gary Library at Vermont College in Montpelier, Vermont, who helped me locate research material, as did the capable reference librarians at Morisset Library at the University of Ottawa and the John Robarts Library at the University of Toronto. As well, I want to acknowledge the fine work, effort and support of Brian Mlazgar, from the Canadian Plains Research Center at the University of Regina, who edited the manuscript, helped in locating photos and managed the publication process.

The genesis for the writing of *False Expectations: Politics and the Pursuit of the Saskatchewan Myth* is rooted in my own perceptions of Saskatchewan drawn over many decades. It also flows, in part, from a thesis for a Master of Arts at Vermont College. My years as a journalist in the province allowed me to witness firsthand the dynamic of Saskatchewan life, expressed in both the expectations of its people and the reality of their lives. It was an immeasurably enriching experience, but one that always left me puzzled about the source of inspiration that was generated by the public dialogue expressed in the rhythms of the province's political debate.

The other motivation is truly personal. Nothing connects me more to Saskatchewan than a sense of belonging to it as a community with a common sense of identity and destiny.

At the risk of sounding maudlin, it is an emotion grounded in family and membership in what is the shared Saskatchewan experience. My wife Louise has been at my side for almost 35 years, and maintains a deep and abiding attachment to Saskatchewan. Today, my strongest emotional connection to Saskatchewan is my daughter Paula, who remains deeply committed to the province and its future. In a way, I feel guilty, like I abandoned her and our home a decade ago when I left the province that had given me so much, to pursue other opportunities and interests. She stayed, married and steadfastly remained true to Saskatchewan and its myth. Somehow I lacked the same fortitude.

Finally, I want to thank Paula and Richard for giving me my granddaughter Madeline. Her innocence has taught me to realize the important things in life—honesty, tenderness, sincerity and love—are what really matter. This book is for her.

Dale Eisler
Ottawa, Ontario
April 2006

Introduction

Saskatchewan is more than a province. It's a state of mind. For people who live there, and those of us who have left, Saskatchewan is about something that reaches deeply into our identity. It is personal. It goes to our sense of self.

For years as a journalist, I wrote about Saskatchewan, its politics, its economy and its people. All the while I thought that I had some insight into the province, that having lived there all my life gave me a measure of understanding into its collective psyche and what motivated its people. But the truth is that it wasn't until I left Saskatchewan ten years ago that I began to realize how little I understood the province and the effect it had on me; how my awareness of my Saskatchewan identity did not emerge until I had left. With detachment came a different perspective. With distance came a new context.

This book is an attempt to better understand my home province, how it sees itself, its past and its future. It is not a personal journey, in the sense of reflecting my own experiences and encounters that have shaped my perceptions of Saskatchewan. It is simply an exploration of the province's history through the lens of myth and the expectations Saskatchewan people have for themselves and their province. As such, it argues that the development and evolution of Saskatchewan's political economy is both the product and expression of myth. It is evident in the psychology of the province, where believing in the myth is central to the Saskatchewan identity.

The starting premise is rooted in the powerful notion Saskatchewan people share the belief there is something unique about their province. That to be from there is special because the bonds of the community we call Saskatchewan are more powerful than in other parts of Canada. That, in some unarticulated way, our commitment to the province, each other and our future together, reaches deeper into our shared identity and is more profound than what most others experience.

It is this sense of belonging, which is central to understanding the emotional and psychological bonds of any community, that lies at the heart of what Saskatchewan means. Quite simply, to belong means to believe. So the question becomes: What do Saskatchewan people believe that gives them their sense of belonging? Why do they believe it? Why does it matter? What is at the core of Saskatchewan? In other words, is there an idea people believe in and all share? This book, therefore, seeks to find a unifying theme to the province's history, an idea or concept that courses through its experience, that helps to explain the way Saskatchewan people see themselves, their province, their past and their future together.

What you are about to read is not intended as an exhaustive history of the province. Nor is it a comprehensive study of its politics, its economy or society. Rather, it is a blend of all those things. It seeks merely to provide a perspective on the province and the contours of its history through the 20th century by understanding the development and evolution of its political economy. It is an episodic journey that tries to capture the relationship between myth, expectations and identity as the forces that have driven the public life of the province. There are large gaps—parts of the province's history, significant events, perceptions and interpretations of others—that are not reflected here. So this should not be read as anything more than one interpretation of the forces that shaped the development and evolution of Saskatchewan's political economy.

In an important way, I owe the emotional impetus for this book to my grandmother. She had the courage to bring my mother and her brothers and sisters to Canada from Russia in 1926. They managed to flee Russia seven years after my grandfather had been shot by Bolshevik militia in front of his family on their farm near Odessa. The shattered family came to Canada seeking a new life and settled near the small town of Mankota in the drylands of southwest Saskatchewan, where others from the same region of Russia had also emigrated. Like countless thousands of other immigrant settlers who came to Saskatchewan in the early years of the 20th century, my grandmother and her children faced enormous emotional and physical challenges in a new land. They had to draw strength from each other, the bonds of their family and their community as they faced the grim reality of the Great Depression, the Dirty Thirties, the Second World War and the often harsh prairie environment.

In retrospect, it is difficult, if not impossible, to imagine the strength of character of the people who settled Saskatchewan and built the province. The prairie that greeted them was often raw and unforgiving, fiercely cold in the winter, unremittingly hot in the summer. They literally had to build a life for themselves and forge a society out of what was a virgin land. As James Minifie wrote in *Homesteader*, the vista of the Saskatchewan prairie made sense only to those who believed in the land:

> As far as he could see, there was neither tree nor bush—nothing to clear before you start to plough, my father reflected. He was already plotting out his farm. A little cluster of low hills suggested a site for house and barn, if only because it was good for nothing else.

Often I have wondered what drew those settlers to Saskatchewan and then what sustained them once they arrived. In its early years, Saskatchewan was a province that offered immense hope to people from around the world. It became a magnet that attracted people to the belief that here was the "last best West," a land that offered opportunity to those willing to embrace it and security for those willing to turn their backs on the repression and persecution they experienced in the old country.

But with the hindsight of history, it is evident that through its first 100 years Saskatchewan has never equalled its original promise. That is not to say the province has not given successive generations the opportunity for a good life, in some cases a life unequalled in Canada for its quality and sense of community. But undeniably, Saskatchewan is haunted by a sense of unfulfillment. The

NA C83564

"The Last Best West." A promotional poster produced by the Department of Agriculture, typical of the idealized promotional material used to draw immigrants to Western Canada.

province and its people are constantly striving for something greater, some rightful destiny that will allow Saskatchewan to take its place among the great provinces of the nation. At its core, Saskatchewan is a hopeful place, its people filled with pride about their home and the determination to unlock a greater potential.

This belief in a greater future is at the core of the Saskatchewan identity. It is rooted in the founding myth of the province, portrayed as a place with boundless potential, where achievement was limited only by the imagination and dedication of those who came to claim their plot of farmland. In some ways, the myth is as strong today as it has always been. It remains a source of pride for those from Saskatchewan whose commitment to their province and country is rooted in the challenges they have overcome, the community they have built and the better future they believe awaits them. The myth, I believe, has been a critical force in sustaining the province, a kind of emotional foundation that has supported its political discourse and the expectations that politics inevitably creates.

As is often the case, the best way to understand an idea, in this case the Saskatchewan myth, is through the lives and emotions of someone else.

Again, I retreat to a personal family vignette. My uncle Frank Schergevitch came with my mother and the other members of their family, arriving on the doorstep of the Great Depression and the Dirty Thirties in the tiny hamlet of Billimum near Mankota. Frank eventually started his own farm, married, and with his wife Phyllis raised six children, most of whom eventually moved to Alberta. Frank never left. His love of the land and Saskatchewan, even through the difficult years, and the opportunity it gave him made him passionate about the province and Canada. When he retired from the farm, he and his wife stayed in Mankota. For years in retirement, Frank had a ritual. In good weather, early in the morning two or three times a week he would walk the kilometre east of town to the Mankota cemetery to visit the gravesite of his mother, sister and friends.

One morning, in the fall of 1999, as he walked in the darkness along the shoulder of the country road to the cemetery, the driver of an approaching car never saw Frank. Struck by the car, he died instantly. My uncle's life spanned much of the last century, and all of it in Saskatchewan had been lived on the land near Mankota. It was his promised land. A few days later, the local Roman Catholic church was packed as family and friends came to say goodbye to their husband, father, grandfather, great-grandfather, uncle and friend.

At the end of the mass everyone rose to sing together the one song Frank had always insisted be played at his funeral, "O Canada."

One   The Saskatchewan Myth

"Official mythologies are common to all countries. All countries cherish one or two particular periods of their histories, which they ennoble and embellish, to justify and give meaning to their present and to give a purpose to their future."
(*New York Review of Books*, October 1972)

So it is with Saskatchewan. From before its birth as a geographic and political entity within Canada, to this very day, Saskatchewan's identity has been in part the product of myth. It has shaped the province's history, steered its politics, and remains a powerful force defining its future.

There is nothing particularly unique or profound to that assertion. After all, myth is an essential ingredient that animates all our lives and inspires our future. We believe in things—ideas, folklore, depictions by others of times we never experienced—that we can't necessarily prove as objective truth. Still, we embrace the belief. Why? Because it helps give meaning to the present. It enriches our lives. As Rollo May, the late American psychologist who studied extensively the role of myth in the emotional lives of people, once said: "Myth is a way of making sense in a senseless world. Myths are narrative patterns that give significance to our existence." Another way to understand the power of myth is explained by Karen Armstrong, who argues that believing in myth is an essential part of being human:

> A myth, therefore, is true because it is effective, not because
> it gives us factual information… If it works, that is, if it forces
> us to change our minds and hearts, gives us new hope, and
> compels us to live more fully, it is a valid myth.[1]

So, in other words, when put into a sociological context, myths are public dreams that can be powerful enough to shape the aspirations we have as a society and the choices we make to achieve what we collectively seek for ourselves.

In that sense, myth can be a powerful instrument in how we interpret the world, our experiences and our expectations for the future. Myth might be an idea or belief that is not be true, but is real. In the words of Mark Schorer,

> myths are the instruments by which we continually struggle
> to make our experiences intelligible to ourselves. A myth is a
> large controlling image that gives philosophical meaning to
> the facts of ordinary life; that is, which has organizing value
> for experience.[2]

So myth is important to all of us because it helps to give greater meaning and purpose to our lives. It provides us with the belief in a better future, if not for us, then for our children, grandchildren and the generations that follow.

When thought of in those terms, it becomes easier to understand why myth matters and, therefore, why its relevance to the political, economic and social reality of Saskatchewan should be at least considered within the context of the province's history. Indeed, myth has provided a powerful impulse that has helped forge the province's identity, sustain its present and animate its future. Attachment to myth has enriched the emotional life of Saskatchewan.

So what is the Saskatchewan myth? How does one describe it? There is no simple answer because no simple, single, easy-to-define myth exists. It has taken many shapes and forms over the past century, adapting itself with the ebbs and flows of the province's history. But two things can be said with certainty. First, at its core, the Saskatchewan myth expresses a powerful and universal attachment to belief in an unrealized potential for the province and a better life for its people. It is an idea with roots in the hearts, minds and spirits of the immigrants who settled the province. Second, the best means to follow the pursuit of the Saskatchewan myth is through the life—the creation and evolution—of the province's political economy. It is at the intersection of the state and market, the juncture of politics and economics, the mingling of private interest and public choice, where the myth finds its clearest and most practical expression.

There are two dimensions to the original Saskatchewan myth. First was an external perception of the province created for the consumption of others. Second has been the resulting self-image. The two are inextricably linked and although the original concept of Saskatchewan that helped form external perceptions of the province has long since been discarded, the self-identity rooted in that founding notion remains. As a result of that divergence, the way others see the province is often far different from how Saskatchewan people see themselves. It is this conflict between the subjective, powerful motivation of myth and the reality of external economic and political control that has been the driving force to the province's history.

The origins of these ideas reach far back into the province's past, intermingling with the idea of Canada itself. History shows us the province was established on a premise that was often overly optimistic and, at times, willfully exaggerated. Thus, the myth was originally rooted in government immigration documents and promotional literature that, in many cases, is more aptly described as propaganda. It was expressed in the notion of Saskatchewan as a land of great opportunity, one that offered a pastoral life and unlimited potential for those the federal government sought to lure to the prairie frontier. Therefore, in the beginning, the conception of Saskatchewan that existed in the minds of many was as a promised land.

The Saskatchewan myth persists today in the province's sense of self. It is a means to reconcile why reality never seems to meet what are considered the legitimate expectations of its people. The modern-day myth remains linked to the imagery of the promised land by rationalizing the ideal with a much different past and present reality. In that sense, it provides meaning by finding value and success in what others would define as failure. As only myth can, it portrays Saskatchewan to itself and to others as a province that is, somehow, more than it seems—a place with a unique identity manifest in an economic, political and cultural ethos embodied in the people who live there and the values they have produced and exported to the rest of Canada. This is the romantic myth of Saskatchewan as a special place with special people. This Saskatchewan spirit is not limited to those who put down deep roots and remained in the province. It persists in the countless thousands who migrated from Saskatchewan to build a better life than the one they left behind. Members of the Saskatchewan diaspora carry with them the indelible imprint of a province that might have failed to meet their economic needs or personal aspirations, forcing them to seek opportunities elsewhere, but somehow still maintains a strong hold over them. Admittedly, this kind of attachment to roots is common for most people, no matter where they consider home. But for people from Saskatchewan, there is a unique quality to the linkage, a deeply felt sense of belonging, kinship and identity with their province.

It is often expressed in an attachment to the land and the geography of Saskatchewan. Indeed, much of the literature Saskatchewan writers have produced expresses an often spiritual reverence for nature on the prairies, specifically the great expanse of land and sky that frame an invisible and ubiquitous wind.

Perhaps the purest expression of rudimentary nature that is part of the Saskatchewan psyche comes from the late W.O. Mitchell, the Saskatchewan-born novelist. Mitchell wrote as his opening words to his classic prairie novel *Who Has Seen The Wind*:

> "Here was the least common denominator of nature, the skeleton requirements simply, of land and sky—Saskatchewan prairie. It lay wide around the town, stretching tan to the far line of the sky, shimmering under the June sun and waiting for the unfailing visitation of wind, gentle at first, barely stroking the long grasses and giving them life.[3]

While it has become almost cliché to cite Mitchell's prose as reflective of nature's psychic power over people from Saskatchewan, the cliché has become accepted as truth. It reflects a dominant, romantic genre in Saskatchewan writing about the prairies that helps affirm the myth of a promised land.

One clear and compelling example of that prairie romanticism is supplied by American-born writer Wallace Stegner, who spent some of his childhood years growing up in the town of Eastend. In *Wolf Willow*, Stegner's acclaimed fictionalized account of his return to his Saskatchewan boyhood roots, he writes with sensitivity and awe of the Saskatchewan prairie, a place that gave him his identity:

> The drama of this landscape is in the sky, pouring with light and always moving. The earth is passive. And yet the beauty I am struck by, both as present fact and as received memory, is a fusion: this sky would not be so spectacular without this earth to change and glow and darken under it... Desolate? Forboding? There was never a country that in its good moments was more beautiful. Even in drouth or dust storm or blizzard it is the reverse of monotonous, once you have submitted to it with all your senses.[4]

Or, consider the writing of Bruce Hutchison, whose 1943 book *The Unknown Country* portrays, in romantic terms, the harsh, prosaic life of his father who settled in Saskatchewan to start farming:

> Acre by acre they broke the land and every year they had a little more grain to trade for the things they needed. Life was hard then and lonely—a sod cabin, a few horses, a sheep dog, and maybe a sweetheart in England who would come out some day. But my father and the others were well content, because they could see the grain growing. Life made sense to these men. They were free men and men can be free only when they feel their own earth under their feet and see the growth of the seed they have planted. These were happy men because they were producing something that the world needed.[5]

But not all Saskatchewan writers romanticize the land and environment. Others, such as Sinclair Ross, provide a much more prosaic, realist perspective of Saskatchewan life. The sense of individual vulnerability and the harshness of the natural environment imbues Ross's classic Depression era novel *As For Me And My House*. Depicting the grim life in the fictional small Saskatchewan town of Horizon during the Dirty Thirties, Ross writes:

There was a hot, dry wind that came in short, intermittent little puffs as if it were being blown out of a wheezy engine. All around the dusk hung dark and heavy, the distance thickening it so that a mile or more away it made a blur of earth and sky; but overhead it was thin still like a film of fog or smoke, and the light came through it filtered and tawny... The dust clouds behind the town kept darkening and thinning and swaying, a furtive tirelessness about the way they wavered and merged with one another that reminded me of northern lights in winter. It was like a quivering backdrop, before which was about to be acted some grim, primeval tragedy. The little town cowered close to earth as if to hide itself. The elevators stood up passive, stoical.[6]

A more recent, but equally powerful example is contained in the writing of Norman Henderson. His book, *Rediscovering the Great Plains*, which chronicles his return to and love for Saskatchewan after years away in Britain, uniquely blends the romantic and realist strains of Saskatchewan writing. What Henderson does is capture the emotional polarities of the Saskatchewan prairie. Recalling his return to the prairies on a train heading west, he writes:

The Plains are not an easy landscape. It is a natural reflex to be awed by mountains; huge and overpowering, they are a beginner's landscape... But the Plains—like the high seas or the desert—are a challenge and a reward for the strong of spirit only. You may sicken and tire here, fall prey to loneliness and melancholy, and be driven out to seek refuge in softer lands. Or you may meet the challenge, your senses may sharpen, strengthen, and thrill, as space and landscape subtlety stretch you out like a transcontinental train at full throttle.[7]

Certainly the majesty of nature as inspiration for writers is hardly distinctive to Saskatchewan. Whether breathtaking in its beauty, cold and harsh, uninviting, or gentle and mild, nature has inspired people through the ages and in all corners of the globe. So nature is an essential ingredient that helps sustain the Saskatchewan myth, even though its expression is anything but unique.

But that doesn't diminish the importance of nature in Saskatchewan literature and the written word to the creation and sustaining of myth. In fact, it is crucial to the definition of identity and the community that shares it. As American sociologist Benedict Anderson maintains in his analysis—some consider it seminal—of nationalism and identity, we live in imagined communities that are defined by mass-produced, printed, vernacular language. How we speak to each other, the ideas, interests and challenges we share, help to define who we are as a community. Therefore, the origins of our collective consciousness, that is, our awareness of each other and shared relevant experiences and common destiny, can be traced to print capitalism. Anderson says it was the convergence of capitalism and print technology that led to newspapers and book production for a mass audience that "created the possibility for a new form of imagined community."[8] Admittedly, Anderson is speaking about nationalism in the sense of sovereign nation-states. But the same logic applies to membership in other imagined communities with a collective consciousness and shared experience, whether they are nation-states or sub-national jurisdictions. Saskatchewan, for example.

The myth states that one way to measure the character of Saskatchewan is through the people it has produced. The list of those who have come from Saskatchewan and gone on to excel in their chosen fields is, without question, impressive for a province that didn't reach a million people until the mid-1980s. Whether it is business, the arts, government, sports or politics, Saskatchewan seems overrepresented. In absolute numbers, no province through the course of the 20th century, other than Ontario, has exported more people to the rest of Canada. Such out-migration, particularly since the Second World War, explains the apparent overrepresentation of Saskatchewan people in Canadian society beyond the province. But rather than an indictment of the province and its failure to retain its own sons and daughters, the outflow has itself become embedded in the belief that maintains Saskatchewan is a special place that produces special people.

To understand Saskatchewan, therefore, you must recognize and appreciate the mythology of the province and how this has become deeply woven into its social and political fabric. The myth is at once both good and bad for the province, a source of psychic strength and emotional cohesion, yet debilitating because too often it also denies reality. Myth has given the province a sense of higher purpose and belief in a greater destiny. The endless pursuit of the unattainable promised land has been the driving force behind the politics of the province. For generations, Saskatchewan people have coped with this distorted notion of themselves and their province. It has shaped their view of the world and themselves, merging to create what has been a distinct political tradition. Thus, Saskatchewan politics is very much rooted in the myth. The political debate in fact depends on the myth, draws from it to motivate and inspire people and, in so doing, creates expectations that sustain the myth.

But the myth upon which Saskatchewan was founded has its dark side. It has led to a kind of identity crisis, where Saskatchewan people have slowly and painfully been forced to confront their beliefs and gradually come to terms with the reality that was denied for generations. In many ways, the problems that confront Saskatchewan more than a century after its birth as a province in 1905 are the result of not only the myth, but the need to make it reality. Government debt, the future of rural Saskatchewan, the immense challenge of a large and rapidly growing underclass of Aboriginal people, the sustainability of the province's economy and its population are all inextricably tied to the myth of Saskatchewan. They are, in a very real sense, products of the constant pursuit of the myth.

Like many false ideas, this did not happen by accident. It has been the result of conscious and calculated effort, the product of a premeditated political plan that began as a crucial element in the nation-building of Canada itself, and has long since taken on a life of its own in the political discourse of the province.

Doubtless, there are those who will be offended by the suggestion of a Saskatchewan myth. It implies something less than genuine about the province's character. Instinctively they see it as an attack on the credibility of a province that has demonstrably carved out a political reputation that, in relative terms, greatly exceeds its place in Canada. For a province with a population that has remained relatively constant for almost seven decades, while Canada itself has tripled in size, Saskatchewan has been able to maintain its status as a special place. It is a province that has produced a reputation for political innovation and progressive social norms, such as universal health care and broader communitarian values, that, in some cases, were eventually adopted by the nation.

Aside from spawning and exporting ideas, Saskatchewan has wielded its influence in human terms through its expatriates. In fact, across Canada and even in cities of other nations, often a social community of people emerges where membership is restricted to those with Saskatchewan roots. The bonds of a common Saskatchewan heritage are so strong and unique that their personal relationships are defined by the home they shared and an instinctive belief in the values that unite them. Still, no one can quite define what it means to be from Saskatchewan, or what makes it especially unique. So, like all myths that have become part of the indigenous culture, you simply believe it to be true, even though you can't quite explain it.

But understanding what makes up the mythology of Saskatchewan is critical to understanding its history and why it unfolded the way it has, and continues to this day. The myth serves as both a starting point and compass, providing a sense of direction in attempting to comprehend the people of a province who believe they have created such a rich and admittedly singular political tradition within Canada, and even North America.

The Saskatchewan myth did not begin there. It was manufactured and planted in the minds of others, some of them thousands of miles away who, in the early 1900s and earlier, knew nothing of the vast and largely empty Canadian prairies. They had only a vague understanding that, as the 20th century dawned, the Canadian West had become one of the last frontiers of the New World.

The seeds of the Saskatchewan myth were carefully sown and nurtured as part of what most historians have considered an act of statesmanship. The settlement of the Canadian West was a final, crucial element in the building of the Canadian nation. When Saskatchewan and Alberta were carved out of the North-West Territories and given official status as provinces on September 1, 1905, the Canadian federation was virtually complete. Although it would be 44 years before Newfoundland joined Confederation, the shape of Canada and its security as a sovereign nation in North America was solidified on that warm, late summer day when Saskatchewan and its sister province became partners in Confederation.

On hand for Saskatchewan's entry into Canada were Prime Minister Sir Wilfrid Laurier and Governor General Earl Grey. Although Saskatchewan became a province on September 1, inauguration day was September 4, with festivities held in Regina to celebrate the christening of the new province. For Laurier, who only a year earlier had declared the 20th century to be Canada's century, the creation of Saskatchewan became a major component in a grand economic and largely non-partisan project. If not the culmination, it was a significant step in a process of nation-building that began long before he and the Liberals took power in 1896 and, indeed, before Confederation itself in 1867.

For decades, stretching back to the early 1800s, the question of what would happen to the great northwestern expanse of British North America was crucial if there was to be nationhood for the colonies of Canada. With the United States frontier established to the Pacific, the largely unpopulated northwest territories of British North America were vulnerable to American expansionism. And there were good historical and political reasons for the concern that if Canada's boundaries did not extend west the region would be absorbed by the United States. There was the lingering strain between Britain and the US that dated back to the American Revolution when the American states fought their war of independence. Tensions between the US and Great Britain had later spilled into conflict involving Canada in the War of 1812, when the Americans declared war on Britain during the height of the Napoleonic Wars. With the British colonies next door, the Americans struck and, thanks to what is generally conceded to be the military incompetence of the American generals, were fought to a stalemate by the outnumbered British colonial forces.

But there were equally compelling economic forces that propelled the Canadian colony towards nationhood. In 1846 Britain moved dramatically towards a policy of free trade, which meant that the Imperial preference Canadian exports enjoyed in Britain was gone. The repeal of the Corn Laws in Britain came as a major psychological blow to the Canadian colony. No longer would Canadian wheat have special access to the British market and the preferences given Canadian timber would also be reduced.[9]

Suddenly feeling economically vulnerable, and with the onset of a recession across Europe and North America, pressure began building in the colony for a trade deal with the US to replace the one lost with Britain. The need for an economic security blanket led to a Canada–US reciprocity agreement in 1854. But it was not to last. The US abrogated the treaty in 1866 at the end of its bloody civil war, won by the northern states. The cancellation of reciprocity with Canada was no doubt in retribution for Britain lending economic and moral support to the breakaway forces of the South. So, having first been cut adrift in Britain's move towards free trade and then denied continued reciprocity with the US, the colonies of Canada looked to each other for some measure of economic security. The threat of American annexation was seen as real and immediate, especially when, in 1868, the US Senate committee on foreign relations passed a resolution in favour of peacefully annexing the British territories in the West. At the same time the US was planning a transcontinental railway running parallel and close to the international boundary between the two countries.[10] Very quickly it became clear that Canada's most secure future rested in nationhood.

But achieving Confederation in 1867 was only the first step in creating a viable nation in the northern half of North America. To secure the union an integrated and self-sustaining economy would have to be forged that stretched from the Atlantic to the Pacific. Implicit in that was the settlement of the West and, with it, the creation of an economic society that would give Canada not only a sense of identity separate from the the United States, but also a commercial reason to exist. The merchant classes of what had been Upper and Lower Canada recognized the benefits of nationhood that would reach westward to the Pacific, creating a market for their goods.

The public policy structure for nationhood is most often defined as a set of economic and social strategies that became known as the National Policy. Historically associated with the return of Sir John A. Macdonald and the Conservatives to power in 1878, the National Policy had three primary components: protective tariffs to build an industrial base in central Canada; construction of a national railway; and, the opening of the West through settlement of the prairies. But limiting the policies of nation-building to Macdonald's and the Conservative's National Policy platform in 1878 is too narrow and gives it an unwarranted partisan tone. In fact, both the Conservatives and Liberals supported common national policies, the key one being the British North America Act itself, which provided for the construction of an intercontinental railway and the removal of internal tariffs to create a national economy.[11] Indeed, during his five years in power during the 1870s, Liberal prime minister Alexander Mackenzie tried to advance the cause of western settlement, although with little success. It was not until the election of 1878, when Macdonald and the Tories' campaign was based on their specific "National Policy," did the role of the West in building a coherent national economy become a clear focus to government policy. In that election, the choice for Canadians was between the expressed free-trade tendencies of the Liberals, and the protectionism of the Conservatives' self-styled "National Policy." The only portion of the generic form of national policy that was clearly associated with Macdonald and the Conservatives was the high tariffs of protectionism. Western settlement, as part of immigration policy, and a national railway were part of the national political consensus.

Thus, settlement of the prairies of the North-West was an integral part of a non-partisan national dream. When British Columbia joined the federation in 1871, the terms of its union were that a national railway would be built to the West Coast and completed in 10 years. It was an enormous commitment for a fledgling nation, but a necessary one to ensure that BC did not become part of the United States. By 1869 the Americans had completed their first transcontinental railway, which meant securing BC's place in Canada was urgent if the nation was to withstand the continental forces of a more powerful neighbour to the south.[12]

With the Canadian Pacific Railway running through the vast, sparsely populated expanse of the North-West to reach the West Coast, the door had been opened to settlement. In effect, the railway gave the prairies an economic and social raison d'être in terms of the larger effort to build a nation. Through immigration, a prairie society would be established to provide a captive domestic market for a tariff-protected manufacturing base in Ontario and Quebec. As well, prairie settlement would expand the nation's agricultural base and Canada would be an integrated national economy and a clearly defined geographic entity that would be separate and sovereign—both economically and politically—from the United States.

So any analysis of Saskatchewan's economic and political history must begin from the context of its place within Canada itself. The settlement of the West, the emergence of a rural agricultural economy and the creation of the province of Saskatchewan were part of a social and economic agenda designed to cement the political goal of nationhood and to help realize Laurier's ultimate dream that the 20th century would belong to Canada. The wheat economy would provide Canada with an export staple that would be the lynchpin not only of the national economy, but the nation itself.

When you realize the social, economic and political motivations that were part of prairie settlement, it is possible to begin understanding Saskatchewan and its myth. In fact, by looking at the origins of the province, you can start unraveling the myth and begin to appreciate why, as Saskatchewan enters its second century, the province's future remains arguably more uncertain and, perhaps, less hopeful than ever.

Two   # The National Policy

"Together, the expansionists wove a thread of utopianism into the western fabric. They described the landscape as 'the largest flower garden on the continent' and the climate as 'very much the same as it was in England 30 years ago...' The images conjured up by immigration leaflets might have been dismissed as exaggerations had they not been embedded in the western mystique by travel literature and popular fiction."

(Gerald Friesen, *The Canadian Prairies, A History*)

It is impossible to understand Saskatchewan without understanding how the idea of Saskatchewan was created, shaped and sold. In other words, exploring what was the genesis of the Saskatchewan myth. More than anything else, for the hundreds of thousands who flocked to the prairies, Saskatchewan symbolized hope. They saw it as a place to start a new life, a life that would offer them opportunity, security and prosperity. It was a powerful, utopian, comforting and, in part, false image.

Consider, for example, the recollections of Maria Adamowska. She was born in the western Ukraine and, at age nine, emigrated with her parents in the early 1900s to a farm near Canora, Saskatchewan. Her family had travelled half way around the world expecting to find a much better life on the Saskatchewan prairies. Like for many others, reality bore little resemblance to the myth that had lured them to the Canadian frontier:

> Our host, who had emigrated to Canada a year or two before, had written us to boast of the prosperity he had attained in such a short time. He said that he had a home like a mansion, a large cultivated field, and that his wife was dressed like a lady. In short, he depicted Canada as a country of incredible abundance whose borders were braided with sausage like some fantastic land in a fairy tale. How great was our disenchantment when we approached that mansion of his and an entirely different scene met our eyes... Later on, father reprimanded the man for writing us such nonsense.[1]

What's interesting, and for the purpose of better understanding the myth, is to examine how the idea of Saskatchewan became such a powerful force attracting people from around the world. It certainly didn't happen quickly. It took years. It was a melange of many factors—partisan politics, geographic revisionism, economic nationalism, exploitation and propaganda.

There were two key building blocks that provided the geographic imperative that eventually led to Saskatchewan becoming a province. The first was in 1869 when ownership of the North-West Territories and Rupert's Land was transferred from the Hudson's Bay Company to the dominion of Canada. The second came two years later, in 1871, when British Columbia joined Confederation. With Canada stretching from the Atlantic to the Pacific, and the federal government in Ottawa in control of the territories of the North-West, the stage was set for the national government to launch the western settlement phase of its nation-building policy. But, for any pioneer settlement plan on the prairies to be effective, it would require a major public relations effort. Basically, people would have to be lured from the relative amenities of life in central Canada, the US or the mature societies of Europe and be convinced a better world awaited them on the endless and largely uninhabited prairies. The job was not going to be easy and, as the years demonstrated, the creation of the Saskatchewan myth would not be done quickly.

The negative image of the prairies as a region of harsh, sub-arctic climate and questionable agricultural potential would have to be reversed. The North-West had to be cast as an agricultural frontier of limitless possibilities. One argument to offset that negative view was that the distorted perception had been created for selfish commercial reasons. In effect, the Hudson's Bay Company had purposefully kept the agricultural and resource potential of the prairies from the rest of the world to protect its commercial fur-trading interests and keep settlement away.[2]

But there were other problems. In the late 1850s a committee of the British Parliament had questioned whether agriculture was sustainable on the Canadian prairies. Sir George Simpson testified negatively before the committee about the prairie northwest, and British scientist J.H. Lefroy said "agriculture settlement can make very slender progress in any portion of that region."[3] Other British MPs agreed. Sir John Richardson, whose opinion of the area was highly regarded, said this about the prairie West: "although fit, probably for sheep pasture, is not soil that I think would be productive for cereal cultivation."

More problematic, if immigration were to be successful, were the reports of two expeditions to the prairie west in 1857–60 period, which came when the expansionist push was starting for Canada to consolidate its western frontier. One survey was sent by the British government, under the auspices of the Royal Geographic Society, and headed by an Irishman named John Palliser. The second was led by University of Toronto professor Henry Hind, who was enlisted by the Canadian colonial government.

Both Palliser and Hind independently came to essentially the same conclusion. They reported that a large area of the prairies was unfit for agriculture. The region was shaped like a triangle that stretched across much of the southern base of the grain belt with the US border and extended to an apex about 300 kilometres north. It covered 16,000 square miles (42,000 square kilometres) and, according to Palliser, was of questionable agriculture potential. The two concluded the area was an extension of a semi-arid, desert-like region in the mid-western United States. Palliser reported that the area was "not in its present condition, fitted for the permanent habitation of civilized man."[4] To this day the area bears his name and is referred to as the Palliser Triangle.

SAB R-A4692-1

John Palliser, the surveyor sent to the Canadian West under the auspices of the Royal Geographic Society.

But not all the news was bad. The Palliser and Hind expeditions also concluded a substantial fertile belt existed that stretched from the Red River Valley at the American border, northwest to the fork in the North and South Saskatchewan Rivers, then west to the Rocky Mountains. The result was that although the two painted a less-than-flattering image of the agricultural possibilities of the prairies, they identified a significant area suitable for farming. At that point, the image of the prairies changed from a fur-trade wilderness, to one with some agricultural potential.[5]

Still, the potential seemed at best limited and not sufficient to justify the grandiose objectives of massive prairie settlement, railway expansion and creation of a vibrant farm-based economy. Reinforcing the image problem was the report of a geologist named George Mercer Dawson, who headed a boundary commission in 1873 and 1874 that surveyed the area north of the US–Canada border from the Lake of the Woods to the Rockies. Dawson talked about the light soils, lack of rain and high rates of frost on the second and third prairie steppes as being far less suited to farming than the fertile belt. Although Dawson believed the more arid regions held greater agriculture potential than identified by Palliser and Hind, he admitted the fertile belt must be the region for settlement and "vast areas of the western plains … must remain as pasture grounds."[6]

For politicians with a national vision, the impressions of the prairies left by Palliser, Hind and Dawson created a major obstacle to western settlement and, therefore, to the National Policy itself. A new, exciting and economically inviting image of the prairies as a promised land needed to be crafted if the

SAB R-A4897

John Macoun, the botanist who surveyed the North-West in 1879 on behalf of the government of Canada.

region were to lure settlers from central Canada and, more importantly, other countries.

The key figure who, perhaps more than anyone else, helped erase doubts about the farming potential of the prairies and the region that was to become the province of Saskatchewan, was a self-taught botanist named John Macoun. Born in the Ulster region of northern Ireland, Macoun's family had emigrated to Ontario in 1850. As a young farmer, Macoun developed a keen interest in native plant life, which he turned into a serious study of botany. He quit farming to become a teacher and continued to devote more and more time to his study of plant life. In summer months, he would rise at 4:00 A.M. to gather plant forms for the collection in his private herbarium, which he hoped would someday be a representative collection of Canadian flora.[7]

Macoun gradually developed the reputation as an expert on plant life. From 1872–81 he made five trips into western Canada to assess the potential for settlement. His first excursion came when he was invited by Canadian Pacific Railway engineer-in-chief Sandford Fleming to be part of a survey for the proposed northerly Yellowhead route for the CPR line across the prairies on its way to the West Coast.[8] It was Macoun who helped convince the CPR to abandon the Yellowhead course and build its rail line across the prairies on a southern route, through a region Palliser, Hind and Dawson had considered to hold limited agricultural potential.

Aside from learning botany by observation and practical experience, Macoun had an enthusiastic personality that bubbled with optimism. After each trip to the prairies, he was more convinced that earlier, less-than-optimistic, assessments of the agricultural potential of the region by the likes of Palliser, Hind and Dawson were flat wrong. At one point, Macoun is said to have told a Winnipeg audience after he had visited the Qu'Appelle Valley that there was "no finer region in the world."[9] But his penchant for embellishment did not go unnoticed. When Macoun suggested there were 200 million acres suitable for agricultural settlement on the prairies he was labelled a "crack-brained enthusiast" by no less than the prime minister, Alexander Mackenzie.

Still, Macoun's profile was such that his credibility was not eroded and he remained an "expert." As a staunch supporter of the Conservatives, his influence rose dramatically in 1878 when Macdonald and the Tories again took power, proposing western settlement as a key element to the National Policy. Macoun was appointed as the official government explorer to the North-West and in 1879 was dispatched as the head of a survey to investigate the southern prairies.

The clear intent was to have Macoun refute the uninviting depictions of the prairies made by Palliser and Hind. Only days after Macoun's party left, the Minister of Railways was already beginning the propaganda campaign. "We believe we have there the garden of the world," he told the House of Commons in May 1879.[10]

Macoun did not disappoint his political masters in Ottawa. His findings were exactly what was needed to help change the image of the prairies as a harsh and desolate region with limited agricultural potential. In his report, published as a book entitled *Manitoba and the Great North West*, Macoun's enthusiasm leaps from the pages. He talks about discovering a land far different from what he had expected:

> I had been led to believe that much of it was little else than desert. Having crossed that part of it north of the Qu'Appelle in the summer of 1879, I can speak with certainty of the fertility of the immense plain sloping towards that river on both sides... No summer frost has ever been reported from this region, and authentic reports say that the spring is two weeks earlier than at Winnipeg.[11]

As for the Palliser triangle, Macoun talked about the arid conditions being "illusory." At a place where "the consequences of aridity appeared the strongest, I came upon ground broken up in the spring, bearing excellent crops of all kinds—oats being four-feet high." Macoun argued that while the uncultivated ground was hard and crusted, simply tilling the land allowed what was sufficient moisture to grow and sustain bountiful crops. "Thus the apparent aridity vanishes before the first efforts of husbandry," he maintained.[12] Almost instantly a new image of the prairies as a lush, fertile region awaiting settlers began to emerge. Indeed, in its 1880 annual report the Department of the Interior seized on Macoun's account and confidently declared: "the portion of the so-called American desert which extends northerly into Canadian territory, is proved to have no such existence." It had been erased by the enthusiasm of John Macoun.

But dispelling an old myth about the arid prairies, or creating a new one about its boundless agricultural potential, was only a small part of a national social and economic strategy. For settlement to proceed there would have to be something concrete to offer people if they were to leave their homes, uproot themselves and settle in the virgin land. The cornerstone to prairie settlement was the Dominion Lands Act of 1872. It was styled closely on a similar United States model and offered anyone who was the "head" of a family, or 21 years of age, 160 acres of free land for the cost of a $10 registration fee. Other lands not reserved for the railway or for schools could be purchased for $1 an acre.[13] So in effect, to lure settlers onto the prairies and create a viable agricultural economy, pioneers were offered what might be termed the ultimate subsidy—free private property.

At the same time, the government passed legislation that created immigration districts and allowed for immigration-aid societies within the districts. The societies were to identify the labour needs in their areas and bring people from Europe, and in particular the United Kingdom, to Canada. On the prairies, large tracts of land were set aside for immigration societies that resulted in the emergence of scattered ethnic colonies.

For the most part these early efforts to settle the area that was to become Saskatchewan met with limited success. The offer of free land meant little when it was in the middle of an isolated prairie wilderness that was bounded by the Canadian Shield on one side and the impenetrable Rocky Mountains on the other.

If the prairies were to be unlocked to settlement and become a viable farm-based economy they would have to be linked to the rest of Canada by the other pillar of National Policy—a transcontinental railway. Thus, railway construction became absolutely key to settlement.

The ultimate cost to Canadian taxpayers for this transportation infrastructure was enormous, in emotional and financial terms. It produced a national political scandal at the time that was a major factor in the defeat of Macdonald's first government in 1873. When it was learned a Quebec-based consortium, one of two competing to build a railway to the Pacific, had contributed heavily to the Conservative Party and been awarded the contract to build the Canadian Pacific Railway, Macdonald's government was forced to resign in disgrace.[14] Ironically the CPR consortium came together seven years later, after Macdonald had returned to power campaigning on his National Policy of high tariffs as part of a national agenda that was linked to prairie settlement and a transcontinental railway.

So, the dream of a ribbon of steel running as the east-west spine of a national economy was born in controversy and, in some respects, remains at the core of Saskatchewan's economic and political debate to this day. The construction of the railway might have amounted to the liberation of the West, but it came at a heavy price. The federal government gave the CPR a cash subsidy of $25 million, land grants of 25 million acres, other land for rights-of-way and stations, exemptions from import duties on construction material, title to already completed sections of track, exemptions from land tax for 20 years, and the guarantee in statute that the CPR would have the railway monopoly in the area south of its line to the American border.[15]

But even with the revised image of the prairies as a fertile agricultural area, the lure of free land and the completion of the national railway by the mid-1880s, there was still no flood of immigration. The world economy was locked in a deep recession that suppressed demand for Canadian exports. More importantly, better homestead land was still available in the temperate, sub-humid areas of the United States. The Canadian prairies were considered less suited to agriculture and therefore the region was largely ignored until homestead land south of the border was gone.

A backdrop to settlement that was inhibiting immigration was the perception of social and political instability. In 1871, Captain William Butler was dispatched by the federal government to investigate and report on the situation on the prairies. In his report to the lieutenant-governor of Manitoba, Butler said: "law and order are wholly unknown in the region of the Saskatchewan, in so much as the country is without any executive organization, and destitute of any means of enforcing the law."[16] The instability ranged from the Cypress Hills massacre of 1873, when 36 Indians were killed in an attack by American and Canadian wolf hunters who accused the Assinboine encampment of stealing a horse, to the Métis rebellions of 1870 in Manitoba and again in 1885 in Saskatchewan led by Louis Riel. Therefore, the need to establish the means and the legal framework to co-exist with the distinct Indian nations on the plains, and for Indian groups to avoid conflict among themselves, was a pre-requisite to settlement.

The basis for negotiations with Indian nations was the British proclamation of 1763, which stipulated that Indian rights must be addressed before settlement could occur. The primary instrument setting out the federal government's obligations, commitments and relations with Aboriginal people was the Indian Act of 1876. Nothing has had a more profound impact on the history of Aboriginal people. The Indian Act effectively established race-based laws that framed the place of Indian people in Canada's society and economy. It gave the federal government, through its Indian agents, immense power over the lives of Indian people, and nowhere was that more evident than on the prairies and in Saskatchewan. As Sarah Carter, an historian at the University of Calgary, argues:

> It [the Indian Act] consigned Aboriginal people to the status of minors; they were British subjects but not citizens, sharing the status of children, felons and the insane, and it established the federal government as their guardians. Those who came under the act were not allowed to vote in federal or provincial elections, and as they were not voters they were legally prohibited from the professions of law and politics, unless they gave up their Indian status.[17]

Concurrent with the Indian Act, was the treaty negotiation process between the government of Canada and Aboriginal bands, which eventually have been declared First Nations. The treaties were a critical element of prairie settlement in that they were seen as the means to ensure peaceful settlement of the West. The Qu'Appelle Treaty, or Treaty 4, which was signed in 1874 and covered much of southern Saskatchewan, and Treaty 6, which included central Saskatchewan and Alberta, were key in helping to open the region to immigration settlement.

In historical terms, treaty making between Canada and the Plains Indians is often portrayed as a "deliberate and wise" policy as part of settlement strategy. But in fact, it was pressure from Indian people, who sought some order and certainty in the face of white settlement, that compelled the federal government to act. First in Manitoba, the Ojibwa Indians of the North-West demanded treaties. Then, the Plains Cree in the 1872–75 period forced the government to do the same for Indians of the Qu'Appelle and Saskatchewan regions.[19]

But there was no mistaking the true intent of the federal government's policy towards Aboriginal people. It was to assimilate them into extinction. "The great aim of our civilization has been to do away with the tribal system and assimilate the Indian people in all respects with the inhabitants of the Dominion, as speedily as they are fit for change," Sir John A. Macdonald said in 1887.[18] That same objective was expressed by Duncan Campbell Scott, deputy superintendent general of Indian Affairs, many years later in 1920 during discussions to amend the Indian Act:

> I want to get rid of the Indian problem. Our object is to continue until there is not a single Indian in Canada that has not been absorbed into the body politic and there is no Indian question, and no Indian Department, that is the whole object of this bill.[20]

It was not until the mid-1890s that the beginning of a tide of immigration to the Canadian prairies—which some have called the greatest migration in world history—was to begin and continue at a more or less even pace for the next three decades. And at the focal point of this massive tide of humanity was Saskatchewan, a province that many believed was truly the promised land.

The final pieces to immigration and the rapid settlement of Saskatchewan fell into place beginning in 1896. It was partly economic coincidence and partly an act of politics that was to launch Saskatchewan into the 20th century. The economic coincidence was that by the mid-1890s, the 20-year global recession was drawing to a close. The political act was the election of the Wilfrid Laurier's Liberal government to power in Ottawa. Although the Liberals had historically been the party of free trade, Laurier did little to the remaining elements of high tariffs and immigration policy that he inherited from the Conservatives. Instead, the Liberals merely built upon the foundation.

Indeed, Laurier underscored his belief in protectionism as being the key to building and sustaining a national economy. Like Macdonald, he saw the West and the flood of immigrants to Saskatchewan as a captive market for the tariff-protected manufacturing sector of Quebec and Ontario. Speaking to the Canadian Manufacturers' Association in Quebec City in 1905, Laurier's commitment to high tariffs and keeping the West an economic colony of central Canada was unmistakable:

> They [the western settlers] will require clothes, they will require furniture, they will require implements, they will require shoes, they will require everything that man has to be supplied with. It is your ambition, it is my ambition also, that this scientific tariff of ours will make it possible that every shoe that has to be worn in those prairies shall be a Canadian shoe; that every yard of cloth that can be marketed there shall be a yard of cloth produced in Canada; and so on and so on...[21]

But surely the promise of high prices resulting from tariff-protected Canadian industry is not the reason for the sudden surge of immigration to the prairies at the turn of the century. People who leave their homes for a strange land, to start a new and uncertain life, are drawn by their dreams and the hope of economic security. The world economy was emerging from its recession, but what Canadian immigration policy needed was a mythmaker to make people dream about living the good life on the Canadian prairies.

The man who took it upon himself finally to unlock the floodgates of immigration was Clifford Sifton. The lawyer from Brandon, and former Manitoba attorney general, was elected to Parliament in 1896 and shortly after appointed Minister of the Interior by Laurier. His primary responsibilities were immigration and settlement.

Sifton was essentially a pragmatist. While sympathetic to business, he believed that government also had a dominant and essential role to play in settlement. For almost 15 years prior to 1896, Canada had more emigrants than immigrants. In fact, the US census of 1900 found that 1.2 million people living in the US had been born in Canada, which was roughly equal to one-third of Canada's total population.[22] Sifton believed the reason was largely due to incompetent government administration and the stranglehold the railway companies had put on settlement because of the "alienated" land that had to be set aside to satisfy their corporate land grants. Across most of the prairies, the odd-numbered sections of land had been withheld from settlement until the CPR selected the land it was granted for building the railway. In total, the reserved land from which the railway could select was 67 million acres. Recognizing the impediment the reserved railway land presented to settlement of the prairies, Sifton quickly began pressuring the land grant railways to select their land. It wasn't easy, but by 1903 the railways had taken title to most of their land.

With the land available for settlement more clearly defined, Sifton set about creating the structure and strategy within his department that would bring immigrants to the prairies. As a westerner himself, Sifton believed the

SAB R-B1863

Clifford Sifton, Minister of the Interior (1896–1905) in the government of Sir Wilfrid Laurier.

previous administration did not understand the problems faced by prairie settlers. He brought in legislation in 1897 and 1898 that simplified regulations for second homestead rights, but he would not succumb to demands that the second homestead be free, arguing that it played into the hands of land speculators. As well, he made provisions for land to be set aside for irrigation and allowed for different regulations governing ranch and farm land.

Wary of private land companies, Sifton believed control of immigration had to be firmly in the hands of government. The only land company he officially sanctioned during his nine years as minister in charge of immigration was the Saskatchewan Valley Land Company in 1902. It obtained a large block of land between Regina and Saskatoon and successfully settled the area around the town of Davidson.[23] Believing the government was key to successful immigration and settlement, Sifton also reorganized the Immigration Branch of his department, establishing immigration offices across Europe and the United States.

Probably the best description of Sifton's approach to luring immigrants to the West comes in his own words. Sifton believed that immigration policy was first and foremost a selling job. It required the committed fervor of a salesman, as he told the House of Commons in July 1899:

> In my judgment ... the immigration work has to be carried on
> in the same manner as the sale of any commodity; just as soon
> as you stop advertising and missionary work, the movement
> is going to stop.[24]

Promotion became the heart of immigration policy. An alluring, even romantic image of the prairies had to be created by government and the gospel of the good life on the western plains spread around the world. The propaganda arm of the government reached into the United States and across the Atlantic to Great Britain and Europe. When Sifton became minister responsible for immigration in 1896, the department produced 65,000 pieces of literature extolling immigration to Canada. By the turn of the century the number had increased to one million. As well, immigration offices were opened in the major cities of Europe and Sifton put heavy emphasis on drawing immigrants from the United States, who he saw as the most desirable. He increased the number of immigration agents in the US from six to 300 and embarked on an aggressive international advertising campaign. To get around the law in some European countries, where immigration advertising by other countries was illegal, Sifton used an under-the-table system with the North Atlantic Trading Company that paid recruiters for every adult they sent to Canada.[25]

A specific type of person was sought by Sifton. For prairie settlement to be successful, he believed immigrants must be ruggedly independent if they were to survive and eventually prosper in the difficult pioneer farming life. He described the ideal immigrant for the prairies as "a stalwart peasant in a sheep-skinned coat, born on the soil, whose forefathers have been farmers for 10 generations, with a stout wife and a half a dozen children."[26] As such, immigration policy under Sifton focused on a specific type of individual to the exclusion of others. Sifton had no interest in attracting entrepreneurs, skilled labourers or people trained for office or clerical jobs:

> We are in a position now to take our choice and we do not want anything but agricultural labourers and farmers or people who are coming for the purpose of engaging in agriculture, either as farmers or labourers.[27]

The same opinion about a specific type of immigrant suited only to agriculture was reflected in a memo Sifton sent to Laurier in 1901:

> Our desire is to promote the immigration of farmers and farm labourers… It is admitted that additions to the population of our cities and towns by immigration [are] undesirable from every standpoint.[28]

The government's propaganda campaign enticing people to the Canadian prairies became the final element in the creation of the myth that helped to found Saskatchewan. Like most advertising efforts, while carrying a basic current of validity, it took great liberties with the truth and sought to fashion the best possible image of the prairies in the minds of those willing to gamble on finding a better life.

By 1902 an immigration advertising campaign launched by Sifton's department was being carried in more than 7,000 local and farm newspapers across the US.[29] The ads often carried a Canadian flag with a headline reading: "160-Acre Farms in Western Canada Free." In one case, an ad was so bold as to make the preposterous claim that western Canada could "support a population of 50 million or more."

But compared to the government's European advertising campaign, the effort in the US usually bore some resemblance to reality. The government realized that many potential immigrants from the US had a better understanding of the so-called "New World" and, in fact, many of them had come to the US as European immigrants. There was apparently less need to be truthful when people from Britain or the rest of Europe, who knew little or nothing about Canada, were being lured to the Canadian prairies.

In the words of one historian, Canada's immigration propaganda was "by all odds the richest, purplest fiction ever written about the Canadian West."[30] While some might argue that was an exaggeration of the original exaggeration, there can be no doubt the immigration strategy was to foster and nurture an image of the Canadian prairies that was uniformly positive and inviting, and also not particularly rooted in reality. In other words, create a myth so powerful that it became a magnet drawing those who yearned for a better life.

This kind of phony imagery was not without its criticism in Canada from those who challenged the ethics of such shameless propaganda. The Toronto *Globe* questioned the policy that rewarded immigration agents "for practising deception." The *Grain Growers Guide*, an influential voice of farming on the prairies, went so far as to ask about homestead policy, saying that "something for nothing is a mighty poor slogan upon which to develop a permanent civilization." Even in the House of Commons in 1907 at the height of the immigration wave, concerns of agricultural societies were being echoed. The reference was to propaganda that made conditions appear better than they really were and that "every immigrant should know the true facts as to the conditions in this country before being induced to come here."[31]

At the turn of the century, London was said to be "plastered with flaring posters representing fields of yellow grain and herds of fat stock tended by cowboys picturesquely attired in costumes." Eager immigration agents handed out pamphlets on street corners inviting interested people to meetings where they could learn how to make their fortune in farming on the western Canadian prairies.[32] If cowboys in costume didn't catch people's attention, then there was the "agreeable" climate to make immigrants yearn for life on the prairies.

One immigration pamphlet shamelessly distorted what were the harsh extremes of the weather:

> The climate of Western Canada, as described by those who have lived there for some years, is said to be very agreeable. Disease is little known, while epidemics are unheard of. Spring commences about the first of April. Some seasons, however, seeding is begun in early March, the snow having entirely disappeared. But spring scarcely puts in an appearance before it is followed by summer and it is almost impossible to describe the delights of that pleasant season, with its long days and cool nights... The climate [of Saskatchewan] is healthy and free of endemic or epidemic diseases. It is

bracing and salubrious and is undoubtedly the finest climate
on earth for constitutionally healthy people.[33]

So, government propaganda was absolutely essential to creation of the
Saskatchewan myth. As prairie historian James Gray has said, the world had
never before witnessed the mass migration that took place in the early years
of the 20th century to the Canadian prairies. While greater numbers of people might have been forced in other great migrations, the settlement of the
prairie west was the most rapid creation of a new society by willing migrants
ever seen. But in many respects it was done for the wrong reasons. Says Gray,
in his book *Red Lights on the Prairies*:

> Nowhere, however, were more people enticed, cajoled, per-
> suaded, induced, gulled and just plain bamboozled into tear-
> ing themselves up by their roots to journey across half a con-
> tinent, or halfway round the world, to a land where not a sin-
> gle constructive step had been taken by anyone to prepare for
> their arrival.[34]

For obvious commercial reasons, the CPR was also deeply involved in fos-
tering the myth of Saskatchewan as a promised land. The commercial calculation for the CPR was self-evident. The more immigrants it could lure to the
province the greater its profits. Not only would the railway make money on
the fares bringing people to the prairies, but every new farmer was a new cus-
tomer who would pay to ship grain by rail or a potential buyer of land from
the CPR and a consumer of products that would be transported by rail to
Saskatchewan. So, as it promoted prairie settlement in its own pamphlets
distributed at government immigration offices overseas, the CPR also created a glorious picture of Saskatchewan and the untapped wealth that awaited
new farmers. Proclaimed one CPR pamphlet:

> It is not easy to forecast the future of wheat in Saskatchewan
> because the extent of the country adaptable to wheat grow-
> ing is so vast that when it comes into production, as inevitably
> it must at no distant time, the output cannot fail to run into
> figures both of quantity and money that imagination can
> hardly reach.[35]

The need to attract immigration and build a prairie community had
become the focal point where the political and economic interests of the
young nation intersected. The prairie west had emerged as key to nationhood
itself and as such, settlement of what was soon to be Saskatchewan could not
fail. For failure would mean the National Policy itself had failed, and with it
Canada.

So in retrospect, these many years later, it is not difficult to understand
why so much energy and unbridled optimism became part of official

government policy and the prairie expansionist movement itself. When you're building a nation, it is natural to be swept up in the fervour of nationalism. But the question remains whether such emotion makes for good public policy. There can be no doubt those promoting prairie settlement were successful in stimulating a positive image of the future. But at some point, image must be reconciled with reality, which would be the real test for those who believed they were building a nation and those lured to the new land.

In his study of the expansionist movement and settlement of the prairies, Douglas Owram condenses the dilemma this way:

> If the great strength of the expansionsists was their ability to evoke an image of the future, their great failure was their inability to maintain any sort of relationship between the myth and the much harsher and more prosaic reality of frontier life... Thereafter the myth worked to distort an understanding of the West rather than to promote its development... The image had been powerful enough to cause Canada to stake its future on the region. The challenge in the years ahead was to subordinate the myth of the future to the policies and problems of present development... The problem was that, as with most utopias, this paradise was unattainable; inevitably those who believed it were disillusioned.[36]

By the dawn of the 20th century, as Saskatchewan prepared to take its place as a province within Canada, the long-sought tide of immigration that was such a crucial part of building the nation was underway. There were great expectations for the province, which quickly took its place at the forefront of what Laurier had so confidently predicted would be Canada's century. The news of Saskatchewan's greatness and potential reached even London, England where a newspaper advertisement placed by the Immigration Department talked of how "the magnificent development of Western Canada since the opening of the 20th century has attracted the attention of the world." It spoke too of how the inauguration of Saskatchewan added "immense impetus to the work of development" which led to rapid population growth. "But there is always room for more in this land of great possibilities, and the Canadian government still offers 160 acres free to every young man over 18 years of age.

Finally Saskatchewan and its myth had arrived. The future looked bright, indeed.

Three   Misguided Economy

"Sir John A. Macdonald gave us our first national policy, and our first lessons in the irrelevance of economics... Macdonald was the first great non-economist."

(John Dales, economic historian)[1]

There seemed every reason for optimism in early September 1905, when an estimated throng of 5,000 people dressed in their Sunday best gathered in Regina to mark the arrival of Saskatchewan. All the signs looked positive. There were high expectations for the new province. Excitement about the future was in the air.

The family farm wheat economy was rapidly taking root. In fact, it was growing faster than anyone thought possible. Settlers, eager to exercise their homestead rights, were flooding into the province by the tens of thousands a year to claim their 160 acres of free land. Already a web of railway branch lines was beginning to spread across the province to meet the demand as people and goods flowed in from eastern Canada.

Granted, the language might have been stilted, but an editorial in the Regina *Leader* adequately expressed the palpable confidence of the new province. There seemed to be limitless possibilities for economic expansion and population growth. Quite simply, in 1905, Saskatchewan was the place to be in Canada. The myth was already flourishing:

> No province in Canada need fear the future, and Saskatchewan above any of them has a future bright with promise... Saskatchewan starts free from debt and with an assured permanent revenue from federal sources sufficient to reasonably meet her local government needs. Saskatchewan enters the provincial state under the most cheering auspices, providence favoring us this year with a bounteous crop to recompense the industry of old and new settler alike. A steady stream of thrifty immigration is directing its footsteps this way and the eyes of the whole English-speaking world and of the European countries are turned towards these fertile plains. Nowhere in the whole realm that recognizes the sovereignty of [King] Edward VII exists today a people living

under more favorable conditions or enjoying prospects more promising than the people in this new province of Saskatchewan.[2]

Clearly, as a centrepiece of the National Policy, the Saskatchewan myth was assuming a life of its own. In fact the moment Saskatchewan took its place within Confederation, it became the symbol of the nation's success. Its mere existence was evidence that the National Policy was working, and working well. In a very real sense, Saskatchewan helped to validate Canada itself. With immigrants streaming to the province, no one questioned the idea of an agricultural frontier as a crucial element in building a truly national economy and independent nation. There was a sense of great potential and incredible economic opportunity.

But what were the economic foundations of the province? Was the notion of Saskatchewan itself well grounded? Did it have the natural endowments to warrant its proclaimed stature as a province with vast economic potential? Was it given the tools it needed to realize its comparative advantage? Was there a long-term strategy for growth, or was one even necessary? Was there an economically coherent plan to guide settlement patterns? How was Saskatchewan being served by the high tariffs, railway expansion and immigration components of the National Policy? Important questions, perhaps, but in the full blush of its status as a new province, and with the future looking bright, those were the questions of cynics and skeptics. Certainly they were not on the minds of people engaged in the work of building a country, or editorial writers swept up in the enthusiasm that is the inevitable by-product of nationalism. Still, the answers to those questions help to explain the foundation upon which Saskatchewan was built and the political economy that resulted. And understanding the original idea of Saskatchewan provides a starting point in a process to eventually reach an understanding of the province's identity and sense of self a century later.

As part of the nation-building exercise of the late 19th century, Saskatchewan was as much a result of politics as economics. It was, in a very real sense, both an expression and a manifestation of the original nationalism that had created Canada as a nation-state in 1867. The arrival of Saskatchewan was merely an extension of that original desire to secure a national identity separate from the United States. It was carved out of the North-West to solidify that yearning for national sovereignty and security.

The fact that the forces of politics should play such a pivotal role in the creation of Saskatchewan was certainly to be expected. By definition every nation, with its component parts, is at its core a political expression of its inhabitants. People identify their shared values and then seek the political institutions to differentiate themselves from others. The values Saskatchewan people would share, giving them a unique identity within Canada, flowed from their singular economic dependence on a farm economy and a sense of

SAB R-A21929-5
Railway construction in southern Saskatchewan.

economic subservience to political and economic forces beyond their control. The need to sustain and nurture a rural economy and society would not only be the central character to the province, but it would be the consensus that was to define its politics.

The relative importance of Saskatchewan to a viable and secure national economy was evident from the outset. Saskatchewan's wheat economy would give Canada two critical economic dimensions: a major export staple to sell on the world market, and a rapidly growing farm population—needing all the necessities of life—to serve as a captive demand market for the manufactured goods of Ontario and Quebec. In other words, the farm economy would create the wealth that would be cycled from abroad into the tariff-protected manufacturing economy of central Canada. In retrospect, the Canada that Saskatchewan joined was a curious and paradoxical economic hybrid. For the prairie region to flourish economically, farmers needed to sell wheat into an open, free-trading world market, and then funnel the wealth into the closed system of a protected Canadian economy. At the centre of this national economic model was Saskatchewan.

There was nothing uniquely Canadian with this kind of approach to economic development. The Americans had used a similar protectionist strategy of import substitution through high tariffs to develop their own industrial sector and were always more than willing to hide behind tariff walls when they feared trade competition from other nations. In fact, the high tariffs of the Macdonald government's National Policy instituted in 1879 were both a defence against similarly high tariff practices in the US and a means to develop an indigenous Canadian industrial base. An offer of reciprocal reduction of tariff levels was explicitly made to the US in the Tariff Act of 1879. In announcing the tariff policy, finance minister Sir Leonard Tilley said many of the imported items from the US that became subject to the higher tariff had been on the so-called "free list" since 1875 "in the vain hope of inducing our neighbour to renew the Reciprocity Treaty." With the Americans unwilling to lower tariffs and determined to protect their economy, Canada responded in kind.[3]

This protectionist mentality was not limited to North America. Even Great Britain, which unilaterally moved to a free trade policy with the repeal of its Corn Laws, did so only when it had used its colonial possessions to create unparalled industrial strength and captive markets that gave it such a massive comparative advantage that it need not fear free trade.

But the Conservatives' new tariff levels as part of National Policy amounted to both a change in tariff theory and practice. Previously the dominion government had used tariffs largely as a mechanism to raise revenue. Under the Conservatives the tariff became an explicit tool for the protection of the national economy. Tilley clearly stated the government's industrial and tariff strategy in his budget speech. The finance minister said the intent was "to select for a higher rate of duty those articles which are manufactured or can be manufactured in the country and to have those that are neither made nor are likely to be made in the country, at a lower rate."[4] The general tariff rate was increased from 17.5% to 20% and duties that previously had been seldom used were applied vigorously. Rates were differentiated based on the degree of processing and ranged from 10% on slightly processed goods to 30% or more on finished products. In the case of agricultural tools and equipment imported from the US, a value-added duty of 22.26% was applied, as well as a tariff of 25%. The tariff on basic hardware items went from 17.5% to 30%, nails went from 17.5% to 32.5% and the wire tariff climbed from 5% to 15%.[5]

Thus, economic development strategy under the National Policy was based on the theory of import substitution. By applying high tariffs on US manufactured goods, an indigenous manufacturing industry would emerge to meet the domestic demand. Government tariff policy would create a comparative advantage for domestic industry over imports. The theory behind tariff-led development was eloquently explained by Thomas White in a speech he delivered to the London, Ontario board of trade in 1877, on the eve of an election campaign when the Conservatives put forward their National Policy of high tariffs. White, who later became minister of the Interior in Macdonald's second government, warned of Canada's manufacturers being "slaughtered" in the Canadian market by American competition:

> Every intelligent man must know that the condition for building up industries is to accumulate capital around them. And how can capital be best accumulated? By the protection of young industries, that they may be able to grow up in our midst. And to tell manufacturers that they are to invest their capital and start their enterprises and then be subjected to

the unfair "slaughtering" of a neighboring nation, is simply to insult the intelligence of every manufacturer in the land… We don't want to be hewers of wood and drawers of water for our neighbours for all time to come. That is not our object. Our aim should be to legislate to build up Canadian interests, that capital may find profitable investment, labour diversified employment and the people prosperous and contented homes.[6]

The idea seemed logical and was certainly compelling, especially given the protectionist proclivities of the Americans. But high tariffs were only to be part of a development phase. Once Canada's manufacturing and industrial sector grew beyond the "infant industry" stage and had reached maturity, the tariffs would be gradually reduced and perhaps eventually even removed. At least such was the theory. In the early years of the National Policy, the stated intention was that tariff protection would only be temporary. Thus, instead of tariff policy creating inefficient and non-competitive industries, it would merely foster a fertile business environment in central Canada that would create breathing space for Canadian industry to reach the point where it could meet import competition.

For that matter, when the high tariff policy was instituted, Sir Charles Tupper of the Macdonald government had suggested that after 15 years of tariff protection, Canadian industry would be in a position to compete. But, what happened was just the opposite and over the years the tariff level gradually increased. By the time Laurier and the Liberals took power in 1896, the average tariff was 30% and had become part of the nation's economic structure. Canada's manufacturing sector was addicted to tariff protection and in no mood to give up its privileged economic status.[7]

Measuring the cost of the tariff on Saskatchewan as it struggled to establish an agricultural economy is not easy. But clearly, if the average tariff was 30% on imports from the US, then farmers were paying 30% more for many of their inputs than if no tariff existed. As Vernon Fowke explained in his analysis of the impact of the national policy on farming, the economic effect of the high tariff is self-evident:

> The prairie economy grew up within a pre-established framework of tariffs which shaped, limited and curtailed its development… Duties on imports into Canada have curtailed a wide range of industrial importations, particularly from the US and have replaced them with high-priced Canadian products.[8]

But aside from blocking development in Saskatchewan and artificially raising the costs of farming, the tariff policy also spawned an inefficient and oligopolistic manufacturing sector in central Canada. What happened was what some economists refer to as the "miniature replica effect," or what is more commonly referred to as a "branch-plant" economy. Faced with tariff barriers that made it unable for them to sell competitively into the Canadian market, many US firms invested in Canada and simply recreated their industry on a smaller scale in Canada as a means to hold or establish their market share. But because of the tariff protection, the branch plants could not maximize the economies of scale of their US parent companies and were therefore less efficient, an economic cost that was passed on to consumers, many of them Saskatchewan settlers. In other words, the economic viability of farming was partially undermined from the outset by a conscious government policy of high tariffs.

By the time Saskatchewan became a province, tariff policy had become firmly rooted in Canadian politics, the economy, and government policy. Although the Liberals had traditionally been cast as a the party of free trade and lower tariffs, after Laurier came to power in 1896 little changed. By 1903 the general tariff rate had been reduced only 3% to 27%. The Laurier government defended its reluctance to lower the tariffs by saying it needed to maintain the high tariffs as a bargaining weapon against similar US tariffs.[9] And the Canadian Manufacturers Association, which wielded tremendous political clout over the federal government, had clearly been able to blunt the Laurier Liberals' free trade instincts. In its publication *Canadian Manufacturer* in 1900, the association gave its blessing to Laurier's decision to continue protectionist policies:

> The party now in power fully recognizes the imperative necessity of maintaining the policy that so strongly attracts manufacturers. As long as those in power maintain the policy of protection, the manufacturers will ask for no change. The existing status is quite satisfactory.

Meanwhile, though, anger was building in Saskatchewan and across the prairies for dramatic relief from the tariff. Farmers were livid over reports that farm machinery and implements manufactured in Canada were selling for less in Great Britain than they did here. The reason was that industry paid a duty on imported iron and steel used in the manufacturing process, but the duty was rebated if their finished product was sold into the export market. Adding to the economic anger of Saskatchewan farmers was the knowledge that farm implements, produced by a company in Chicago with a branch plant in Hamilton, were selling for more than 25% less in Idaho than in Saskatchewan.[10]

The Laurier government only marginally attempted to deal with some of the economic disparity created by the tariff on the farm economy. In 1907 it lowered the tariff on the "main class" of farm machinery from 20% to 17.5%.

But this gesture was rebuked by farmers as of little or no value. Indeed, farmers argued that higher prices for machinery meant the effective duty—which was based on price—had gone up, not down.

There can be little doubt that the tariff policy, as envisioned by the National Policy, created an artificial environment that fostered the growth of a central Canadian manufacturing sector that otherwise would not have developed as fast, or to the degree it did. At the same time, it extracted high costs and redistributed income from the West, which meant Saskatchewan was born into an economic environment consciously designed against its parochial interests.

Thus, the political economy concept of the tariff, which helped to create the economic foundation for Saskatchewan, in fact ensured a lower standard of living for the people who lived in the province. It is part of what economist John Dales calls "the mercantalist contradiction" that proposes a country can increase its wealth by making its citizens poorer. Says Dales:

> In Canada, this contradiction has been enshrined in a beautiful piece of word magic that would surely have delighted Macdonald himself. The tariff, historians have taught us, is "the price of being Canadian." In reality, of course, it is the price we pay for our protected manufacturing industry—very often the bribe we pay foreigners to establish manufacturing capacity in Canada.[11]

In economic terms, Dales points to a paradox contained within the National Policy. While Gross Domestic Product (GDP) was growing because of tariffs, and thus the nation itself was becoming richer, just the opposite was happening at the level of individuals. Specifically, the GDP per capita was declining while the GDP itself was increasing.

If the tariff undermined and weakened the infant Saskatchewan economy, then what about the other two pillars of the National Policy, namely railway development and immigration policy? Each was intimately dependent on the other for its viability. Without people on the prairies there could be no market for tariff-protected industries to exploit and without a railway there could be no settlement or means to develop an east-west economic flow.

To this day the railway—specifically the CPR—remains close to the emotional source of Saskatchewan's political and economic debate. Little wonder. No private industry, in constant dollar terms, has received the government largesse of the CPR, nor been granted by the state the pervasive economic power the railway has enjoyed over the province and its economic destiny. In many ways the history of railway development, or more specifically federal and provincial government policy towards railway development, is crucial to understanding the roots of Saskatchewan's economic distress and its political culture of alienation.

From the outset there has been a basic emotional and intellectual contradiction to the CPR. It was a private company that was essential to the public policy of government. In that sense the interests of the CPR were seen by many as being identical to those of the nation. What gave the railway company its tremendous clout and seduced generations of politicians and governments was the idea that the CPR embodied the notion of public-spirited capitalism.

Think of it in these terms: with a transcontinental rail line indispensable to the idea of a nation-state itself and a viable east-west economy, the company that built the line across the prairies and through the Rocky Mountains to the West Coast was building a nation as much as it was building a business empire. The only logical alternative to a national railway would be the expansion of American railways north into western Canada. Clearly the inevitable result would be a north-south flow of commerce that would threaten a national economy and the nation itself. So the CPR, from the moment the dominion government awarded it the task of building a line to the West, became a private company that could not fail because Canada itself depended on its success.

It was this mixture of private and public interests that allowed successive governments to become virtually captives of the corporate interests of the CPR, as well as other railway companies that ultimately failed. More importantly for Saskatchewan, this unequal relationship, where the public good was seen as inextricably linked to the welfare of the CPR, helped to undermine the economic foundations of the province. The fact that the railway could not fail, because the fate of the nation itself was seen to hinge on its commercial viability, meant that Saskatchewan's economic interest had to be subordinate to the larger interests of the CPR and the nation. It is that logic which was at the core of the 19th century National Policy.

Still, in retrospect, it is difficult to imagine anything but a private syndicate, such as the CPR, taking on the daunting task of building the transcontinental line. The project was so massive that it did not seem logical, in the last half of the 19th century, for the government of such a young nation to assume the financial burden, let alone the monumental engineering and business challenge, of building a railway to the Pacific. Besides, private railway interests—in particular the Grand Trunk Railway—were well established in Canada and a brief attempt by Mackenzie's Liberal government of the 1870s to let the public sector expand the rail line west from Ontario had been less than successful.

A Royal Commission in 1880 that studied government efforts to take on railway construction, after the Pacific Scandal had scuttled Macdonald's first attempt at a national railway and cast a cloud over private railway interests, was less than enthusiastic about the results. The commission found the government experiment in railway construction was riddled with patronage and waste. In its report, the commission concluded: "That the construction [of the railway] was carried on as a public work at a sacrifice of money, time and efficiency."[12] But it's worth noting that the commission was appointed by the recently reinstalled Macdonald government, which was eager to get on with private interests completing the railway to the Pacific and probably just as eager to discredit the former Liberal administration.

The legislation establishing the Canadian Pacific Railway was passed on February 15, 1881, and the private company received its charter the following day. Even by today's standards, the amount of government subsidy given to the CPR is staggering. The company received $25 million of taxpayers' money in cash and 25 million acres of land. Portions of the transcontinental line already built by government and valued at $37.8 million were given to the CPR. It also got another 6,000 acres, much of which was to become prime downtown Vancouver real estate, when it agreed to extend its western terminus from Port Moody to Burrard Inlet.

Also, the land granted to the CPR was handed over free of taxes for 20 years and taxes were waved in perpetuity on property used for railway purposes. All equipment needed to build the railway was brought into the country duty free and the CPR was given a statutory monopoly in the area south of its mainline to the US border. The monopoly clause, however, was rescinded in 1888 following western protests. By its own estimates, the CPR by 1916 had net proceeds from land sales, much of it used in the settlement of the prairies, totalling $68.25 million and unsold lands worth $119.25 million.[13] The total aid from federal, provincial and municipal governments given to the CPR for construction of the railway, not counting the value of granted land, was estimated to be $106.3 million.[14]

Other than the outright subsidies from taxpayers, the CPR had many of its loans and bond issues underwritten by the government. So, what emerged from the government's financial entanglement with the CPR was a parallel political fusion between the Macdonald government and the company. It was a relationship succinctly stated by Macdonald himself in an 1889 letter to George Stephen, CPR president: "My own position as a public man is as intimately connected with the prosperity of the CPR as yours is as a railway man."[15]

This union of government and private interests inevitably spilled over into overt partisan politics when the CPR used the government to protect its corporate interests against the Liberals and others who professed the merits of free trade and business competition. When the Laurier Liberals were campaigning on a platform of unrestricted reciprocity with the US during the 1891 federal election, then-CPR president William Van Horne wrote to a prominent Montreal businessman and the letter ended up in the Montreal *Gazette*:

> I am well enough acquainted with the trade and industries of
> Canada to know that unrestricted reciprocity would bring

prostration or ruin. I realize that for saying this I may be accused of meddling in politics, but with me this is a business question and not a political one, and it so vitally affects the interests that have been entrusted to me that I feel justified in expressing my opinion plainly.[16]

In 1911, when Laurier again campaigned on the promise of signing a reciprocity treaty with the US, Van Horne was quoted as saying: "I am to do all I can to bust the damn thing."

Although the Laurier government had failed to slash tariffs like many in the West had expected, it did recognize the economic inequity of tariff policy on prairie farmers. To offset the imbalance, Laurier and the CPR negotiated the Crow's Nest Pass Agreement in 1897. In exchange for a $3.4 million subsidy to help the CPR build a 330-mile line from Lethbridge to Nelson, BC, where the smelting and mining industry was rapidly growing, the CPR agreed to reduce its freight rates on grain and flour and to keep them at those levels permanently. The rates were approximately a half a cent per ton per mile. The railway also agreed to reduce freight rates on a specific list of settlers' effects and accepted the principle of rate regulation by a federal commission.[17] In a very real sense then, the Crow Rate itself became part of the National Policy as the Laurier government saw it as compensation to the prairies for the higher costs built into the wheat economy because of the National Policy's high tariffs. For Saskatchewan farmers, the Crow Rate became hugely important as an economic offset to the monopoly power of the railway. At the same time, it acquired the political symbolism of explicit recognition by the government in Ottawa that many of the prairie farmers' grievances were legitimate.

But government largesse certainly wasn't limited to the CPR. Indeed in the early years of the 20th century, the Laurier government sought to break the CPR's stranglehold on transportation and in 1903 passed legislation sanctioning two new transcontinental railways—the Canadian Northern and the Grand Trunk Pacific. As usual, Ottawa helped bankroll the new railroads, issuing guarantees of Canadian Northern bonds to a maximum of $13,000 a mile for 620 miles from western Manitoba to Edmonton and another 100 miles from Manitoba to Prince Albert.

The emergence of the two additional transcontinental lines triggered an era of feverish railway expansion that was to extend until 1914 and the onset of the First World War. The CPR quickly moved to meet the competition and began expanding its branch lines in Saskatchewan to maintain its dominance of the mushrooming prairie grain market. Before long it became apparent that the massive investment in transportation infrastructure was a mistake and three national railways, along with countless smaller lines that were, for the most part, leased to the large companies, could not be economically sustained, even with massive taxpayers' subsidies.

In the meantime, however, construction of railway branch lines in Saskatchewan could not keep up with the demand as wave after wave of settlers rolled into the province. During Saskatchewan's first 10 years as a province, railway construction moved at a frantic pace, with total rail mileage increasing from 1,551 to 5,980.[18] The feverish railway construction in the province further stimulated a rapidly expanding farm economy. It created a huge labour demand that attracted migrant workers and also helped to prop up the farm economy by providing off-farm income for farmers in the winter.

Even before it became a province, Saskatchewan's population was growing faster than anyone had anticipated and there was no sign of it slowing. More than half the total increase in Canada's population from 1901 to 1911 occurred on the prairies, with Saskatchewan the hotbed of development and immigration. The prairies' population increased by 169% during that period, but Saskatchewan's climbed by almost 440%, going from 91,279 to 492,432. And the people kept coming by the trainload. In 1921 Saskatchewan's population was 757,510 and in 1931 it was 921,785, making Saskatchewan the third most populous province in Canada, behind only Ontario and Quebec.[19]

Now, in the context and perception of Saskatchewan 100 years later, all this seems incongruous. But by the end of the first decade of the 20th century, it was evident that Saskatchewan was the boom province of Canada. So when Saskatchewan was proclaimed "the banner province of the dominion" to Laurier when he stopped in Regina during a tour of the West in 1910, he did not dismiss the suggestion, or patronize it. He merely acknowledged it, and the fact Saskatchewan was indeed challenging Ontario as the most dynamic province in the dominion, by saying: "Ontario will find no fault with your aspiration. It will be a worthy incentive to her greater efforts to retain the title."[20]

Clearly then, in its early years, Saskatchewan's population and economy grew at a rate never seen in Canada, either before or since. As with any migration of people, there were push-and-pull factors that led to the rapid influx of people. It was the convergence of those forces that accounted for Saskatchewan's truly remarkable emergence as a province that quickly took its place as a hothouse of development.

The push factors were obviously exogenous to government efforts such as the National Policy. In fact, there are some who have maintained the National Policy was largely irrelevant to the settlement of the prairies. The argument is not easily dismissed. It states that forces beyond the reach of government policy in this country account for the influx of settlers and, if anything, the National Policy was not only irrelevant, but ultimately harmful to national development.

A compelling case can be built to support the theory. The fact is that the National Policy was essentially in place for 20 years before the great wave of settlement finally arrived. The tariff structure was established by 1880, the railways had reached the prairies by 1883 and free homestead policy was on the books in its final form by 1882. Yet it was not until the turn of the century that immigration finally caught fire on the prairies.

The argument is that outside forces—the so-called push factor—were what triggered western settlement. It was not until the prime US farmland had been settled, wheat prices started climbing in the final years of the 1890s, transport costs on wheat exports started to decline, labour and capital flows became mobile, and dryland farming techniques were developed, that settlement became economically and socially feasible on the Canadian prairies. Thus, the National Policy was, at best, of secondary importance and did not in any substantive way trigger the development of Saskatchewan.[21]

Clearly those external factors were crucial. But rather than one or two key factors, the combination of many determinants created the conditions for Saskatchewan's rapid growth. Free farmland and rail transportation helped to make prairie farming possible, as did rising wheat prices which climbed from 74¢ a bushel in 1900 to $1.10 in 1908 and $2.24 in 1918. The advent of summerfallowing techniques, and faster maturing Red Fife and Marquis wheat also helped to fill in the economic equation for Saskatchewan.

There was also a convergence of other outside forces, mostly related to the world emerging from a long recession, beginning in the last years of the 1800s. Political upheaval and economic dislocation in Europe, coupled with the aftermath of what some describe as a second Industrial Revolution in Western Europe and the US, were pushing people to emigrate from the growing urban slums of industrial Europe. Population growth during rapid expansion in industrial output meant people were crowding into cities and raising the demand for food, in particular cereal grains. Wheat prices, which by 1890 had fallen 40% since 1875, were beginning to rise, and a major gold discovery in South Africa raised world gold stocks by 50%, suddenly renewing world investment capital flows. Meanwhile interest rates were at record lows, which spurred overseas investment.

With that set of circumstances in place, public policy in Canada further accelerated the pace of settlement. Clearly, government-created incentives and a largely taxpayer-financed transportation infrastructure helped create the conditions that led to the rapid migration of people to what was to become Saskatchewan.

As a harsh critic of national policy, John Dales dismisses the argument that government had to create the infrastructure so people would seize the economic opportunity:

> Economic man does not need to be prepared by government policy before he reacts to opportunities for making profits. Is it crude hero worship, or an unconscious human predisposition to human explanations of history that leads Canadians to believe that what success they have enjoyed "must" reflect

Macdonald's wise nation-building policies? Or are we all merely prisoners of our own history—as it has been written?

It is true that people will respond to economic opportunity. But the rate they react depends on other factors, which in the case of Saskatchewan's explosive development in the first three decades of the 20th century relates directly to government policy. So if government did not create the economic opportunity, it certainly made the realization of it more readily available to people. In that sense, what the railway and immigration components of the National Policy did for Saskatchewan was supply the pull factors that sped up development once the other economic and social forces were pushing immigrants to Canada.

What cannot be disputed is that settlement of Saskatchewan from 1905 to 1930 was nothing short of astounding. Not only did population grow from 257,763 to 921,785 during that 25-year period, but homestead acreage mushroomed from 12,488,200 to 30,729,100 acres.[22] The pace of settlement and quality of land that was turned into farms related directly to government actions, specifically its economic-development strategy. It was the free homestead policy, the system of land grants to railways and the sanctioning of private land companies by the Dominion government that account for both the rhythm and pattern of Saskatchewan's settlement. The question that needs to be answered is whether the long-term economic and social well-being of Saskatchewan people was served by this manner of rapid immigration and settlement.

When the tide of people started arriving, pulled by government propaganda, free land and infrastructure investment, and pushed by economic and social forces in their homeland, what happened was that settlement took on a life of its own. It created its own inertia that quickly fostered an environment fertile for those seeking to profit from the situation. But, there appeared to be no overall plan to Saskatchewan settlement or the development of its economy beyond how it complimented railway expansion and a tariff-protected manufacturing and industrial sector in Quebec and Ontario. It was hardly surprising, then, that settlement in Saskatchewan, and the economy it produced, was distorted by a combination of public and private factors, both operating on short-term agendas. There was the political expedience of government seeking to "develop" the West and the greed of private commercial interests that sought to profit from the settlement.

Obviously, growth in the young Saskatchewan economy hinged on expansion of cultivated wheat acreage. Initially that meant settlement was restricted to the more fertile, darker soil areas of the province, an area that stretched along the park belt in an arc northwest from the Red River region of southern Manitoba. But with immigrants flooding into the province, pressure was building to open the more productively marginal semi-arid regions to homesteading.

The turning point came in 1908 when the federal government ended the railway land grant process. Up to that period, all odd-numbered sections had been set aside for railway land grants. The railway companies were allowed to select their land from areas "fairly fit for settlement" and, not surprisingly, they took land in the more fertile, darker brown soil region of the parkland. Left largely untouched was the vast arid portion of the province that stretched west, northwest and southwest from Moose Jaw to the Alberta border. With the CPR having claimed its land, the federal government opened to homesteaders the area that Palliser had called an extension of the Great American Desert.

With the demand for land growing, Mother Nature also played a hand in rapid settlement of the arid regions. The four years after 1908, other than 1910, were periods of "super-normal rainfall" in the dryland district, which gave people a false sense of security that would come back to haunt them. Says historian Vernon Fowke:

> The indiscriminate settlement of the dry belt—or dry triangle—which took place under the false stimulus of abnormally favourable moisture conditions after 1908 had serious regional consequences a decade later.[23]

But private greed also played a role in the rapid overdevelopment of the Saskatchewan farm economy. A key factor in the settlement of the drier portions of the province, that begin north of the Regina plain and reach to south of Saskatoon, was the privately owned, but federally sanctioned, Saskatchewan Valley Land Company (SVLC). According to historian and prairie settlement expert Chester Martin, "the organization and success of the Saskatchewan Valley Land Company reads like a tale in the Arabian Nights."

Led by Colonel A.D. Davidson and owned by a mixture of Canadian and American shareholders, the SVLC bought almost 940,000 acres of land grant property from smaller railways in the province. The company then launched an aggressive advertising campaign centred in Minneapolis, which included a two-page ad in the Minneapolis *Journal* proclaiming the great potential of the land in Saskatchewan. More than 30,000 copies of the newspaper were distributed at the state fair in 1902. American journalists, politicians and interested farmers were brought to Saskatchewan free of charge and given a tour of the land for sale. Prior to the arrival of the SVLC, settlers had been ignoring this arid region and "the whole district was becoming a by-word throughout the whole section and settlers invariably crossed this desert, went through it by the thousand, to more eligible lands at Rosthern, Duck Lake and beyond."[24]

However, in a matter of a few years, the SVLC had settled the area and become one of the few private land company success stories, other than the

SAB R-A2
Empty grain wagons leaving the elevator, c. 1913.

CPR, in the province. The company's success in settling the area was duly noted by Clifford Sifton in the House of Commons in 1906:

> In going over this tract [of land] a year ago, I saw villages, elevators, stores, hotels and the largest wheat field I ever saw in my life… I shall be content, when the history of this country shall be written, to have the history of the last eight or nine years, as far as western administration is concerned, entered opposite my name.

Success, of course, is always relative. At the time, it was only proper to consider the settlement of Saskatchewan as a success. After all, this was a vast virgin land that almost overnight was turning into what seemed to be a burgeoning vibrant economy. Towns were springing up, homes, schools and churches were being built and an entire prairie society was emerging, populated by people from far away who could not resist the push-and-pull factors that brought them to their new home.

A key goal of the National Policy for decades had been to settle the West, so when it finally started it was difficult not to assume that such rapid development of Saskatchewan was a sign of success and economic progress. It seemed to make perfect economic sense. There was growing demand on the world market for wheat, an abundance of land to be cultivated that would grow the wheat to meet that demand, and a shortage of labour to do it. Obviously, wealth was being created and a new economy established as settlers converged on the province to begin farming.

But, if on the surface the rapid settlement merely reflected the untapped economic potential of the province, underlying it were questions about what was sustainable, what was the optimum level of population growth and what settlement patterns were sustainable for a rural economy and society like Saskatchewan. Unfortunately those questions were neither asked nor answered in the early years of Saskatchewan's development. The settlement of Saskatchewan and the creation of a widely dispersed farm economy and society were seen as virtues in and of themselves.

It wasn't until three decades later, in the final years of the Great Depression, that the folly of unthinking and unplanned settlement in Saskatchewan was becoming apparent, at least to some. The weakness of development in the wheat boom years was cogently addressed in the final report of the 1940 Royal Commission on Dominion-Provincial Relations:

> In a period of rising prices, rising land values and cheap cred-
> it, the lure of free lands in the "last, best west" was irre-
> sistible… By the end of 1913 the rapid phase of western set-
> tlement was over. In so short a time the frontier was pushed
> to its limits in almost all directions.The occupation of prairie
> lands proceeded with little discrimination. There was no clas-
> sification of resources, no soil surveys, no climactic records to
> guide either the government or the unwary settler. The
> policies and methods of the Dominion were mainly designed
> to serve the national purpose of filling the Northwest at once
> with as many people as possible. The selection of land was
> left largely to chance and to the devices which colonization
> agents, railways and land companies employed in their own
> immediate interests.
>
> The sectional survey, the railway land grant scheme and pre-
> emptions [homesteads] illustrate a system designed for indis-
> criminate mass colonization and it worked with almost
> mechanical perfection. Adjustment to the vagaries and fail-
> ings of nature was left to time, and bitter experience.

In retrospect then, the three pillars of the National Policy—tariff protection for industry, railway development, and settlement of the West—did not serve Saskatchewan well. Each played a part in creating what were false expectations predicated on a vulnerable and partly false economy that rapidly produced a far-flung society.

What started as part myth had suddenly become a perverse sort of reality. Here was a flourishing province, with a rapidly growing economy and population. The time was at hand for people to deal with the reality they encountered in Saskatchewan as best they could.

Four   # The Illusions of Growth

"It would be wise of you to treat the big profits of this year as capital and not income. Nature has a way of averaging her favours, and is apt to follow her sunniest smiles with the blackest of her frowns."

(Governor General Earl Grey, 1909, in Regina)

In retrospect, the advice of the Governor General was sound. In fact, maybe even prescient. The rapid emergence of Saskatchewan's economy and rural society was clearly one of the more remarkable events in 20th century Canadian history. In the span of little more than 20 years Saskatchewan went from a vast, sparsely populated prairie wilderness to the third most populous province in the nation. But with the unharnessed growth came the inevitable problems—social and economic dislocation, ethnic tensions, divisions between Aboriginal people and settlers, agrarian political protest and a unique brand of prairie populism—which, in time, would help revise and reshape the myth of Saskatchewan as a promised land.

In spite of the difficulties, Saskatchewan still seemed poised on the threshold of economic greatness in Canada. While there were years when the wheat economy suffered from drought or falling world wheat prices, or both, the provincial economy showed no outwardly apparent, or potentially fatal weakness. In fact, there was no denying that agriculture, and more specifically the wheat economy, was a powerful engine driving spectacular economic growth for not only Saskatchewan, but for the nation.

The dominance of wheat to the national economy was most apparent when compared to other major wheat-exporting nations in 1925. In Canada, the average wheat production per capita was 43.7 bushels. Meanwhile, wheat production in Australia was 24 bushels per capita, Argentina was 22.6 bushels and in the US wheat production was 7 bushels per capita.[1]

The social and economic pressures created by the first signs of rapid development were a key reason behind the campaign for provincial autonomy in the years prior to 1905. When immigration flows, which for years had been barely a trickle, suddenly turned into a tide, territorial premier Frederick Haultain pushed hard for provincial status. The territorial government's dependence on financial support from Ottawa, and its severely limited ability to raise money through taxation, meant that it was virtually

Frederick Haultain, premier of the North-West Territories, 1897–1905.

impossible for the local government to meet the needs of a fast-growing population.

A resolution calling for provincial status was passed in the territorial assembly on May 2, 1900. The impetus was largely financial, as the territorial government found it difficult to meet burgeoning demands for public services that came with the increasing immigration flows. Requests for more money from Ottawa to pay for construction of schools in the territories had met with little response, which made provincial status the only logical alternative to deal with the escalating number of immigrants.[2]

An editorial in the Regina *Leader* on December 28, 1904, summed up the rationale behind the push for provincial status:

> Our autonomy demand was never due to any grievous lack of home rule, it was due to a grievous lack of money … could we be assured of adequate money grants for 10 years to come we should be better off without constitutional change for 10 years to come.

Of course the two issues were linked. The lack of home rule meant the territorial government had severely limited taxation powers, which was at the root of the financial pressure on the region.

The problems created by the rapid influx of people for the territorial government were outlined in a letter from Haultain to Laurier in December 1901. In it, Haultain emphatically stated the strains being felt by the immigration policies of the federal government. Aside from the rate of immigration being promoted by the Department of Immigration, Haultain noted the special kind of problems that rural, farm-based settlement created for government:

> The increase in the population has increased our work and expenditures by a rate far greater than can be measured by the mere increase in the number of people. Immigration in

> other parts of the Dominion has resulted largely in adding only to the population in settlements and towns previously in existence. In the Territories it is not so.
>
> New settlers in the North-West seem desirous to pass by the settlements already opened up and to become pioneers in districts removed as far away as practicable there from. The new settlements are too small and the settlements are too widely scattered to bear the burdens which necessarily go with the opening up of a new country, and the fact cannot be disguised that they must be assisted to do so if the people are to become contented and prosperous, or even retained in the country.

As Haultain explained, the unique social and economic problem that came with rapid, largely unplanned settlement of the prairies was that virtually every group of new settlers sought to establish its own new community.

After first being sympathetic to the idea of provincial autonomy, Laurier rejected Haultain's request as premature. To force the issue, Haultain called a territorial election in 1902 on the question of provincial status and won a large majority. Laurier could not ignore the result. Thus, in the 1904 federal election, the Liberal prime minister said he would deal with the autonomy question, which set the stage for the Saskatchewan Act of 1905.

When Saskatchewan finally arrived, the birth was not entirely painless. The political controversy largely revolved around two components of the legislation making Saskatchewan a part of Confederation. One related to the separate school issue. The other was Ottawa's decision to retain control of public lands and resources rather than transfer them to the province, as had been the case with the formation of Ontario, Quebec, New Brunswick, Nova Scotia and British Columbia.

The separate school controversy hinged on the belief that the Saskatchewan Act rolled back the clock to the same situation as the North-West Territories Act of 1875, which had explicitly allowed for the operation and administration of a separate school system. But subsequent amendments had created a system where the Roman Catholic schools were governed by the Territorial Education Department. The Saskatchewan Act, some argued, regressed the new province to the law of 1875 and gave control of separate schools back to the Catholic Church.

Aside from leading to Clifford Sifton's resignation from cabinet in 1905, the separate school controversy underscored the religious tension evident in a fast-growing immigrant society. Simultaneously, the province was attempting to blend diverse ethnic, religious and cultural forces, while forging a rural, farm-based economy.

From the outset, this religious tension became a major and lingering force that, for years, would be an undercurrent to Saskatchewan's provincial politics. Many saw Laurier, himself a Catholic, as succumbing to the pressure from the church in Quebec and elsewhere. Then, when former Liberal MP Walter Scott was selected the province's first premier instead of Haultain, the die was cast for the shape and tone of provincial politics in the decades ahead.

Scott had resigned as an MP to become leader of the provincial Liberals before being appointed premier. Many expected Haultain, who had led the non-partisan territorial government since 1891, would be named the province's first premier. He was, after all, experienced in the administration of government and respected by most citizens. But Haultain was accused of abandoning the non-partisan tradition of Territorial politics when he attended a 1903 convention of Territorial Conservatives in Moose Jaw that had passed a resolution saying the party should place candidates in every constituency in the next Territorial election. Although he opposed the resolution, Haultain accepted the position of honorary president of the newly formed Territorial Conservative Association, which undermined him with his own non-partisan government in Regina and the Liberals in Ottawa.[3]

Haultain also grew more alienated from Laurier and the Liberals over the Saskatchewan Act itself. The Territorial premier opposed the separate school provisions, Ottawa's continuing control of natural resources and the decision to create two provinces instead of one between Manitoba and BC.

The public division between Laurier and Haultain on basic issues relating to the new province was all the reason the prime minister needed to name Scott as Liberal premier of the new province. In defence of his decision not to select Haultain, Laurier said:

> The language he [Haultain] made use of … left no doubt at all that if he had the power he would do everything he could to destroy the constitution which we have given to the provinces of Saskatchewan and Alberta.[4]

When Scott was chosen premier, Haultain formed the Provincial Rights Party to fight the first provincial election in December 1905. But Haultain's new party was no match for Scott and the provincial Liberals, who had the advantage of forming an interim government during the three months before the province's first election could be called. The Liberals ended up winning a comfortable majority of 16–9 seats and, in the process, laid the foundations for a quarter century of political hegemony by the Liberal Party.

What's most important about that first election was how it shaped the political landscape. The Liberals took great advantage of being the party in power federally and provincially during a time of massive immigration. In fact, the Department of Immigration itself became an influential partisan tool that, in not-so-subtle ways, urged immigrants to identify themselves politically with the Liberals. It gave the Liberals an enormous edge and a

Walter Scott, first premier of Saskatchewan, 1905–1916.

virtual monopoly over claiming the loyalty of new people flooding into the province.

Meanwhile, Haultain's Provincial Rights party was seen as a provincial offshoot of the Conservatives. Although Haultain argued that Saskatchewan's terms of entry into Confederation were unjust, the greatest distinction between himself and the Liberals appeared to be on the separate school issue. As a result, in its early years of development, provincial politics in Saskatchewan were drawn as much on religious as ideological lines.[5]

Although far less emotional, the issue of Ottawa maintaining control over public land and natural resources was immeasurably more relevant to the future development of Saskatchewan's political economy, than debates over separate schools. By retaining control, and paying Saskatchewan an annual grant of 80¢ per capita as compensation, the federal government was asserting its continuing jurisdiction over immigration, settlement and railway development. The belief in Ottawa was that responsibility for settlement and the distribution of homesteads must remain part of the federal government's Dominion Lands policy. In short, the parochial interests of the provinces could not be allowed to dictate the course of national development.

This clash of interests over control of Crown land between the federal and provincial governments went to the heart of how development proceeded in Saskatchewan and the public policy theory behind it. The conflicting federal-provincial views on lands policy and the competing federal and provincial interests were expressed quite eloquently and accurately by Frank Oliver, who followed Sifton as minister of immigration, in a 1905 House of Commons speech. In effect, he explained how immigration and settlement resulted in a conflict between Ottawa and the province:

> The prosperity this Dominion is enjoying today is to a very large extent due to the fact that the lands of the Northwest Territories have been given away and that people have taken them. I say that the interest of the Dominion is to secure the

settlement of the lands, and whether with a price or without a price makes little or no difference.

It is worth the while of the Dominion to spend hundreds of thousands of dollars in promoting immigration to that country and to spend thousands of dollars in surveying and administering these lands, and then to give them away.

But the province is not in that position. The province derives no revenue from the customs duties or from the wealth which the settler creates. Every settler who goes on land in the Northwest Territories is a bill of expense to the provincial government. That settler requires good roads made, he requires a school supported, he requires the advantages of municipal organization, so that as a matter of fact the tendency of the provincial government is to get such money as it can out of the land and to prevent settlement from spreading any further than can be helped. On the other hand, the interest of the Dominion is to get the settlers on the land, to scatter them far and wide, so long as they are good settlers and they get good land.[6]

In theory, federal control of settlement, while a nation-state was being formed, made good sense. But in practice, history suggests otherwise. While undeniably Ottawa had a keen interest in settlement and could take a national view in terms of its policy, results indicate Ottawa could only see the big picture and, as a consequence, paid little attention to the detail necessary to craft economically and socially responsible settlement patterns. As the province at the centre of settlement in the early decades of this century, Saskatchewan bore the benefits and damage from the federal government's broad-brush approach to immigration and settlement.

As noted earlier, even before Saskatchewan became a province, pressures created by an ill-planned federal immigration and settlement policy on the prairies were obvious. In his letter to Laurier in 1901, Haultain outlined the social and economic problems created by rapid immigration, arguing the need for a new province to be created:

Put in the briefest possible form the position is simply this: The population of the Territories has been and is increasing so rapidly as the result of the efforts put forth by the Immigration Branch of the Interior Department that the means at the command of the Territorial Government are far from being sufficient to enable it to properly administer the affairs of the country.[7]

He talked about how the population was becoming ever more widely dispersed, with "the certainty that nearly every small group of new settlers, united by any tie whatever, means practically the opening up of a new settlement.

The lack of any clear strategy by Ottawa that was sensitive to the climate, topology and economic sustainability of the semi-arid regions of Saskatchewan left an indelible imprint on the province's economy and politics. While no one can know with any certainty if provincial control of settlement would have altered the course of history, some had been left to wonder. Certainly the fiscal pressures on the province resulting from a rapidly expanding population, and the concurrent infrastructure demands, would have been an inhibiting factor that conceivably would have affected the scope and speed of settlement.

Historian Cecil Lingard raises the point that settlement would have been more sustainable had greater influence been exerted at the local, rather than federal level:

> One wonders whether the federal government was not, after all, ill-fitted to cope with the many problems of immigration, especially those of homestead selection and supervision, and whether the homesteading of semi-arid tracts, necessitating the untold hardships and sacrifices of recent years, could have taken place under local administration?[8]

As for the question of provincial control over natural resources, it was to be a recurring issue in Saskatchewan. It was finally addressed with the Natural Resources Transfer Agreement of 1930, but the issue of compensation owing to the province from Ottawa would not be resolved until a 1935 Royal Commission assessed the situation and ruled that $5 million should be paid to Saskatchewan in compensation.

But such issues and doubts were only to become apparent many years later when the problems of an economy, built almost exclusively on a single, staple export such as wheat, became a reality. In the meantime Saskatchewan was to become the economic hothouse of Canada, growing faster in real and proportional terms than any other province in the nation.

There are many ways to measure the spectacular growth of Saskatchewan's economy. Likely the most easily grasped measurement is raw population data. In 1901, the population of the area of the North-West Territories that was to become Saskatchewan was 91,279. In 1906, less than a year after Saskatchewan had become a province, the population had mushroomed to 257,763. The population explosion continued in the coming years, reaching 492,432 in 1911, an increase of almost 440% in 10 years. The flood of people continued, reaching 647,835 in 1916. Although the growth rate slowed somewhat from that point, the best way to describe the change is from a torrent to a steady stream of people flowing into the province. In 1921 the total number of people had reached 757,510, in 1926 it was 820,738 and by 1931 there were 921,785 people in the province. In percentage terms, during its first 26 years, Saskatchewan's population grew by approximately 260%. If the starting point of the measurement is extended four years earlier to 1901, the population increase to 1931 was a colossal 910%.[9]

But the growth didn't stop in 1931 with the advent of the Depression and the Dirty Thirties. Even though the province suffered severe economic and social trauma through much of the 1930s, its population continued to grow, peaking at 931,547 in 1936 before going into decline. It wouldn't be until the 1960s that Saskatchewan's population would recover to its level at the height of the dust bowl years in the Dirty Thirties.

Coupled with rapid population growth was a mushrooming farm economy. No matter what measurement is used, the growth of Saskatchewan's agriculture economy during the province's first two decades was nothing if not phenomenal. For example, in the 12 months ending June 30, 1906, 27,692 homestead entries were registered in Saskatchewan, representing 66% of homestead entries for the entire nation that year.[10] During the most intense decade of expansion from 1906–16, homestead acreage in the province went from 12.48 million to 29.08 million acres, a 133% increase.[11]

The total number of farms climbed from 55,971 in 1906 to 136,472 by 1931. Growth in the number of family farms was constant throughout the boom, but it was the most intense in the 1901–11 decade when 81,568 new farms were started in Saskatchewan. In the first five years after the province was created, 39,042 farms were established. By 1916 the number of farms was 104,006. The total climbed to 119,451 by 1921 and actually declined slightly to 117,781 in 1926.[12]

As one would expect, the acreage of field crops grew at a similarly spectacular pace. In 1901 there were only 655,537 seeded acres in what was to be Saskatchewan. By 1931, with the drought and deprivation of the 1930s only just beginning to grip the province, the seeded acreage had gone up by an astonishing 5,020% to 33.54 million acres, about 85% of which was spring wheat. The total value of the crops had also gone up exponentially. But it is important to realize the value of crop production did not increase at an even pace with the addition of new cultivated farmland each year. The entire crop for the province in 1901 was valued at $4.6 million and by 1931 it was worth $105.53 million. But within that time span were wrenching periods of huge fluctuations in value.

For example, in the five years between 1911 and 1916, the value of the crop leapt from $79.95 million to $273.35 million. However the total value declined to $249.31 million in 1921, then exploded to $368.27 million in 1926 before collapsing with the wheat market in 1931 to $105.53 million.

Still, on the surface and up to the downward spiral in farming that began in 1930, the agricultural economy seemed sound. The growth in aggregate wheat production had been astounding, going from 26.1 million bushels in 1905 to a pre-Depression peak of 321.21 million bushels in 1928. This

1,130% increase in production was clearly related to constant expansion of seeded acreage driven by immigration. But there were other factors related to improved farming methods, such as the introduction of more rapidly maturing Marquis wheat and the use of summerfallowing to retain greater subsoil moisture, which helped to improve production. As well, higher productivity through early labour-saving forms of farm technology were beginning to make inroads in what was a labour-intensive industry. Oxen used to pull plows were replaced by draft horses. By 1908 there were 3,219 threshing machines in the province, compared to 368 for the entire North-West only 10 years earlier. And, by 1915, small gasoline tractors were common.[13]

But within this framework of spectacular growth were symptoms of the fragility inherent in the Saskatchewan economy. The fact was that massive inflows of people were fuelling aggregate growth in the province's Gross Domestic Product. However, when growth was assessed on an income-per-capita basis, there were reasons for concern. In effect, while the province was generating more wealth, individually people in agriculture were often not doing as well from one year to the next. It was the same economic reality that had happened nationally under the high tariff policies of the National Policy. While the total economic output of the province—its GDP—was growing, at an individual level, people were often getting a smaller share of a larger pie. The reality was that the population was growing at a faster rate than the economy.

At the root of the problem was the inconsistent price of wheat, which was effectively the single underpinning to the province's young economy. For example, in 1906 the average wheat price was 76¢ a bushel, while in 1892 it had been 80¢. By 1909 the price had gone up to $1.08 a bushel and fell to 95¢ in 1911. During the war years, the price skyrocketed 155%, going from 91¢ a bushel in 1915 to an amazing $2.32 in 1919. The following year it dropped by almost 50% to $1.55 a bushel.

Beneath these price fluctuations was a disturbing long-term trend in price. From 1885 right up to the Great Depression when prices collapsed, the movement of the world wheat price in absolute terms, and relative to other commodities, was down. As well during this period when the Saskatchewan wheat economy was expanding, so too was the oversupply of world wheat stocks. Basically wheat production far exceeded world demand. The annual carryover from one crop year to the next went from an average of 695 million bushels in the mid-1920s to 1,187 million bushels in 1934. That excess amount equalled 40% of the total world demand for human consumption and seed use.[14]

This overproduction of wheat could be seen in the growing gap between actual wheat acreage and "necessary" acreage, as defined by human consumption and seed requirements. In 1903–04 the excess between actual and necessary acreage was 11 million acres. By the mid-1930s surplus wheat acreage had climbed to 31 million acres.[15]

Coupled with price instability was the unpredictability of Mother Nature. With much of the semi-arid regions settled by homesteaders, yields varied as much or more than the price. What resulted was a situation where farmers faced two key input variables beyond their control, which lengthened the odds of attaining any measure of economic security or predictability. Wheat yields bore no relation to supply or demand and were, for the most part, external to the factors of production.

From 1905 to 1931, wheat yields per bushel in Saskatchewan fluctuated wildly. In 1905 the average yield was 23.1 bushels an acre, in 1907 it was 13.5 bushels to the acre, in 1915 it jumped to 25.2 bushels, plummeted to 8.5 bushels in 1919, recovered to 23.3 and then spiraled down to 8.8 bushels an acre in 1931. In the aggregate, those yields are reflected in spring wheat production that varied from 224 million bushels in 1915, down to 115 million bushels in 1920, back up to 235 million bushels in 1925 and then back down to 183 million bushels in 1930.

As you would expect, the roller coaster variables of price and yield were reflected in net farm income figures. In 1926, the first year that such statistics were compiled, realized net farm income in Saskatchewan was $170.48 million, which equaled an average of $1,457 per farm. A year later it was $144.45 million—or $1,188 per farm—and in 1928 it had jumped to $188.68 million before beginning a steep descent into economic chaos. Over the next four years, net farm income went from $122.19 million to *minus* $12.79 million, which translated into an average deficit per farm for the year of $93.[16]

Yet the problems and instability created by such wildly changing values, production and income levels were largely hidden in the macroeconomic appearance of an economy that appeared to be growing by leaps and bounds. It seemed incongruous to suggest there could be anything seriously askew in the Saskatchewan economy during a time when population growth was surging and an entire agriculture sector had emerged from a meagre base to dominate the entire province. This phenomenon is what economic historian W.A. Mackintosh refers to as "pseudo-prosperity." He says that "as long as settlers pour in, as long as capital is expended, all the appearances of prosperity are present."[17]

But if you look more closely at the wheat economy in those boom years, there were clear reasons for concern about the sustainability of the type of growth that was taking place. From a per capita value of $50.48 for all field crops in 1900, by 1911 the per capita value had increased to $162.37 and to $422.49 in 1916. However, by 1921 the value of grain production per person had dropped to $329.34, and although it recovered to $449.11 in 1926, by 1931 it had plummeted to $114.58.

Equally telling during these boom years was that during the 10 years before the advent of the Dirty Thirties, the total value of farm property, as well as the average value per farm, was declining. In 1921 total farm value, which included land, buildings, implements, machinery and livestock was $1.65 billion. By 1926 it had declined more than $300 million to $1.3 billion and by 1931 it had sunk by another $300 million. Over the same period the average value for each farm fell from $13,814 to $9,325. During the decade 1921–31, the value of farm property in Saskatchewan actually fell by 22.9%, while in the previous 10 years it had increased in value by 98.1%.

And, while the farm equity base was eroding, the level of debt was increasing to keep pace with the capitalization of new farms being established. Although the rate of expansion peaked in 1913, it remained strong for the next 20 years. By the advent of the First World War, the farm debt problem was already on the public agenda in Saskatchewan and for all intents and purposes has been there ever since. After staging a series of public meetings across the province, the Saskatchewan Commission on Agriculture Credit found the total mortgage indebtedness of Saskatchewan farmers to be $65 million, or an average of approximately $1,500 per farm. With Saskatchewan at the peak of its economic boom, the commission sounded a warning about the emerging problem of debt on Saskatchewan farms. In its report, the commission stated:

> At an early stage in our investigation at home and abroad the
> conviction was borne in upon us that we were concerned with
> a question no less fundamental than the entire problem of
> rural life. We are face to face with a serious situation.[18]

The commission found that in the preceding 15 months, 1,723 farm foreclosures or forced mortgage sales were underway in the province.

Still, the level of debt and the foreclosure rate were neither unmanageable nor even surprising. There was a great deal of equity in Saskatchewan farms because of free homesteads and a significant number of foreclosures were to be expected in a pioneer economy where many homesteaders would fail. However, the situation became more severe when wheat prices collapsed after the war and the provincial government was forced to create a farm debt adjustment bureau that assisted more than 9,000 farmers in four years.

Beyond the economic uncertainties inherent in the farm economy, there was a whole other dimension to the challenges created by an immigrant settler farm economy. Although not readily apparent at the time, major structural problems were also being built into Saskatchewan's social and economic society that so rapidly emerged from ground zero. On one hand a widely dispersed rural population required the necessities of life on the prairies and the elements of a civil society, such as education, health care and a system of justice, that could only be delivered by government. On the other hand, the cost for this new society would have to come from an economy that would live or die on the success of its wheat production. And, by the 1920s, the wheat economy had largely reached its geographical limits, which meant that unplanned growth, or more precisely growth for growth's sake, had brought large tracts of marginal, semi-arid land into wheat production. The fact was, the combination of demands from a pioneer society that brought high fixed costs as it established itself on the prairies, and a variable and unpredictable farm economy, left Saskatchewan from its inception in a constantly vulnerable state.

This incompatibility between the nature of the rural society created and the economy to support it, was acknowledged in the midst of the Dirty Thirties when governments turned their attention to the collapse of Saskatchewan's farm economy. In his analysis of the situation, economist W.A. Mackintosh pointed to the inherent irrationality of Saskatchewan's economy and the rural society it spawned.

Mackintosh, who was one of Canada's foremost public policy economists and economic historians, said rapid growth in a virgin region that is peopled by pioneers and farmer-entrepreneurs rather than a tradition-bound peasantry, must bring demands for community services and for public improvements that add to the community and regional overhead costs. Something of a vicious circle results. Expansion of agriculture stimulates expansion of other businesses that support farming, which merely raises the already tenuous economic stakes by putting more dependency on agriculture, which itself is volatile. Implict in this is permanent instability:

> It is an axiom of finance that heavy fixed charges and highly fluctuating income are incompatible. The rapid expansion of agriculture settlement leads to the assumption of heavy fixed charges; highly fluctuating incomes make them difficult to carry.[19]

The pressures on government created by this rapid influx of people were evident at the provincial and local level. Among the first major spending initiatives of the Walter Scott government was an attempt to facilitate development by speeding up railway expansion within the province. With, in many cases, settlement moving ahead of railway lines, the government was under constant pressure to support the construction of branch lines to ensure that farmers were able to get their wheat to market. It was fully understandable. Without rail service, farmers had no economic lifeline either to transport their wheat to export positions, or acquire the goods necessary to operate their farms. If not economically incapacitated, they were severely disadvantaged.

In the first session of the provincial legislature a Department of Railways was established and five regional railways were chartered under provincial law. The importance of the railways to the political economy of the province was vividly apparent and reflected in the fact that Scott named himself as the first provincial railway commissioner, a post he held until 1908.[20]

Like the federal governments, which had poured vast sums into railway development, the Saskatchewan government was more than eager to use public money for what it perceived as a public good—expansion of branch lines. In 1909, legislation was passed to guarantee the principal and interest on bonds for both the Canadian Northern and Grand Trunk Pacific. The guarantee covered what was to be 1,050 new miles of rail line for the province to a maximum of $13,000 per mile.[21] Aside from meeting the needs of the growing farm population, the railway construction also created off-farm employment that helped to further stimulate what was already an overheated economy. By the end of 1913, more than 60% of the Grand Trunk Pacific's lines in the province had been guaranteed by the Scott government, and 30% of Canadian Northern's operation was backed by provincial guarantees.

Before long, however, it was apparent that the railway investment was doomed. By the start of the First World War, both the Canadian Northern and Grand Trunk Pacific were near a state of collapse. So bad was the financial condition of the railways that even with a federal government guarantee of 50% of the $100 million it sought, Canadian Northern was unable to raise the capital it needed to stay afloat. By 1919, the Canadian National Railway was formed to absorb all the lines in Canada of the Grand Trunk Pacific and Canadian Northern, to go with the Intercolonial Railway and the National Transcontinental that had already passed into federal government hands.

It had become apparent that railway policy, which was such an integral part of the National Policy, had been terribly miscalculated. A 1932 Royal Commission that looked into the railway debacle clearly linked the over-expansion of the railway to an unrealistic attitude about immigration and development on the prairies:

> The decision to add to these lines and to the western lines of the Canadian Northern, such additions as would create in total three complete transcontinental railways, changed the whole aspect of the railway situation in Canada. The policy of expansion was determined upon and construction begun in the atmosphere of the early years of the century, when almost unlimited growth was predicted for Canada… It was not long, however, before less favourable conditions made it apparent that railway construction had too far anticipated national growth… In a little more than 10 years, the whole railway situation had passed from a position of manageable cost and moderate expansion to one of financial confusion and over-extension.[22]

The story in Saskatchewan was little different. Even with its debt guaranteed by the provincial government, the Canadian Northern and Grand

Trunk Pacific were financial disasters waiting to happen. And the signs of trouble were apparent long before the federal government intervened.

After getting provincial guarantees in 1909 on branch lines to be built in the province, the two railways were granted a series of extensions on the guarantees when they failed to meet the deadline for construction of the lines. Each year from 1912 to 1915 the legislature extended the time the railways had to meet their commitments. As well, the government also guaranteed railway debt of up to $3.8 million for construction of terminals and bridges.[23]

But railway development also went hand-in-hand with the pattern of settlement and the structure of Saskatchewan society that resulted. While in many cases settlement was established first and the railway followed, the symbiotic relationship between the two is self-evident. In his historical analysis of the wheat economy, George Britnell says: "Railways and continually improving transportation were as essential as rain and sun to progressive settlement on the Canadian prairie."[24]

As a result, the speed of immigration and railway development produced a widely dispersed rural society in Saskatchewan. Rural communities usually formed at rail line sidings, which the railway companies positioned seven or eight miles apart as collection points for grain shipments. Elevator companies followed by building collection facilities at the sidings, which provided the economic focal point for communities to emerge.

A consequence of this settlement was the need for an extensive and expensive system of local government. The Rural Municipality Act came into force in 1909, giving local government responsibility for collection of school taxes, road building, some health care functions, welfare support and telephone service. By 1916, 302 rural municipalities, each representing a separate local government structure, were in place.

Each RM included nine townships, which might have provided geographic balance but bore little relationship to population distribution or, therefore, cost-effective public administration. Settlement was based on homestead quarters within sections of land. However, interspersed with the free land were sections and quarter sections owned by the railroad, the Hudson Bay Company or reserved for school purposes. The result was often wide distances between homesteads, which combined with the arbitrary location of railway sidings, created a rural settlement hodge-podge.

Thus, from its earliest days, Saskatchewan found itself burdened by a settlement structure that aggravated the costs of the new society, which was already strained by high tariffs and the precarious nature of a single crop wheat economy.

In a report to the provincial legislature many years later, the local government continuing committee identified the problems that came with settlement in Saskatchewan:

Perhaps the most serious and long-lasting effect of our isolated settlement pattern has been to maximize the cost of local services, particularly roads. It would be hard to devise a pattern which requires more road per farm. The effect on other dispersed services, such as power and telephones, is similar.[25]

Trying to keep pace with all the problems associated with development was a constant challenge for both provincial and local governments. In 1910 the Public Works Department instituted a 50–50 shared-cost road construction program with municipalities. Of the 74 RMs in existence, 59 received provincial grants which were limited to $5,000 per municipality. By 1919, the federal government had set aside $20 million for highway construction over five years, with Saskatchewan's share $1.8 million. Two years later, the provincial government spent $430,000 on "main market" road construction that was contracted through RMs and another $369,000 on direct government crews. When there were regionalized crop failures, the government often implemented a road-construction program to provide off-farm jobs and income for farmers. As Premier William Martin explained in 1919: "There is nothing [that] will do more to develop a new country like Saskatchewan than the construction of good roads."[26]

Similar challenges were faced to meet the health care and hospital needs of the population. In 1916 the Rural Hospital Act was passed that allowed for two or more municipalities to form a union hospital. With no logic to population density among the RMs, the legislation was changed two years later to allow the formation of hospital districts. The next phase was the creation of municipal doctor plans that allowed an RM to hire a doctor who was paid a flat salary to care for local residents.

But nowhere were the strains of growth more acute than in education. The number of school districts, each with an area of up to 25 square miles, exploded from 1,190 in 1906 to 3,838 in 1916 when school population reached 125,590. By 1930, the number of pupils was 220,352. On a year-to-year basis, spending on elementary schools only in the province went from slightly more than $1 million in 1905, to $16.5 million in 1920. Throughout this period finding qualified teachers for rural schools was a huge problem and often exceptions had to be made and the underqualified were granted teaching certificates.[27]

Making matters worse was the turnover of teachers, who simply could not cope with the number of students, their vast differences in ability and the conditions of life they faced in rural Saskatchewan. In 1916, for example, 188 rural schools changed teachers three of more times during the year, and 937 schools had at least two teachers. The effect was duly noted:

> This has a most disastrous effect upon the progress of the children in these schools. The numerous changes of teachers,

the short term schools and the irregular attendance in our country districts explain the backward condition of the children in many of our rural schools.[28]

All of these pressures from growth were converging on government at the provincial and local level. But as long as population and wheat production were increasing, the fiscal demands seemed manageable.

The only time when there was reason for doubt were years, such as immediately after the First World War, when wheat prices fell by almost 50%, and on the doorstep of Depression in 1930. In each case the provincial government found itself running deficits in its operating account; a deficit of $298,000 in 1920–21, followed by deficits of $1.4 million in 1921–22, $246,446 for 1922–23, and $518,178 for the 1929–30 fiscal year.

Meanwhile on the municipal front, cracks were also beginning to show as immigration was grinding to a halt and the realities of the wheat economy were taking root. By 1930 the cumulative tax arrears for all RMs were $15.1 million, which was more than 75% of the total RM tax levy for the year of $19.55 million. There were clear signs of trouble:

> Because of increasing tax arrears, rural municipalities were forced to borrow to meet their payments to school districts and telephone companies and to carry high interest charges. The vulnerability of the RMs to short-term price declines was clearly manifest.[29]

So, from its earliest days, Saskatchewan was a curious dichotomy. It was a province absorbing enormous numbers of people, all the while trying to cope with the phenomenal growth of a wheat economy and the rural society it spawned.

As the product of political forces driven equally by mythology and cold, cruel economics it was not surprising that Saskatchewan people would try to moderate and control, if not re-create, their world.

"If there'd been a bridge across the ocean, we would have walked home. But there
was no bridge and no money, so we stuck it out. What else could we do?"[1]

(A Saskatchewan immigrant)

The economic dilemma confronting Saskatchewan was quickly apparent to
the thousands drawn by the myth of a promised land. As they arrived, to
stake out their homesteads and begin the arduous task of building a new life
for themselves on the land, one can only assume many couldn't help but
wonder if they had made a terrible mistake. Ironically, people who came
seeking security, economic freedom and opportunity, instead often felt precarious and vulnerable to forces beyond their control. The hope that drew
them often turned into a reality that disappointed them.

For some, it ended in failure. During the years 1911–31, when
Saskatchewan was at the zenith of its prowess within Canada, 57% of the
homesteads failed. Unable to sustain a life on the farm, settlers who came to
what they thought was a land of hope and opportunity were often forced to
abandon their dream. For agricultural historians like Vernon Fowke, the dis-
crepancy between the number of registered homesteaders and those who
stayed long enough to get patent on their land "is so pronounced as to indicate a wastefulness little less than shocking."[2]

From this harsh reality grew a conviction people were not in control of
their economic destiny, that they were the captives of a difficult, sometimes
hostile, natural environment and perverse economic forces. This notion was
to become a central and unifying theme to Saskatchewan life and politics.
The belief that more powerful interests elsewhere were exploiting
Saskatchewan and its people became the common instinct to the political
culture of the province. The same view has remained virtually unchanged to
this day. It is a notion of external control that is at the core of Saskatchewan's
political psyche and the fuel of populist sentiment on the prairies.

As we have seen, there were good historical reasons for Saskatchewan
people to see themselves as victims of economic subjugation. The whole
notion of the prairies, and their place within Canada as part of the National
Policy, was as a region subservient to the interests of the business and political classes of central Canada. Immigration and settlement in Saskatchewan

were conceived as the means to a captive market for the benefit of industry in Ontario and Quebec. As such, the east-west economic structure of Canada was explicitly designed to effectively treat the prairies as an economic colony of central Canada.

Clearly, the primary control of Saskatchewan's economy was in other hands. The tariff structure of the Canadian economy, which was designed to exploit the immigrant farm economy, was itself an expression of the political control that the manufacturing and industrial sector in central Canada had over the federal government. If there was any doubt about the political influence of those business classes, it evaporated after the Laurier Liberals had taken power in 1896 espousing free-trade policies, and then proceeded to continue and defend the high-tariff policies demanded by central Canadian business interests. Indeed, before being elected, Laurier's anti-tariff rhetoric could hardly have been more categorical and unequivocal, leaving no doubt about the strength of his opposition to protectionism. "I denounce the policy of protection as bondage—yea, bondage; and I refer to bondage in the same manner in which American slavery was bondage," Laurier said in an 1894 speech in Winnipeg.[3]

This sense of western alienation against outside influences was rooted in other grievances as well. While perhaps not analogous with the economic issues of tariff policy, when the Métis attempted to assert their religious, cultural and language rights in the 1870s and 1880s, it was from the perspective of defending themselves from incursions by central Canada. When Canada annexed the North-West in 1869, it was seen as compensation to the merchant and industrial class in Ontario for accepting a lowering of tariffs as the price for bringing the Maritimes into Confederation. Recognizing the prairies were being cast as an economic chattel of Ontario, Louis Riel sought protection from the imposition of Protestant English values and institutions on the Métis: "Tell them our great thought is to resist being made Irishmen of."[4]

In more concrete terms, what added to this sense of Saskatchewan people not being in control of their economic destiny was the structure of the prairie farm economy they encountered. It was dominated by the large and powerful interests of the railway companies, the Winnipeg Grain Exchange and a small number of elevator companies. In the hands of such oligopoly interests, the system was seen to be stacked against the interests of individual farmers. Farmers saw themselves as economic captives in an industry they believed was willfully, and even maliciously, treating them like pawns.

Complicating this unequal relationship for the individual farmer was the nature of the prairie wheat economy. Unlike most manufactured commodities, demand for the commodity that comes from a renewable resource such as wheat, namely bread, is inelastic. That means demand for wheat is quite stable and largely unresponsive to price changes. In other words, unlike other goods or products, if the price of wheat falls it has little impact on demand for bread. Conversely, and to the benefit of farmers, when wheat prices rise, demand for bread does not decline because the cost of wheat is such a small component in the bread price.[5]

When put into the context of an economy where thousands of individual farmers operate on an independent basis, compared to another sector where only a few producers exist, the market dilemma the farmers face becomes obvious.

A small number of producers in a specific market who face elastic demand for their product are able to recognize the benefits of mutually curtailing output. They realize that, rather than flooding the market with a product few want, they are better to reduce production to the point they can sell what they produce at a price they find acceptable. The lower price thus gets absorbed, in large measure, through less production and resulting unemployment. The key is that the erosion in return on capital investment can be shielded, or at least moderated, from price and market fluctuations by cuts in production and jobs.

However, there is no such luxury in an atomized family farm economy. Thousands of farmers who are independent operators are the exact opposite of an oligopolized market. Their instincts, when prices are down, are to produce and sell more wheat, often in the belief that things are only going to get worse. So, as a result, by acting individually the problem is made worse for everyone. As well, with the family farm a social as well as an economic unit, the option of externalizing the costs through unemployment is not viable. In economic terms for farmers, unemployment is not an abstraction that affects others, as is the case in other industries.

This dilemma for individual farmers was Saskatchewan's dilemma. If grain growing was inherently unstable, then so too would be Saskatchewan because the economic foundation for the province was the wheat-dominated agricultural sector. In effect, the social and economic well-being of the province was directly linked to the ups and downs of agriculture. Just how intimate the link was between grain and the viability of Saskatchewan was identified by a 1910 provincial study into a proposal for government-owned grain elevators:

> The grain is the gold of the province, the gold that is divided between the growers and all other classes. Upon the grain falls the largest share of the burden of the railways, telegraphs, telephones, roads, etc. of the province; of the educational and religious institutions; of the professional classes; and of the machinery of administration and government... The grain of the province needs to be a large and rich crop to be able to pay these tolls, bear these burdens and give the growers a return for their labour, and a profit for their investment.[6]

This economic insecurity was quickly expressed in political terms. It became a powerful and omnipresent force that permanently shaped Saskatchewan's value system and embedded itself in government. With the province's economic well-being intimately linked to agriculture, what emerged was a political economy whereby the interests of farming became synonymous with what were perceived as the common good of all Saskatchewan people. What evolved around this political-economic consensus was a series of farm groups, some imported and others unique to Saskatchewan, that became the means to advance the concerns of agriculture. In fact, the US influence in shaping Saskatchewan's political culture was crucial. As American historian Paul Sharp points out, more than a million Americans migrated northward to Canada and the "last best West" in the early years of the 20th century. "American farmers carried with them an agrarian political experience which had a profound effect upon the political life of the prairie provinces," says Sharp.[7]

One of the first such farm groups was the Grange, which initially surfaced in Ontario in 1872. Originally started in Washington, DC, the Grange opposed monopolies, tariffs and profiteering that lowered farm income. It was seen by some in the US as "a mysterious and secret society."[8] Although the Grange never became a significant force on the Canadian prairies and by 1900 had vanished, it sowed the seeds for farm activism of the future.

In the pre-Saskatchewan days of the North-West, farmer interests were expressed through a series of other groups that rose briefly into prominence before fading from the scene. The Manitoba and North West Farmers Alliance emerged in the early 1880s and lasted long enough for the Prince Albert chapter to draw the ire of the federal government by supporting the land claims of Louis Riel in 1885.

A far more influential farm group was the Patrons of Industry, another US-based populist movement that by 1895 claimed 5,000 members on the Canadian prairies. It also opposed monopolies, specifically the CPR and grain elevator companies, and its agitation spawned a federal Royal Commission that led to the Manitoba Grain Act in 1900, which attempted to break the railway and elevator company control of the grain-handling system.

In terms of shaping farm politics in Saskatchewan, a key movement was the Non-Partisan League, another populist American farm movement that became a factor in Saskatchewan politics immediately after the First World War. Although the League, which formed the state government in North Dakota, never achieved the same magnitude of political success in Saskatchewan, its influence should not be underestimated. As the direct political arm of the populist farm movement, the League did manage to elect one MLA in the 1917 provincial election. Recognizing the Non-Partisan League's farm support, both the Liberals and Conservatives decided against contesting the seat and supported the candidate put forward by the farmers. But the important long-term significance of the League was less overt and far more important than the election of a lone MLA.

What the League did was plant the seeds that grew into the farm-based political parties that followed. The key was its non-partisan nature. By distancing itself from partisan politics and speaking for the interests of farmers, the League undermined both the Liberals and Conservatives and began the process of breaking down provincial political allegiances. In time the situation would be fluid enough that a new party could emerge to challenge the two traditional parties. Although it was unable to break the party discipline of Canadian-style politics, the League did help to energize and inject populist militancy into the farm movement.[9]

In terms of shaping Saskatchewan's political economy, undoubtedly the most important farm group was the Territorial Grain Growers' Association, which formed in 1901. It was renamed the Saskatchewan Grain Growers' Association (SGGA) when the province was created and, for the next 20 years, held far-reaching influence over the provincial Liberal government and the emerging political culture of the province.

The list of farm grievances was long, and almost exclusively directed at the perceived control and manipulation of the grain trade by the corporations that dominated it. The farmers' villains included the railway companies, banks, the grain exchange, terminal and line elevator companies, and the tariff-protected eastern implement and machinery manufacturers.

One of the first successful attempts to break from the grip of such domination was the Manitoba Grain Act, which became known as the Magna Carta of the grain industry. It was adopted in 1900 by the Laurier government in the face of farm protest against monopoly control by the railway and line elevator companies. Farmers believed they were being gouged and unfairly treated by private elevators that the CPR had allowed to be built along its lines. The companies operating country elevators and the CPR were seen to be in collusion, taking advantage of a disorganized farm population. In effect, these elevators had a monopoly because the railway refused to allow farmers to bypass the elevators and load their grain directly. The Manitoba Grain Act, which came as a result of a Royal Commission responding to complaints of farmers, sought to break the monopoly by requiring the railways to build loading platforms so that farmers could load rail cars that they ordered for delivery.

The change failed to resolve the issue and farmers complained the railway was maintaining its control by making loading platforms inaccessible and rail cars for individual farmer use unavailable. Still, the fact that the federal government had responded to farmers demands helped to give impetus to the farm movement.[10]

In Saskatchewan, a direct challenge to the Winnipeg Grain Exchange was mounted in 1906 when the Grain Growers' Grain Company (GGGC) opened an office in Winnipeg and bought a seat on the Grain Exchange. The GGGC was a farmer-owned grain elevator company in the town of Sintaluta that attempted to give farmers greater control by breaking the monopoly of the grain trade. It had been formed by Edward Partridge, an outspoken, mercurial and controversial farm radical, after he was unable to convince the SGGA to become involved in co-operative grain handling and marketing.

In terms of farmer participation and support, the GGGC was very successful and by 1910 as many as 9,000 farmers were marketing their grain through the company.[11] But the farmer-owned company was also a threat to the existing private grain trade and soon lost its seat on the Grain Exchange because it was paying dividends to its members, which contravened the Exchange's regulations. However, such attempts by the private grain trade to banish the farmer-owned company from the Exchange only helped convince farmers they were being exploited.

What provoked the anger of farmers the most about the Winnipeg Grain Exchange was its trading in grain futures. They believed it amounted to gambling and profiteering that had the effect of driving down the price they received for their wheat. Farmers could see no useful purpose for the exchange and believed five companies were controlling the price of grain to the disadvantage of producers. The speculation that came with hedging of grain purchases for the futures market on the Grain Exchange was believed to depress the price so that the profit margin would be larger when the wheat futures purchased from farmers by speculators were sold later.[12]

These sentiments against corporate interests seen as exploiting the Saskatchewan economy were merely extensions of the psychology that opposed high tariffs protecting industry in central Canada. When farm anger with the grain trade and railway monopoly was joined with the deeply rooted opposition to the tariff policy, a powerful populist force was unleashed that became the foundation for Saskatchewan politics.

The focal point for farm sentiment was the Saskatchewan Grain Growers'Association. It was acknowledged as the voice of farmers and held far-reaching influence over provincial government policy until the mid-1920s. Even federal politicians had to pay homage to the SGGA or else risk alienating a powerful grassroots organization.

In the summer of 1910, when Prime Minster Laurier travelled across the prairies, Saskatchewan had 6,000 members in 263 local organizations of the SGGA. The appearance of Laurier served as a rallying point for farmers, who massed at every stop on Laurier's Saskatchewan tour demanding a reduction in tariffs as part of free trade with the US. Saskatchewan farm anger over the tariff had been reignited in 1909 when the secretary of the Canadian Manufacturers Association (CMA) boasted of the organization's economic muscle. G.M. Murray said the CMA was: "like a young giant, ignorant of its power … it could, if it chose, bring several millions of people to the verge of starvation and paralyse the industry of the whole Dominion."[13]

Laurier's tumultuous trip through Saskatchewan was a turning point in farm politics. Although Laurier seemed to heed the opinion of farmers and negotiated a reciprocity agreement with the US in 1911, his government lost the election of that year and the free trade deal died. Again the West had been denied the economic justice it sought. Completely opposed to a reduction in tariffs, the industrial and business interests of Ontario and Quebec had worked to defeat Laurier, free trade and the concerns of prairie farmers. The result reconfirmed the belief in Saskatchewan that the interests of farmers were marginalized by more powerful forces that dominated federal politics. The farmers' unhappiness with Laurier's failure in government to make good on his original promise of reducing the tariff had given way to hope that a Liberal re-election would finally bring free trade for the West. Instead the business class of central Canada had prevailed yet again.

SAB R-A249

William Motherwell, Saskatchewan's first minister of Agriculture, and formerly first president of the Territorial Grain Growers' Association.

What made the 1911 election result even more aggravating for the West was that industrialists rallied to the defeat of a reciprocity deal that would have allowed for free trade in natural products only. In other words, Canadian farm products could have been sold tariff free in the US, but cheaper manufactured US goods would still face a Canadian tariff. The central Canadian business class fought reciprocity not because of what it would do, but because they feared it might eventually lead to wider free trade, where they would lose their economic privilege.

But if the economic needs of Saskatchewan farmers were expendable at the federal level, they certainly weren't for the Liberal administration in Regina. The provincial government paid close heed to the wishes of the SGGA, which was seen as the expression of what farmers wanted from government. Each year the government would adjourn the Legislature so that cabinet ministers and MLAs could attend the annual SGGA convention. To maintain the support of farmers, the government would often quickly turn SGGA resolutions into policy.

It was common for senior officials of the SGGA to become prominent cabinet ministers in government. W.R. Motherwell, the province's first minister of Agriculture, was also the first president of the Territorial Grain Growers' Association, forerunner of the SGGA. At one point, former SGGA president J.A. Maharg left federal politics to accept an invitation to become a provincial cabinet minister. As well, both George Langley and Charles

SAB R-A9093

John A. Maharg, minister of Agriculture in the Martin government, and formerly president of the Saskatchewan Grain Growers' Association.

Dunning were prominent in the SGGA and also served in the Liberal government cabinet. In 1922, Dunning took over from William Martin and spent four years as premier.

Officially, the SGGA declared itself as non-partisan. But clearly it had close ties to the provincial Liberal government, a fact that made some of its members uneasy. As an organization, it recognized the enormous power it wielded over the provincial government and constantly sought to avoid doing anything that might undermine its influence. For example, attempts to get the SGGA involved in commercial activities were blocked because they could jeopardize the organization's unity and sully its image as reflecting the most important and unassailable aspects of life in Saskatchewan. In opposing such commercial activities, Motherwell, writing to his deputy minister in 1914, perhaps best explained how the upright moral qualities of the SGGA were central to life in early Saskatchewan:

> The SGGA should bear much the same relation to the economic life of Saskatchewan and the West as the church bears to the moral and spiritual life of the country. Once a church becomes wealthy and prosperous in material success, the tendency is for its influence in moral and spiritual matters to wane. I cannot but feel that the same would be true of the SGGA. With any organization that exists to mould public opinion and educate the people, it has got to be a case of "root hog, or die."[14]

While the political influence of the farm lobby from the earliest days of Saskatchewan was immense, it was not so great that the SGGA could always dictate policy to the government. An example of how the Walter Scott government did not merely accept the SGGA's position on all agriculture issues came with the so-called elevator issue of 1908–11. When the SGGA called on the province to create a government-owned elevator company as had happened in Manitoba, the Scott government formed a Royal Commission to look into the issue. The elevator commission held public meetings across the province in 1910 to investigate farmers' allegations against the system.

The accusations were aimed at the privately owned country elevator system, the banks, the railway companies and the Winnipeg Grain Exchange. Levelling their sights on the elevator system, farmers complained of artificially low weights and grades, excessive dockage, unfairly low prices for their grade, "skimming" of prices by the mixing of wheat grades, and unduly high freight rates because wheat was not cleaned until after it was shipped. The banks were accused of restricting farm credit and imposing high interest. The railways were said to be making it almost impossible for farmers to use loading platforms so they could bypass the elevator entirely and the Winnipeg Grain Exchange was said to be little more than a disguise for a grain trade controlled by the powerful few.

These issues went to the core of farm political sentiment and could not be ignored by government. With the SGGA demanding the government form a publicly owned elevator system, Scott appointed a commission to study the issue. But, from the outset, Scott opposed the idea of a government-owned system and SGGA officials had told the premier privately that they would be willing to consider alternatives.[15]

In its report, the three-member commission unanimously recommended against a government-owned elevator system. In rejecting the idea, the commission raised doubts about the feasibility of public ownership:

> The government would be at a disadvantage arising from the fact universally admitted that there is a general disposition to exact the utmost possible from the public treasury while not giving the utmost return... The government would be at a disadvantage arising from the fact that political influences would tend to make themselves felt. Whatever party happened to be in power would be tempted to run the system in its own political interest.[16]

But in historical terms, more important than the rejection of a government-owned system was the commission's endorsation of a farmer-owned elevator company. It said "a solution must be sought along the line of co-operation by the farmers." As for the government's role, it should be limited to making low-interest capital available for the farmers co-operative.

In March 1911, less than a year after the commission's report, the Saskatchewan Co-operative Elevator Company Act was passed by the legislature. It gave the new company the "power to construct, acquire, maintain and operate grain elevators ... to buy and sell grain and generally to do all things incidental to the production, storage and marketing of grain." The legislation

SAB R-B3514

Farm labourers at harvest time (no date). During the settlement era, and for years afterward, the provincial economy of Saskatchewan depended almost exclusively on wheat production.

also provided for the government to loan money to the co-operative for up to 85% of the cost of purchasing or building the elevators it needed.[17]

The co-operative elevator act was a major effort by government to meet economic problems of individual farmers. But it certainly wasn't the only example of government attempting to deal with the economic insecurities readily apparent in the farm sector during the height of immigration to the province. Before long, a body of statutory evidence was amassed showing how the Saskatchewan government recognized the problems faced by farmers and sought to alleviate, if not eliminate, them.

There was the Seed Grain Act of 1908 that provided up to $250 for seed grain to farmers suffering crop failure. By 1912, the Hail Insurance Act was in place, based on draft legislation presented by the SGGA. Another crucial effort to deal with farm financial problems was 1913 legislation setting up the Saskatchewan Co-operative Farm Mortgage Association. It provided mortgage money at interest rates equal to the cost of money raised by government guarantees of the mortgage bonds. The Farm Implements Act of 1915 was drafted to protect farmers from implement salesmen acting as agents for the manufacturer. As well, homestead legislation was changed to protect wives losing homestead rights when their husbands used the homestead for security.

In the wake of a 1914 crop failure in the southwest, the government passed legislation that put in place a federal-provincial agreement providing money to ease the situation, "owing to the severe drought which prevailed during the past summer and that the crops in those districts were almost a total failure and that the settlers are in many cases destitute."[18] In the same year, the government passed legislation to create the Saskatchewan Co-operative Creamery that provided government loans at an interest rate of no more than 6%. The Saskatchewan Farm Loans Act, in place in 1917, created the farm loan board. It provided 30-year loans at interest rates based on the cost of money to government for use by farmers on permanent improvements to their farm property. With special consent, the subsidized loans could be used to purchase additional property.[19] As well, there were the extensive statutory loan guarantees extended to the railways as an incentive to expand the rail network to all corners of the province's grain-growing region.

While far from a comprehensive list of government efforts to moderate the economic reality of farming, such legislation reflected the omnipresent influence of farming in the economic, political and social life of the province. This dominance of agriculture was acknowledged and accepted as what should guide the public policy of Saskatchewan from its earliest days.

Nowhere was this expressed more as an article of faith than in the 1914 report of the provincial grain markets commission. It had been established by the government to study the wheat economy and determine what could be done by government to support and strengthen the lot of farmers.

Ironically, the report acknowledged that grain farming, at the time, was not economic. Among its conclusions, the commission stated: "exclusive grain raising in Saskatchewan as generally practised by even our best farmers is not remunerative at the present time."[20] But at the same time time, the report concluded Saskatchewan's future was inextricably bound to farming:

> The prosperity of Saskatchewan depends and always must depend on agriculture. This is a pioneer province and pioneer agriculture must with us consist principally in grain production. Under our conditions of soil, climate and markets, grain production offers at once the simplest, easiest and quickest means to permanent agriculture development.[21]

In setting out its remedies, the commission pointed to ways of shaping the farm economy to better serve the economic interests of farmers. Among the remedies: credit being "supplied at cost instead of at a large profit"; elimination of the tariff; reduction in the freight rate on manufactured goods imported to the province; continued improvement of country roads; extension of co-operative grain marketing companies; and, extension of railways to districts "not yet adequately served." Among the more bizarre suggestions of the commission was its call—if deemed feasible by engineers—for a system of navigable inland canals and waterways "from the heart of the grain-growing areas to the head of the lakes."[22]

Clearly, it had become apparent to the Saskatchewan government and farm activists alike that the wheat economy had significant structural deficiencies that were the product of nature, politics and outside economic forces. While the natural endowment of the province—its distance from export positions, the risks of drought or early frost—could not be changed, the structural problems perceived to be man-made, could be adjusted by people. The question, of course, was how could the agricultural interests of individual farmers in Saskatchewan be brought to bear on what was seen as a predatory system explicitly designed to exploit the province?

Out of this sense of victimization grew the realization that, to counter-balance more powerful political and economic interests that controlled the province's destiny, the farm population had to somehow unite. Individually, farmers had no power to determine their fate and were entirely disposable within the grain-marketing system. Only if they co-operated and pooled their efforts could they hope to take some control over their economic fate and enhance the financial sustainability of the family farm.

In a real sense, the provincial elevator commission report helped to define this emerging political culture. By rejecting a system of government-owned elevators and proposing a farmer-owned co-operative system, the idea that farmers could take responsibility for, and control of, their economic lives was formally legitimized. The idea of co-operation was proposed and endorsed as a means to empower the farm population.

Two years later, the Saskatchewan Agriculture Credit Commission reiterated the belief that co-operation was the principle that should determine the shape of the Saskatchewan farm economy. In looking for solutions to credit problems faced by farmers, the commission travelled to Europe and studied the structure of agriculture. It pointed to co-operation among farmers as the model to apply in Saskatchewan:

> In their attempts to grapple with similar problems, European countries have profoundly changed their whole rural economy. They frankly recognized that under modern complex conditions, organized industries preyed upon the unorganized. And the agricultural industry, being unorganized, suffered. In every country in Western Europe, farmers have organized after the same fashion, namely the application of the co-operative principle to agricultural production and distribution and finance. This has, without a single exception, contributed not only to the economic improvement of the farmer and the conservation of agricultural resources, but also to the educational development of the individual and the progress and integration of rural society.[23]

While farmers had long since recognized the need to work together in formal associations, their efforts primarily had been directed at getting government to respond to their needs. The next phase in that maturation of the farm movement in Saskatchewan was to embrace co-operation as a means for power in the market, rather than just in government.

The clearest example of this was the emergence of the notion of orderly marketing and, concurrent with it, the formation of the Saskatchewan Wheat

Pool in 1923. Although the Saskatchewan Co-operative Elevator Company was operating by 1911 and a year later had 139 elevators, it failed to adequately meet the perceived needs of farmers. In spite of generous government aid, high volumes and, ironically, larger storage fees than private companies, the Co-operative Elevator Company profits were declining. As well, it was viewed as less than democratic, unresponsive to farmers and too closely tied to the SGGA and the provincial government.[24] The SGGA was itself seen as part of the establishment, controlled by Anglo-Saxons to the exclusion of non-English-speaking immigrants. When a rival and more radical farm group called the Famers Union of Canada, Saskatchewan Section emerged in 1921 to challenge the SGGA, support was building for a more aggressive market approach by farmers that eventually led to the creation of the Wheat Pool.

Giving crucial impetus to the pool movement were the lessons learned from a one-year experiment in pooled selling of wheat under a Wheat Board created by the federal government in 1919. The board was created under terms of the War Measures Act as a monopoly to supply wheat to Canada's allies during the war. By pooling all Canadian wheat, farmers received a stable price. And even better for Saskatchewan farmers, prices reached record highs because of the war, which had disrupted production throughout Europe. When the board was disbanded in 1920 and the Winnipeg Grain Exchange, which had suspended operations, was reopened, prices quickly began to fall as equilibrium returned to the market as supply increased in the wake of the war. Wheat that in August 1920 was selling for $2.73 a bushel had fallen to $1.11 by 1921. For farmers, the idea of the Winnipeg Grain Exchange being a den of thieves was again confirmed. The evidence seen as proof was that prices collapsed when the government-controlled Wheat Board died and grain marketing fell back into the hands of profit-seeking speculators. Not surprisingly demands for the Wheat Board to be reconstituted grew across the prairies. The federal government was willing to act, but wanted all three prairie provinces to endorse the move. When the Manitoba legislature voted the idea down, the plan for another Wheat Board disintegrated.

Convinced that pooling wheat was the solution, the newly formed Farmers Union began pushing for a co-operative wheat company that would buy and sell Saskatchewan farmers' wheat. Quickly a consensus formed around the idea, much of it fuelled by the charismatic figure of Aaron Sapiro, an American from California brought in by the Farmers Union to espouse the wonders of co-operation. Sapiro was a powerful figure who spoke with a religous fervour that transfixed rural audiences as he barnstormed the province.

The SGGA, which was losing members to the Farmers Union, endorsed the wheat pool idea, as did the provincial government. The campaign for the pool took on almost a religious fervour and created a disparate coalition of interests that included banks, boards of trade, 20 life insurance companies, service clubs, retail merchant organizations and municipal councils. The provincial government pitched in by publishing posters backing the pool idea and urging farmers to sign contracts for delivery of their wheat to the pool.[25]

But the coalition of interests was still not enough for the organizing drive to reach its goal of getting signed contracts covering 50% of the province's wheat production by a deadline of September 1923. It would be another year before the Saskatchewan Wheat Pool would meet its target and begin buying and selling wheat under contract from members of the Pool.

Running throughout this period of rising prairie farm activism was a parallel political process that reflected the clamour for change. The election of the Conservatives and defeat of Laurier's platform of free trade in 1911 had convinced many that the "old-line parties" could not be trusted to support the interests of farmers. The farm unrest spilled into direct political action with the rise of the loosely knit Progressive movement and spectacular, if transitory, success in the election of farmer-based governments at the provincial level. Meanwhile in Ottawa, a wave of western farmer MPs arrived as a force on the floor of the House of Commons. In 1919 the United Farmers of Ontario formed government in that province. The United Farmers of Alberta took power in 1921 and a year later the United Farmers of Manitoba were elected to govern. At the federal level in the 1921 election, farmer candidates ran under the title of Progressives and won 23% of the vote and took 65 seats, including 15 of 16 in Saskatchewan.

As a coalition of mostly farm interests under the Progressives' umbrella, the collection of farmer MPs shunned party politics and refused Opposition status, even though they were the second largest political grouping in the House of Commons. As populists, they sought to somehow remain above politics by renouncing any official status in the Commons, or in government. Their sole aim was to influence government policy in the interests of agriculture.

The focal point for this rise of farmer-based political parties was the Canadian Council of Agriculture (CCA). It produced what amounted to a farmers' platform in 1916 that became known as the New National Policy. The platform took dead aim at the high-tariff policy, which the CCA said spawned combines and trusts that exploited farmers and led to rural depopulation. The western, farm-based Progressive movement became the political vehicle that carried the CCA platform into federal elections.

It was no accident that Saskatchewan, a province with the biggest economic stake in agriculture, somehow avoided the wave of provincial farmer governments that emerged throughout this period. A key reason was that the SGGA served as the Progressive movement's entry point into the province. Moreover, the close ties between the SGGA and the provincial Liberal government tended to defuse farmer anger in the provincial political arena. By being careful to heed farm interests in the province expressed through the SGGA, the Liberals were able to maintain their hold on power as a rising cacophony of farm revolt reverberated across the nation.

In 1917 the SGGA endorsed the CCA's Farmers Platform. The Progressive movement in Saskatchewan kept its focus on federal politics and assumed the posture that "we've always got what we demanded provincially and where we need to press for power is at Ottawa."[26]

Still, it took deft political maneuvering by the provincial Liberals to avoid being swept aside in the political tide that had led to the rise of the Progressives in federal politics. In fact provincial Liberals were livid with provincial agriculture minister W.R. Motherwell in 1919 when he left provincial politics to run for the Liberals in a federal by-election in Assiniboia. His adversary was independent farmers' candidate O.R. Gould, who was backed by the likes of farm leaders such as Edward A. Partridge, Henry Wise Wood of The United Farmers of Alberta and J.A. Maharg. Mortified by the prospect of being associated with a candidate running against the farmers' candidate, the provincial Liberals did not go near the by-election, which Gould won handily. Then, in 1921, prior to provincial and federal elections, Premier Martin officially severed the provincial wing of the party from the federal Liberals in a bid to distance himself as much as possible from the national party.

Clearly, then, the reason the Saskatchewan Liberal government remained relatively immune from the spreading political farm revolt was because it was able to maintain its image as a government faithful to the interests of farmers. While there were signs of erosion in the provincial Liberals' political base by the early-to-mid 1920s, the party had done much over the years to institutionalize a political economy that was deeply rooted in the ethics of a rural farm society.

There could be no doubting that as the 1920s drew to a close in Saskatchewan, the convergence of politics and the farm economy had shaped a unique society on the prairies. In little more than two decades, the province had been flooded with immigrants. To cope, it had produced an expensive and elaborate social and economic structure that hinged entirely on what was demonstrably a tenuous and unpredictable wheat economy. But cracks in the Saskatchewan promised land myth were clearly evident in the later years of the 1920s. Outwardly, there was impressive growth and reason for optimism. But beneath the surface were signs of economic trouble and social tension. At celebrations around the province on July 1, 1927, marking the 60th anniversary of Confederation, the theme was "unity in diversity," in recognition of the many ethnic groups—including Indians and Métis—who made up the province. But earlier that same year the Ku Klux Klan had entered the province and began organizing. Less than a month before the July 1 celebrations, a crowd estimated at 8,000–10,000 attended a Ku Klux Klan "Konclave" in Moose Jaw, the largest KKK event ever in Canada. At the same time, the economic decline of Saskatchewan in relative terms to the rest of Canada was underway, as resource production in Ontario, Quebec and British Columbia surpassed the growth of the wheat economy.[27]

SAB R-A1641

Postcard of a cross burning by the Ku Klux Klan, May 24, 1928.

It was the recognition of this economic vulnerability and underlying social tensions that animated the politics of the province and drew people into the debate over how to reconcile the vagaries of the farm economy with the instinctive need for a sense of personal and collective security.

But this emergence of farm activism spawned over many years brought with it a fundamental shift in the ideological underpinnings of Saskatchewan. A society that originally was free-market oriented, galvanized by the fight against the tariffs of the National Policy and the monopolistic and oligopolistic nature of the grain trade, embraced a different model for itself than it preached for others. The move towards farmers' co-operatives, the pooling of wheat and demands for a government-controlled wheat board were attempts by farmers to cartelize the wheat market and inhibit price competition. As economist Abraham Rotstein noted: "With nary a blush, virtue had turned into vice and vice into virtue; competition and monopoly had changed places."[28]

In retrospect, this change is not surprising and is even logical, given the realization that the economics of Saskatchewan's wheat economy were fragile. A combination of instinct and fear was driving economic and political life in Saskatchewan. People knew the wheat economy was a house of cards. Instinctively they feared that someday it would collapse. They wouldn't have to wait long for their fears to be realized.

Six	The Changing Myth

"Thirty per cent of Saskatchewan soils may be considered either first class or moderately good wheat lands and a further 25 per cent as fair for purposes of wheat production. Forty-five per cent of the settled area is poor or very poor wheat land, incapable, over a period of years and with normal prices for wheat, of yielding sufficient to cover the costs of production."

(Government of Saskatchewan brief to Royal Commission
on Dominion-Provincial Relations, December 1937)

No event, or era, has done more to permanently shape Saskatchewan's political economy than the twin calamities of drought and depression of the 1930s. The "Dirty Thirties" have become so deeply embedded in the psychology of Saskatchewan that those years haunt the province still. If there was a defining moment, a time when the modern Saskatchewan ethos, as we know it today, was born, it came during the economic and social tragedy of the 1930s.

With the lost years of that decade, Saskatchewan underwent a fundamental change. The seeds of false expectations and optimism that had been so carefully planted and nurtured as part of National Policy, finally withered in the bleakness of the Dirty Thirties. The apparent prosperity of a new society that was sustained by a flood of people seeking the economic opportunity of free farm land that lured them to Saskatchewan, turned into a mirage. The founding myth of Saskatchewan had been shattered.

It was a cruel way for the dream to die. The toll in terms of suffering for Saskatchewan people during the drought and depression of the 1930s was enormous. At one point in 1937, fully two-thirds of the province's population was receiving relief from the government. The depth of economic and social deprivation in Saskatchewan was unmatched anywhere in Canada during what was a period of economic upheaval throughout the nation, and the world.

Although the scars left by the dust bowl years reflect the pain of that time, they also represent an important point of departure in the province's political and economic history. Not only did the original, defining mythology of Saskatchewan perish with the Dirty Thirties, but a new identity, this one deeply tempered by a sense of vulnerability, rather than consumed and driven by false hope, emerged from the depths of the Great Depression.

Curiously this new sense of self, a Saskatchewan *zeitgeist* if you will, has had a paradoxical impact on the province and its people. While the 1930s brought a realization that the original notion of Saskatchewan as a promised land for those seeking a new life was unattainable, the province has never been able to completely let go of its original hope. Thus, the politics of the province have since become an effort to sustain what the 1930s told us was a mythological view of the province as a place with vast economic potential. In many respects, one myth was merely replaced with another. The new myth is deeply rooted in a belief that institutional reform and economic control through political means would allow Saskatchewan to achieve its full potential. The promised land would be politically redefined by Saskatchewan people themselves, rather than imposed on them by others.

If the 1930s demonstrated in the harshest terms that the original promise of the province was unrealistic, it also produced a gritty kind of survival instinct. The Depression experience made Saskatchewan people determined to deal with reality, hostile and threatening though it might be, and to survive and thrive in spite of it. The people of the province became infused with the notion that the Dirty Thirties added a strength of character, and dedication to overcoming the odds, that further strengthened the pioneer spirit of perseverance and community in Saskatchewan. The fact is that suffering is a critical element in helping to define a community and shape its sense of shared identity and destiny. It is most often expressed at the national level, in terms of nationalism, but the same is true for sub-national units like a province. As the French scholar Ernest Renan argues: "the nation, like the individual, is the culmination of a long past of endeavours, sacrifice and devotion. Suffering in common unifies more than joy does."[1]

In that sense, the Dirty Thirties have become an emotional anchor and political reference point for the province. The trauma of those years has endured down through the past seven decades and is evident in every facet of Saskatchewan life, whether politics, the arts, business, our social structures or the general world view of people from Saskatchewan.

So great was the social turmoil, economic dislocation and psychological trauma that the Dirty Thirties have become part of Saskatchewan folklore. Virtually every family in the province has its own oral history of that decade. Grandparents and parents pass down the bleak stories of the grim reality of Saskatchewan in the 1930s, when countless men climbed aboard empty railway boxcars to "ride the rails" looking for work. There are stories of days so dark from dust storms that a brilliant midday sun was transformed into an eerie moon in a depressing sky cloaked by a suffocating gray haze. Parched lips, throats choked by dust, and a sky alive with grasshoppers have become part of the vivid images of the Dirty Thirties. They are etched in the minds of those born many years later, but have grown to understand what the Dirty Thirties meant to Saskatchewan's soul.

Unable to escape the memory, we have tried to reconcile ourselves with it. It has been manifest in a reverence for nature that has deep religious undercurrents. We recognize the power of nature and our vulnerability to forces greater than ourselves that are beyond our control. It has forged a sense of community and a recognition of our interdependency as crucial to the province's economic and social stability.

This awe of nature in Saskatchewan can be either exhilarating or foreboding. Before the 1930s there was an awareness of nature as crucial to Saskatchewan's well-being, but there was not the sense of respect that exists today. In the 1930s we were humbled by nature, and ever since we have treated it with the esteem worthy of a power that controls our economic destiny.

The sense of our fate being inextricably bound to nature has been a powerful theme running through Saskatchewan literature since the Dirty Thirties. It is part of our conscious and subconscious awareness that flows from that pivotal time in our history. It is reflected in both romantic and realist terms by many Saskatchewan writers.

There are countless examples of nature as the theme that unites the Saskatchewan consciousness in writing about the prairie ethos. Nature and God are at the core of W.O. Mitchell's classic *Who Has Seen the Wind*. In personal accounts of growing up on the prairie the relationship of man and nature is key, whether it's James Minifie's *Homesteader* or James Gray's depiction of life in Saskatchewan and the struggle to reclaim the land laid waste by the 1930s entitled *Men Against the Desert*. Sharon Butala's writing is filled with the same fusion of people and nature in her novels about the Saskatchewan southwest. In *The Gates of the Sun* she talks of the sun beating down on the land:

> There was never enough rain. All summer long the sky was endless, clear blue, high, empty clouds, and from its quarter of the sky, the sun burnt down, turning all growth to yellow, then to brown, and finally to a dead grey."[2]

But perhaps nowhere is the role of nature in the Saskatchewan spirit captured better than by Robert Collins in *Butter Down the Well*, his tale of a prairie childhood:

> That was my Saskatchewan—cruel and sensual by turns. Our living room walls were hung with cutout pictures from calendars and magazines; woodland streams, English stone bridges, billowing oaks—the kind of landscape we wished we had. Outside the naked telephone poles marched single file beside tedious dirt roads, and grey fence posts leaned crazily into the double-strand barbed wire, like drunks tottering home in the arms of friends. Yet deep down—I know it now—I loved our prairie best. It was uncompromising. It was magnificent.

The wind and sky orchestrated our moods. The wind played the tunes, the sky lit the stage. Together they could make us laugh or cry. When the sun shone, our spirits turned to green and gold… The clouds came, legion upon legion, darkening the pasture sloughs and casting shadows on our souls. We looked to the sky for portents. Did that black cloud carry rain or dust or hail?

And the wind? It never rested… Some people were driven to suicide by the wind. Some of us were soothed by it, and still are.

I knew so intimately the smells and tastes, the language and rhythms of the land that even now if I were dropped there not knowing the time or date, I could say "this is a February afternoon because the long shadows always slant off the sharp snowdrifts, just so, at four o'clock" or "this is August because August smells of sage grass and ripening wheat." The seasons ran their cycles, as sure as life and death."[3]

But all the romantic literature that has evolved from the Dirty Thirties still does not hide the truth. It merely seeks to romanticize it and make it less painful by transforming it into a source of emotional strength. For almost a decade, Saskatchewan was filled with visible suffering. Nowhere is the emotional bleakness and the stark reality of the Dirty Thirties more palpable than in the writing of Sinclair Ross. In his acclaimed novel *As For Me and My House*, Ross captures the grim truth of life in small-town Saskatchewan, through the diary entries of a Mrs. Bentley writing about life with Philip, her frustrated clergyman husband in the fictional town of Horizon.

The psychological impact of the drought and dreary life on the prairies is evident throughout Ross's book. In his analysis of *As For Me And My House*, Henry Kreisel sees "two polarities" in the pitting of man against an often-hostile environment. One is man as "giant-conqueror," the other is "insignificant dwarf" that form the two polarities of the prairie state of mind.[4] The two come together in one particular passage from Ross's novel:

The last hymn was staidly orthodox, but through it there seemed to mount something primitive, something that was less a response to Philip's sermon and scripture reading than to the grim futility of their own lives. Five years in succession now they've been blown out, dried out, hailed out; and it was as if in the face of so blind and uncaring a universe they were trying to assert themselves, to insist upon their own meaning and importance.[5]

But to understand fully the economic, social and emotional toll the 1930s had on Saskatchewan, it is important to get beyond the filter of romantic and realist literature and examine the harsh facts of life. One must understand the dismal science of economics, the impact of the Great Depression on Saskatchewan, its root causes and how Saskatchewan was essentially power-less to significantly alter its fate in the face of global forces. Specifically, that means exploring how the attempt by farmers and government to use their collective market power to influence the price of wheat often only made the economic situation even worse.

If statistics don't lie, then from 1930–38 there was no worse place in Canada than Saskatchewan. In its exhaustive final report released in 1940 that explored the problems confronting Canada in the 1930s, the Royal Commission on Dominion-Provincial Relations—known best as the Rowell-Sirois Report—referred to the "well known Saskatchewan debacle" when it spoke of the economic chaos of the 1930s. It admitted there was no point doing statistical analysis between Saskatchewan and other provinces because the situation in Saskatchewan was so bad that it rendered such comparisons "unrealistic."[6] Still, the litany of economic data helps to put the extent of the problem Saskatchewan faced in some perspective.

The situation in December 1937 was explained by provincial attorney general T.C. Davis, who presented the provincial government's brief to the Royal Commission during hearings in Regina. Davis said that the combination of drought and depression, coupled with "oppressive national policies" such as high tariffs, had created a financial burden for the province that was "well-nigh unsupportable."[7]

It is worth noting that the sense of grievance against the federal govern-ment, and specifically its tariff policies, still animated the political debate in Saskatchewan. The economic suffering of the province in the 1930s was seen as intensified by high tariffs. As Davis told the Royal Commission hearings:

> For the province of Saskatchewan in particular, where it is almost completely true to say that everything is bought in a protected market and everything is sold in a free market, the consequences of the protectionist policy have been more disas-trous perhaps, than for any other political division of Canada.[8]

In arguing Saskatchewan's case against the tariff, the provincial govern-ment relied on an analysis of the tariff by Professor N.M. Rogers, who pre-pared an economic brief for the commission on behalf of the Nova Scotia government. The Saskatchewan government argued the tariff amounted to a "dead-weight burden" that was felt disproportionately by Saskatchewan:

> The nature of our economy, characterized as it is by intensive specialization in the production of an export staple and by the absence of secondary industries, makes this inevitable.[9]

Based on Rogers's analysis of the provincial distribution of tariff subsidies, only tiny Prince Edward Island fared worse than Saskatchewan. He found the proportional distribution of the tariff subsidy per capita in Saskatchewan was $3.55. The per capita tariff benefit to Ontario was $64.42 and $46.23 for Quebec. By comparison, the three other western provinces received far more economic benefit from the tariff than Saskatchewan. The subsidy per capita in BC was $32.03, in Manitoba it was $28.44 and in Alberta it was $11.22.[10]

To make matters worse, in the midst of the Great Depression, Saskatchewan's staple export economy was further squeezed by the protectionist response to the economic dilemma. Facing a depressed wheat market, it was crucial that farmers be able to cut their input costs as a means to offset their falling income. However, just the opposite was happening because tariffs were being increased, which added to the cost of farming.

But clearly the tariff was not the cause of the collapse of Saskatchewan's economy in the 1930s. It only aggravated the problem.

So what did cause the economic downfall of Saskatchewan? There is no one answer, but rather a complex web of factors that together help to explain what happened. They include the structural faults in a one-crop farm economy; the recurring drought of the 1930s; the collapse of the world economy in an era of rampant protectionism; and, the ill-fated and misguided attempts of Saskatchewan farmers to manipulate the price of wheat. Underpinning it all was the Saskatchewan myth, which had provided the psychological foundation for the province's economy and society.

Of all those factors, the most significant—in terms of understanding Saskatchewan's political economy—was the belief that economic problems could be resolved, or at least moderated, by farmers taking control of the marketing of their wheat. That notion had become the theology of farm activism, especially after the First World War when high wheat prices created by the war had collapsed. As noted earlier, during the latter stages of the war, the Canadian government had suspended the operations of the Winnipeg Grain Exchange and created a Wheat Board to market all prairie wheat. The high world price for wheat became associated in farmers' minds with the orderly marketing of the Wheat Board and not the economic fallout of war in Europe. Thus, when the war ended, the Wheat Board was disbanded and prices fell, the idea became entrenched that the key to maximizing price was through orderly marketing, such as a wheat board.[11]

But in terms of Saskatchewan coming to terms with its own inherent and fundamental economic weaknesses, the issue became how to deal with a congenitally volatile world wheat market. At the core of the solution, people believed, was to take more control of their economic destiny by exercising greater market power. The problem was not the rapid immigration and unsustainable growth of Saskatchewan. It was the greed and external control of capitalists. Thus, what emerged from the depths of the Dirty Thirties was the socialist belief that the economic collapse was proof the capitalist economic system itself was deeply flawed and needed to be replaced. It accepted the premise that the one-crop economic society produced by immigration-driven rapid expansion was sustainable if the economic structure was fundamentally changed. In other words, because Saskatchewan was the product of politics in the form of the National Policy, its economic problems could be fixed through political action that redesigned its economic structure.

Ironically, evidence the Saskatchewan wheat economy was not economically sustainable, at least in terms of maintaining a predictable and acceptable level of family farm income, came from the experiences of the Saskatchewan Wheat Pool. Organized to maximize returns to farmers by eliminating profit-taking by others as part of the grain trade, the Wheat Pool was unable to achieve its goals. The theory behind the Wheat Pool, which joined with the pools in Alberta and Manitoba, was to form a mini-cartel called the Canadian Co-operative Wheat Producers Ltd. that would attempt to affect, or force up, the price for grain on the world market. In other words, the objective was to use a collectivist business model to pursue the maximization of profits for the benefits of farmers. The instrument was the Central Selling Agency (CSA), which pooled prairie wheat and sold it directly to customers in the US or Europe, or on the Winnipeg Grain Exchange.

In world economic terms, the beginning of the Great Depression is considered to be Black Tuesday, October 29, 1929 when the stock market crashed. But for Saskatchewan, the decade of the Dirty Thirties and Depression took its stranglehold on the province on July 10, 1930. That was the day when the CSA set the initial price for wheat at 70¢ a bushel, down from $1 a year earlier. A few days later, the initial price had fallen to 60¢.[12]

This price collapse came after more than a year of effort by the Pools, through the CSA, to prop up the world price by withholding wheat from the market. In the meantime, the CSA was selling modest amounts on the higher-priced Winnipeg Grain Exchange and buying wheat futures in attempts to bolster prices. All the while cheap wheat from Argentina was flooding onto the European market and displacing Canadian wheat, which the CSA was holding back in the belief that Argentine wheat stocks would diminish and the price rise.

This attempt at price manipulation by the pools was doomed. A key reason was because the pools refused to hedge the wheat they bought from farmers. It had long been a basic tenet to the pool movement that speculation in wheat futures created a downward pressure on price, especially in the early delivery months of the crop year when most farmers were selling their wheat to grain elevator companies. As such, the pools carried the entire risk should the price fall from the time they purchased wheat from farmers to when it was sold.[13]

The $1 a bushel advance of 1929, even though it came at a time when the Winnipeg exchange spot price was $1.44, proved to be a disaster. Before long the pools were trapped in a dilemma at least partly of their own making. The debts of the CSA reached record highs of $74.9 million, while it held unsold wheat inventories of $105.3 million, in part due to a huge 1928 crop that was of low quality and difficult to market. With world prices already low, the pools could not unload their backlog of wheat because it would push prices down even further.[14]

At the same time the CSA was being attacked for its attempt to control the market. In January 1930, *Barron's* magazine in the US criticised the pools for "this most audacious and most gigantic speculation in the history of the grain trade."[15] Even the mayor of Winnipeg was blaming the growing unemployment rate in 1930 on the Pools, saying that by not shipping grain the Pools were forcing the railways to lay off workers.

Trapped in a downward spiral of wheat prices, the Pool found itself stockpiling wheat it bought from its members. And as its inventory of wheat grew, its value declined steadily. At the same time, the Pool was under mounting pressure from the banks, which extended credit only if the Pool paid farmers 15% less for their wheat than the current street price on the Winnipeg Grain Exchange. With prices falling, clearly that differential was evaporating, and with it the banks' line of credit to the CSA. Refusing to hedge the wheat it purchased by offsetting it with future sales, the CSA was carrying the full risk of loss should prices fall before the wheat it purchased had been sold.

A crisis was briefly averted in November 1930 when the provincial and federal governments agreed to guarantee bank credit to the CSA. But in return, the three prairie Pools gave up control of the CSA to the federal government and prime minister R.B. Bennett appointed John McFarland, a veteran of the private grain trade, as general manager of the CSA. McFarland quickly closed CSA sales offices abroad and announced:

> The only possible permanent solution of the depression in the world wheat situation is a proportionate reduction of acreage by all wheat producing countries.[16]

By late December 1930 wheat prices fell to a record low of 50¢ a bushel. A few months later the CSA was officially out of business, the three Pools reverted to being elevator companies only, and the Saskatchewan Wheat Pool's share of the CSA's $22.1 million loss was $13.3 million.

The experience of the Wheat Pools demonstrated that while there are benefits to collective and orderly marketing of wheat in smoothing the market's daily ups and downs, it has no impact on the global market situation. The cyclical fluctuations are beyond the collective action of prairie farmers, who lack the market power to have any price influence in terms of either supply or demand.[17]

More pointedly, the 1930s demonstrated how Saskatchewan's one-dimensional farm economy was tied to forces beyond merely Ottawa and the business interests of central Canada, but the world economy itself. What had happened was that the growth of protectionism after the First World War laid the foundation for the world economic collapse that would eventually swallow Saskatchewan. It's important, therefore, that Saskatchewan, with a wheat economy so intimately tied to the global economy, be seen in the context of the world economic forces at the time.

The nature of international economic relations changed dramatically after the war. The new national boundaries in Europe resulting from the Treaty of Versailles, the technological advances spurred by the war effort, and Europe's return to agricultural production created an entirely new economic order. Not only did wheat prices fall from artificially high levels during the war, but competition increased.

SAB R-A4823
Horse pulling wagon along road filled by drifting soil, during the Dirty Thirties.

However, instead of meeting the competition, nations turned inward and sought remedy in the old, nationalist, protectionist solutions.

For its part, the US in the 1920s followed a policy of protectionism and inflation. While the US money supply remained constant, credit mushroomed by 61%, going from $45.3 billion in 1921 to more than $73 billion by July 1929. As well, the US followed a parallel policy of protectionism, first with the Fordney-MacCumber Tariff Act of 1922 and then the infamous Smoot-Hawley Tariff of 1930 that effectively triggered a world depression by bringing the global trading system to a halt. By 1931, bank failures were spreading throughout Europe, and in 1931–32 there were 5,096 bank failures in the US, with deposits of more than $3 billion. Simultaneously, countries were forced off the gold standard, credit evaporated and international monetary chaos ensued.[18]

Ominously, during the 1925–30 period, world agricultural stocks increased by 50%. Although such a market overhang looked worrisome, it had no immediate impact while money was being pumped into the reconstruction of Europe. It wasn't until that artificial stimulus was played out that the economic consequences of protectionism came down like an avalanche on the world trading system. Then, when the stock market collapsed, nervous international lenders called in their loans at a time when debtor nations faced rising tariffs and were unable to increase exports to deal with their balance of payment problems.

SAB R-A3368
Great Depression, drifting soil near Cadillac, Saskatchewan, 1937.

A rapid, chain-reaction crisis unfolded. Europe's ability to export into the US and earn the foreign exchange to import wheat and other foodstuffs was blocked by the Smoot-Hawley Tariff. To protect its farm population, Europe responded by drastically raising its tariffs and restrictions on food imports. The result was predictable. Increasing world agricultural supplies, higher trade barriers and falling consumption due to contracting world investment led to historic declines in prices for agricultural products and raw materials.[19] The entire international economic system, which requires a hegemonic nation to ensure discipline, was descending into chaos. Great Britain was in a period of decline and no longer willing, or able, to act as the economic leader it had been for almost a century. The United States had emerged from the war as the world's new economic power, but it followed its isolationist instincts and was unwilling to assume the role of a hegemon to stabilize the world economy.

In his analysis of the root causes of the Great Depression, Charles Kindleberger points to a number of factors, including the overproduction of primary products such as wheat in the last half of the 1920s. But more critical was the US unwillingness to step in to stabilize the world economy when Great Britain withdrew from that role after the First World War:

> The world economic system was unstable unless some country stabilized it, as Britain had done in the 19th century and up to 1913. In 1929, the British couldn't and the United States wouldn't. When every country turned to protect its national private interest, the world public interest went down the drain, and with it the private interests of all.[20]

As a result, nations attempted to resolve problems by imposing their own national policies and controls, each seeking to protect its own interest at the expense of others, the classic "beggar-thy-neighbour" approach to economic crisis. But in what had become an ever-more interdependent world after the First World War, individual interest did not add up to collective welfare. Every weapon in the arsenal of economic autarky was used. Economically untenable positions were protected, high-cost producers were kept in business and obsolete equipment was preserved by rising tariffs, import quotas, cartels, government subsidies and stabilization of prices.[21]

Sucked into this international vortex was the fragile Saskatchewan farm economy. But lest we consider ourselves the innocent victims of sinister economic forces, it is worth noting the efforts by the wheat pools to control prices were very much part of the perverse international economic pattern—and problem—of protectionism during the pre-Depression period. Like other economic sectors, the Saskatchewan farm economy failed to recognize that inflated wheat prices during the First World War were the aberration of a market distorted by war. The record prices of 1918–20 were certain to collapse when world wheat production grew in peacetime and the productivity effects of growing mechanization were brought to bear on farming.

But no amount of retrospective moralizing diminishes the harsh impact of the Depression and drought of the 1930s on Saskatchewan. Their effects were felt in every aspect of public and private life in the province, whether it was a rapidly growing government debt, skyrocketing unemployment, farm abandonment or simply the loss of hope.

One way to put the economic crisis in context was from the perspective of rural municipal governments. In its annual report for 1937, the Department of Municipal Affairs summarized the situation this way:

> The year 1937 proved one of the most disastrous from an agriculture point of view that the province has ever experienced... In 1937 approximately 85% of the arable area of the province failed to produce a marketable crop. The result in tax collections in rural municipalities was immediate and arresting.[22]

The accumulated tax arrears for all municipalities in the province climbed from $22.31 million in 1929 to $62.44 million in 1936, a 180% increase. The situation was so bleak that in 1937 the government canceled $13.57 million in tax arrears, realizing the money was not collectable.[23]

Another method to get an overview of just how far the Saskatchewan economy fell in the years from 1929 to 1937 is by looking at farm income figures and total income for the province. In 1929, net agriculture income was $51.32 million, down dramatically from $184.66 million the previous year and $168.64 million in 1926. In 1930 farm income had plunged to

SAB R-B2465-1
Relief certificate issued by the Saskatchewan Relief Commission, April 15, 1933.

$38.2 million. In 1931 it was *minus* $31.11 million and minus $1.4 million in 1932. In 1933, farm income plunged to minus $14.48 million and by 1937 had fallen to minus $36.33 million.[24]

During this same period of 1929–37, total income for all occupations in the province—which included relief payments from Ottawa—went from $380.1 million, to a low of $125.6 million in 1933 and to $194.9 million in 1937.[25] Total relief expenditures in the province from 1930 to 1937 were $110.6 million, with the peak of $21.74 million reached in 1934–35.[26]

Aside from the obvious economic problems of the Dirty Thirties and the suffering they spawned, this period also demonstrated the structural weakness of fiscal policy in Saskatchewan. However, it would not be accurate to say the problem of public sector finance sustainability was brought into focus during the Dirty Thirties. Over the years in Saskatchewan, and especially in more recent times, the general view has taken root that public sector debts and deficits have become a contemporary problem only. In fact, there were signs that the provincial government was unable to meet its financial obligations as early as the 1920s, well before the advent of the Depression. In the years 1921–23, for example, there was an aggregate deficit in government revenue over expenditure of $2.26 million.[27]

It is hardly surprising these fiscal danger signs would have emerged. A quickly established settler society brought with it immediate demands for services that could only be met by the public sector. By far the greatest responsibility to meet these growing needs fell to the provincial and municipal governments. Everything from welfare, hospitalization, old age pensions, mothers' allowances, education, free school textbooks, and highway and road construction was the responsibility of either the provincial or local government. As a provincial taxation commission noted in 1936, expenditures grew not only with the population, but more than in proportion with the population. In 1921 per capita provincial spending, not including capital expenditures, was $15.96 and 10 years later it was $19.75.[28]

At the same time, the provincial government's revenue base was significantly limited. Its primary sources of income were an annual federal subsidy in compensation for Ottawa's control of lands and natural resources, interest on advances to other agencies such as the Power Commission, Co-op Creameries or the Wheat Pool, interest on money earned from the sale of school lands, liquor board revenues, and a property tax that had been instituted in 1916 as a "Patriotic Tax" to support the war effort. To meet growing fiscal pressures, the government brought in a gas tax in 1928 and a provincial income tax in 1932. When control of natural resources was finally transferred to the province, a Department of Natural Resources was created in 1933 to begin collecting royalties for the sale and leasing of provincial natural resources.[29]

By the 1930s, the abuse of public sector finance—that has become a common outcome of overly politicized fiscal policy down through the years—was evident. In effect what began happening was that the provincial government disguised its revenue shortfall by charging more and more of its expenditures to capital, when in reality the money was being used for the day-to-day operations of government.

While the concept of capital budgeting was perfectly sound, its implementation often failed to meet its theoretical basis. Expenses are charged to capital when the money is being spent on assets of long-term or more permanent value. Thus, when a government spends money on a highway or a building that will be used, and the benefits derived over many years, it is costed over many years. The problem with capital budgeting was twofold: it tended not to present a clear picture of the growing public sector debt, and it opened the door for government to "reduce" its expenditures and therefore appear to balance the budget. This was done by allocating some spending to capital, rather than expenditure, that is funded from annual tax revenue.

In its 1936 study of Saskatchewan's fiscal situation, a provincial Royal Commission on taxation spoke of this kind of capital-budgeting abuse. The report said capital budgeting was creating a false impression of the state of public finances and that to balance the budget, both prospective revenues and expenditures must be equal on both the revenue and capital accounts:

> A dollar spent on a building is "spent" just as completely as
> a dollar spent on payroll in the sense that an equal respon-
> sibility is created on the part of the province ultimately to
> find revenue [other than borrowed money] to meet either
> expenditure.[30]

With capital budgeting one way to finance the public sector and avoid the
appearance of deficits, being able to borrow money quickly and easily
became politically important. The key legislative tool was, and is to this day,
the Saskatchewan Loans Act.

Originally, the act allowed for borrowing by cabinet when the approval of
the legislature was not required, or when it was for the payment of principal,
interest or renewal on an existing security or previous loan. In 1932 the provisions were amended to allow for borrowing to meet the pressures created
by the Depression. Two years later the way was cleared for borrowing on
expenditures "proposed to be made or incurred" and in 1936 the act was
made even more discretionary for cabinet. It allowed borrowing to meet
deficits or repay debt in any fiscal year.[31]

Still, up to the advent of the Depression, the province did not seem over-
burdened by debt. The total net bonded and treasury bill indebtedness of the
province to April 30, 1929 was $62.87 million. As the Saskatchewan brief to
the Rowell-Sirois Commission noted some nine years later, that amount
could hardly be considered "reflecting wanton extravagance" when such capital expenditures were used to provide the infrastructure to a widely dispersed rural society.[32]

But the debt position of Saskatchewan changed dramatically over the next
eight years. By 1937 the funded and treasury bill indebtedness of the
province had climbed to $199.8 million, an increase of more than 200%.[33]
Much of that increase was due to $110.6 million in relief expenditures spent
in the province from 1929 to 1937, $35.7 million of which came from
Ottawa and $4.3 million of which was raised by municipalities. Of the
$70.58 million provided by the province, all but the slightly more than $6
million that came from revenue, was raised through borrowing. The bulk—
$57.84 million—came in the form of treasury bill sales to Ottawa. With the
province unable to repay its debts to Ottawa, the federal government ultimately agreed to cancel and write down the Saskatchewan debt it held to
$28.4 million.

Underlying all these numbers was a clear message as the Dirty Thirties
slowly drew to a close in Saskatchewan. It had become painfully obvious that
the province's farm sector could not supply a foundation for consistent economic growth. In effect the province had developed along patterns that gave
it the worst of two interdependent worlds, one economic and the other social.

A high-cost rural society patterned on small, individual family farm units
was the economic backbone to the province. But it was based on the volatile

and unpredictable income of a wheat economy that, on one hand, carried high fixed costs and on the other was at the mercy of uncontrollable variables, such as weather and world trade flows that influenced price. Adding to the economic dilemma was the nature of family farming itself, which was an attempt to integrate a social institution with an economic unit.

When, by the 1930s, there were almost 140,000 such social and economic entities, owned and operating independently in Saskatchewan, the province had an economy that was completely vulnerable to volatile world market forces. The sheer number of farm units meant the effects of downward pressure on price would be played out entirely in farm income. With so many independent producers there could be no cuts in production to offset dropping demand. And, with the family farm a social unit with little or no wage labour, losses due to falling prices could not be moderated by shifting the cost through the creation of unemployment.

This resulted in an export-staple economy based on wheat production that was inherently unstable. Not only was it unable to deal with changing market conditions—whether the effects of world wheat production and consumption or the uncertainties of weather—but it could not adjust internally because of the farm being as much a social as an economic unit. The result was boom-or-bust. An example of just how narrow the margin was between good and bad years was actually played out in the years just prior to the darkest days of the Dirty Thirties.

For example, from 1925 to 1929 the wheat crop in Saskatchewan averaged a vibrant and encouraging 260 million bushels a year and the price hovered around the $1 a bushel mark. Then, in 1929, a partial crop failure brought a yield of only 160 million bushels. But in spite of the "remarkable prosperity" of the preceding four years, the provincial government had to spend $750,000 on agriculture relief in 1929 to deal with the effects of one below-average crop.[34]

This precarious economic situation brought with it an obvious fiscal paradox for government. On the one hand government faced the demands of meeting the social needs of a far-flung rural society. On the other, it had to raise revenues from an economy where income was unpredictable and often not accessible because of the narrow taxable margins inherent to the family farm economy.

The vulnerable state of an entire society built on a highly variable one-crop economy, that had been recognized for years, wasn't finally realized until the 1930s. Clearly, hostile weather had been a factor in turning the dilemma into reality during the Dirty Thirties. But as the government of Saskatchewan itself noted, the problem of drought was only exacerbating the "fundamental weakness" of the Saskatchewan economy.

In its report to the Rowell-Sirois Commission hearings, the provincial government argued the drought was more a symptom of the problem, than the problem itself, that confronted Saskatchewan:

It is distinctly arguable that the financial crisis of the last eight years has been due quite as much to the fundamental weakness of an economy which is based almost entirely on the production of a single commodity, namely wheat. It is contended therefore, that the claims of this province cannot be dismissed in the belief that prosperity will return when production of wheat on a large scale is resumed. The long-term economy of the province must be examined and this examination must include the effect of national policies on it.[35]

What the Dirty Thirties really did, therefore, was confirm what previously had been feared. The one-dimensional Saskatchewan wheat economy left the province in a state of constant vulnerability, where the fear of economic collapse was always at hand. The political question became, what to do about it.

Seven   Keeping Hope Alive

"Gunfire blazed out in relief-torn Regina tonight leaving one policeman dead and a striker dying as steel-helmeted Royal Canadian Mounted Police and city constables clashed with 3,000 relief-camp deserters and sympathizers."

(Toronto *Globe*, July 2, 1935)

It was appropriate, even logical, that the dangerous mixture of frustration, economic hopelessness and anger spawned by the Depression should explode in the Regina Riot of 1935. If there was a vortex for political and economic disillusionment, it could be found in Saskatchewan. The province that had been born in such great hope, attracting a flood of people with high expectations, was socially, economically and emotionally shattered by the havoc of the Dirty Thirties.

The founding myth of Saskatchewan—forged by the National Policy's potent mixture of politics, economic nationalism, and the private commercial aspirations of a central Canadian business class—had dissolved in the pain of those years. For a quarter century, the optimism of the original Saskatchewan had been slowly eroding to the realization of a province that was built on false expectations. But it wasn't until the Dirty Thirties that how we viewed ourselves and the future of the province changed, both fundamentally and permanently.

In place of the promised land myth emerged a much different identity, this one deeply rooted in hardship, suffering and economic alienation. The attempts of earlier years to take greater control of Saskatchewan's economic destiny were further radicalized. A new consensus emerged, one that sought to create a more just and egalitarian society where hostile economic forces would be tamed for the common good. It was a fusion of the numbing reality that came with the 1930s and a belief that Saskatchewan people were victims of an unjust economic system. From the economic distress grew the intensely political belief that we could build a better society on the prairies. All it would take was the will to change the system that had failed us. A stronger sense of community was established where people saw their interests and needs intertwined. So, the Saskatchewan myth was not dead. Instead, it was refashioned and reborn, sustained by a new political culture that itself was dependent on maintaining the myth's existence.

Thus, the new Saskatchewan identity that emerged in the 1930s was a product of harsh reality. It altered, but did not bury the Saskatchewan ideal that had been such a crucial dimension to the National Policy.

In its place a new set of political expectations emerged, based on an even more radical notion of victimization. These held that Saskatchewan was denied its true destiny because of outside forces that were part of an economic and political system that was preventing the attainment of the promised land myth. While a sense of economic exploitation and alienation was at the core of the province's identity from the beginning, the disillusionment was always accommodated, more or less, within the economic and political system itself.

In the 1930s that began to change. What emerged was a growing sense that the problem was capitalism, and the only way to change economics was through politics. We could overcome our problems and still achieve our goals if there was the political will. We could build a "New Jerusalem" on the prairies out of the economic and social tumult of the 1930s.

Whether or not this new myth was attainable did not matter. The purpose of politics is to create a vision of the future that motivates people to that end. The fact the so-called New Jerusalem might never be reached was irrelevant. What counted was that people believe it was possible and would work towards a goal that was always beyond their grasp. In the process of reaching for what can never be attained, there is progress. It is defined in political terms through improvements to the human condition, either real or imagined.

Such political myths have two elements. Historian George Melynk says they are made up of the merging of identity and image. The sense of ourselves that comes from within us is our identity; the idea of the self that comes from the way others see us results in our image. Melynk says myths are created from the interaction of identity and image:

> Myth as a synthesis of image and identity retains both identity's sense of truthfulness and image's sense of falseness. So myth could be considered both an illuminator and a deceiver, a speaker of truth and of falsehood.[1]

But, in political science terms, myths are also essential to help understand the world and our place in it, particularly as members of an identifiable community. They help to attach people to others based on a common past and perceived destiny. We are unified by our belief in a shared myth.[2] In that sense, politics is very much about myth making and believing.

The roots of modern-day Saskatchewan politics can be traced directly to the refashioned myth that emerged from the 1930s. It was a time that left deep emotional scars and a perpetual sense of vulnerability as its legacy. But it also produced fertile ground for a belief that the destiny we identified, which was rooted in the founding myth of Saskatchewan, was still attainable.

SAB R-B171-1
Picture taken during the Regina Riot, July 1, 1935.

The dream had not died. We only sought to attain it through different political and economic means.

By the time the Regina Riot erupted on July 1, 1935, at the depth of the Depression, the province's distinct political culture that had evolved over the previous three decades had distilled into a new political movement. The riot was triggered when Prime Minister R.B. Bennett ordered an end to the On-to-Ottawa Trek of the unemployed, who had started in Vancouver and stopped in Regina as part of their journey. Two years to the month before the riot, the Regina Manifesto had been issued by the Co-operative Commonwealth Federation (CCF). By Canadian political standards it was a radical socialist document that called for dramatic and fundamental change to economic society.

The final words of the manifesto echoed the frustration of people and reverberated across the nation by vowing "no CCF government will rest content until it has eradicated capitalism." Ironically, the polemical statement that gave the CCF a revolutionary image was added almost as an afterthought to the manifesto. Curiously, the manifesto did not define what it meant by capitalism, nor did it give any clear definition of socialism, which it proposed to replace the existing system. Thus, from the beginning, there was no well-grounded sense of what the CCF stood for. Was it a radical socialist party in the image of the growing tide that embraced many of the ideals of Marxism and communist Russia? Or was the CCF a watered-down form of agrarian socialism, driven more by pragmatism than the often blind faith of ideology.

In fact from its beginning, the CCF was uncomfortable with itself and unable to reconcile the often incompatible interests of the disparate groups that came together to create the party. At the founding convention in Calgary, and then a year later in Regina in 1933, there were some who strongly rejected the use of the word "socialism" when describing the CCF.[3]

The rise of the CCF was the culmination of a long process. Its roots were in the protest farm politics of the prairies that were a response to the political and economic dominance of central Canada. Farmers had created a sense of group consciousness that was manifest, as we have seen, in an array of farm organizations that included the Grain Growers' Grain Company, the Saskatchewan Grain Growers' Association, the radical United Farmers of Canada (Saskatchewan Section), the Farmers' Union and the Saskatchewan Wheat Pool.

This collective consciousness took various political forms, much of it a Canadian version of the populist farm politics in the United States. The US influence was directly imported from North Dakota in the form of the Non-Partisan League. As previously noted, although the Non-Partisan League had only minor electoral success in Saskatchewan and the West, it laid the political foundation for the Progressives, who burst onto the federal scene in the 1921 federal election with 65 seats in the West. At the same time farmer governments won power in Alberta, Manitoba and Ontario under the name of the United Farmers. It's interesting to note that in Saskatchewan, the Canadian heartland of farming, provincial politics remained relatively immune to the rise of farmer governments, such as the United Farmers of Alberta and the United Farmers of Manitoba. The inability of farmer-based parties to take root in Saskatchewan provincial politics was a testament to the provincial Liberal Party's ability to be seen as the voice of farm politics even as it held power.

Ironically, it was the failure of the farmers' movement to seize political power in Saskatchewan that undoubtedly helped propel the rise of the CCF. Slowly, the alliance between the provincial Liberals and farmers was considered more politically manipulative than substantive, especially as more and more members of the SGGA executive were co-opted into positions within the Liberal government.

The tipping point, in terms of the province's political psychology, came with the advent of the Dirty Thirties. When the farm economy in Saskatchewan collapsed in the early 1930s, the belief took hold that a new political movement, which sought to change the system and which would be controlled by farmers and other victims of the system, had to be established.[4] For years farm groups in Saskatchewan had tried to work within the political system by using the provincial Liberal Party as the means to political and economic influence. But by the 1930s the strategy had failed and the ground became fertile for a political movement with roots in the economic alienation of the Great Depression.

The common thread that bound the western-based farmer movements was a powerful emphasis on democratic control. Much of that impulse came from the American populist influence and it reflected the strong sense of individualism that was so central to family farm life. But what the farm movement lacked was an ideology to unite it. The Progressives, for example, were bound by little other than their opposition to tariffs and a sense of economic exploitation by central Canada. Moreover, the Progressives rejected party politics and remained purposefully aloof from the party system. By contrast, labour had a very clear political and class identity. It shared with farmers the same sense of alienation from the economic and political establishment.

Still, the two groups were wary of each other and didn't see their interests as naturally compatible. It wasn't until the Depression that a political bond developed out of the common destitution faced by farmers and labour. This convergence is described by Walter Young:

> [In] Saskatchewan there were many workers who saw farmers as proprietors and employers, and many farmers who viewed labour's agitation for the eight-hour day as some kind of a sick joke. But when the mills of the Depression ground out destitution and misery on the farm and in the cities alike, there was no real difficulty in bringing the farmers' groups into close liaison with the labour parties in the cities.[5]

What happened was that shared economic hardship faced by farmers and labourers helped create a single class consciousness that, at least for a time, helped diminish if not completely overcome the conflicting economic interests between land-owning farmers and those who sold their labour.

But more importantly, in terms of the CCF putting down roots in Saskatchewan, two crucial factors were at play. One was the lack of any class distinctions, and therefore conflicting economic and social interests, among farmers. While there was some differential in income among farmers, rural Saskatchewan was a one-class community. As Seymour Martin Lipset, who has written extensively on the CCF, says: "The wheat farmers of Saskatchewan have more in common with each other economically and socially than any other groups in the population." The other key reason for the CCF taking hold in Saskatchewan was a political and economic culture of external control and exploitation. In other words, long before they heard anything of the CCF or socialism, farmers in Saskatchewan believed they were being economically oppressed.[6]

By the early 1930s, the alliance between farmers and labour was already taking form, based on links between the two camps over the previous decade. J.S. Woodsworth was an Independent Labour MP from Winnipeg who worked closely with the "Ginger Group" of Progressive MPs in Ottawa. By 1926 a teacher named M.J. Coldwell had organized the Independent Labour Party (ILP) and been elected to city council in Regina on a distinctly socialist platform. Using weekly radio broadcasts to spread his message, Coldwell had become a well-known and popular figure. The Farmers' Political Association was formed in 1930 as a provincewide organization by George Williams, who had been a key figure in the United Farmers of Canada (Saskatchewan Section). The same year it held a joint convention with the ILP. By 1932, a Baptist preacher named T.C. (Tommy) Douglas in Weyburn had formed the Weyburn Labour Association to assist the unemployed. After Woodsworth put Douglas in contact with Coldwell, the Weyburn association became a branch of the ILP.

These growing links between farmers and labour set the stage for the creation of the CCF as a new political voice. The final piece was the League for Social Reconstruction (LSR), a group of Ontario and Quebec academics founded by F.R. Scott from the University of Toronto and Frank Underhill of McGill University in Montreal. Other early members of the LSR included Eugene Forsey, J. King Gordon and Graham Spry. The LSR was formed by Scott and Underhill in January 1932, based on the belief that Canada needed a third party that wouldn't be absorbed by the Liberals, as the Progressives had been. It was to be a Canadian equivalent to the British Fabian Society, providing intellectual stimulus, research and policy direction for a new socialist movement.[7]

So the people who gathered to establish the CCF in 1932 in Calgary, and then a year later congregated in Regina to hammer out the Regina Manifesto for the party, were a strange lot. They were farm activists, labour radicals and socialist intellectuals. Not surprisingly, they did not all share the same socialist view of the world.

For his part, Woodsworth alluded to the problem of farmers finding a common cause with labour in his speech to the 131 delegates at the 1933 Regina convention:

> The Canadian farmers have inherited an individualistic tradition and formed such a homogeneous bloc that it has been difficult for them to realize their new and wider social relationship. Gradually they have been drawn into the capitalist machine.[8]

The ideological divisions separating farmers and labour were also identified by Scott himself. The co-founder of the LSR said the Regina convention demonstrated how the farmers did not agree with or understand the radical Marxist views expressed by labour:

> Amongst the delegates, the farmers represented probably the most solid body of opinion. On the whole it was right-wing opinion—right-wing, that is, according to CCF standards ... it never indulged in and was sometimes baffled by the Marxian phraseology of the socialist labour delegates, and it

vigorously supported the principles of constitutionalism and compensation for owners of nationalized industries. It clearly would have voted against nationalization of the land had that proposal been made.[9]

The Regina Manifesto, which became the CCF's detailed policy statement, was itself a compromise between the radical labour and intellectual factions and the more moderate and pragmatic farm wing of the party. It called for a much greater role for the government, including state health insurance, public pension plans, unemployment insurance and direct government involvement in the economy through Crown corporations. It set out 14 planks in the CCF program, seeking to end the concentration of economic power through social ownership and called for "the supplying of human needs and not the making of profits."[10]

On the issue of Aboriginal people, the Manifesto was silent. In retrospect, as a movement that proclaimed itself as socially progressive and driven by egalitarianism, it is remarkable that the conditions faced by Aboriginal people in Saskatchewan at the time were not even mentioned. The CCF policy on Aboriginal people ultimately was rooted in the liberal view of individual rights and equality, rather than group or collective rights. It saw Aboriginal people as equal, but without any specific or unique inherent rights beyond those legal rights identified in treaty.

For the most part, the manifesto was more an attack on the capitalist system than a proponent of a socialist society. It contained 17 negative references to capitalism and only one positive mention of socialism.[11] As such, it fit the populist traditions of agrarian politics.

But what has stood out over the years, and dogged the CCF and eventually its successor, the New Democratic Party, was a statement added to the main document at the last moment. The manifesto closes with the call:

> No CCF government will rest content until it has eradicated capitalism and put into operation the full programme of socialized planning which will lead to the establishment in Canada of the Co-operative Commonwealth.

Such language allowed the CCF to be cast in many minds as a communist-like threat at a time when many eastern Europeans were fleeing the unspeakable communist atrocities of Stalinist Russia. The communist accusation would follow, and in many respects haunt, the CCF for years. In fact, for 10 years after its founding convention, the CCF found itself at odds with the Roman Catholic Church. At the crux of the issue was the 1931 papal encyclical *Quadragesimo Anno* that declared socialism to be contrary to the principles and tenets of Christianity. The Church acknowledged there have been abuses when "property, that is, 'capital' has undoubtedly long been able to appropriate too much to itself." But the role of the state was not to take away ownership because of misuse of property. It noted that

> when the State brings private ownership into harmony with the needs of the common good, it does not commit a hostile act against private owners, but rather does them a friendly service ... it does not destroy private possessions, but safeguards them.[12]

Although delegates had voted to include a statement opposing change through violence, the mere fact that the pros and cons of violence as a legitimate tool for change were debated at the Regina convention raised questions about the CCF. Indeed, William Moriarity, a labour delegate from Toronto, seemingly spoke in favour of violence:

> The methods suitable to capitalism are those of force. If the ruling class opposes the will of the people, we must use a method suitable to the occasion.[13]

The arrival of the CCF as a political party spawned harsh reactions. Federal Liberal leader Mackenzie King told a Winnipeg audience the day after the Regina Manifesto was approved that the CCF's aims were revolutionary. In spite of the CCF renouncing violence, Mackenzie King questioned how the party expected to achieve its end of state control without the use of violence. "Do you realize what it means? How is this socialistic state to be brought about?" King asked, suggesting that if the CCF's plan was to seize control of industry, it would be nothing short of Communism.[14]

Not surprisingly, with the rise of Communism in Russia and the repression that resulted seen as a major threat, the CCF was portrayed as a dark force by the establishment. The editorial opinion towards the new party was uniformly negative. The co-operative commonwealth was characterized as misguided, impractical and dangerous. The Toronto *Globe* editorialists took dead aim:

> The CCF manifesto is nothing more or less than a 4,000-word expression of a wish, without giving any explanation of how it can be attained.[15]

The thought of the CCF in power was almost too bizarre to be contemplated, the *Globe* editorial page suggested:

> Should the CCF, by any stroke of ill fortune, become the ruling political power, the people would have to expect either closely co-ordinated force compelling adoption of a policy or utter chaos.[16]

In spite of what seemed like a radical tone, the CCF that emerged in Saskatchewan as a political party was eventually to become more pragmatic than ideological. The influence of farmers, who were wary of labour's Marxist, class-oriented view of society and its often volatile rhetoric, ensured that the CCF in Saskatchewan did not end up on the radical fringes of politics.

Over the next 10 years, what the CCF achieved was to dramatically change the way Saskatchewan people viewed themselves and their economic and social future within Canada. The CCF was the political expression of frustration that grew out of the belief that the Saskatchewan myth had been denied because of the capitalist economic forces that where lined up against the province. It's important to recognize that this new political movement did not accept that the notion of the province itself was somehow flawed from its inception. It did not question the fundamentals of a society that was the product of the National Policy's distortive effects that resulted from economic protectionism, ill-planned immigration and an unsustainable single-crop farm economy. Rather the CCF, like political parties before it and since, believed that Saskatchewan could become the land of opportunity and hope that had lured immigrants by the hundreds of thousands through the first two decades of the century.

The belief that things can be made better is, of course, the very essence of politics and the motivation around which political parties operate. Many in the CCF believed the economic collapse and social turmoil wrought by the Great Depression and the Dirty Thirties was, in large part, an inevitable result of a capitalist system that put the interests of corporate profits before those of people. It did not believe, nor even entertain the idea, that the economic failure of Saskatchewan was rooted in the unrealistic and ill-founded expectations of the people drawn to the province by the illusory hope of prosperity.

Clearly, the political landscape was ideal for the emergence of a new political movement like the CCF in the 1930s. The drought and depression created fertile ground for a populist party with its roots and psychological appeal in the cult of economic victimization. By its nature, political debate tends to distort reality for the sake of effect and often what results is a caricature of reality. In some ways, that was what happened in Saskatchewan during the 1930s, and the result was a overly negative picture of the economic and social condition of the province.

The late James Gray, a journalist who wrote extensively about the effects of the Dirty Thirties on Saskatchewan, noted that depictions of hardship in those years of drought were at times more in the realm of fiction than fact:

> More lies have probably been told about the weather of the Dirty Thirties than about any other subject except sex; yet most of the lies could have been true. There was the legend of the children reaching well into school age before they had

ever seen rain; of children running terror stricken to their mothers when they first felt rain on their heads.[17]

Moreover, the lament of Saskatchewan farmers that the farm economy was in a state of collapse did not always sit well with others, who saw the tales of woe as excessive. Some noted the incongruity of the political argument that farmers, on one hand, sought protection from the banks and creditors and, on the other, said the farm economy was bankrupt. One editorial in *Saturday Night* magazine touched on what it perceived as an illogical debate in Parliament about the economic problems of farmers:

> In one breath members are saying that the West is bankrupt and that the farmers are in a hopeless mess, and then in the next have been berating the financial institutions for not taking a long chance by extending further credits.[18]

Still, there is no denying the economic hardship of the 1930s on Saskatchewan; clearly it was a period of tremendous economic and social upheaval. Many people faced misery. But the public debate of that time, as is so often the effect of politics, also tended to generalize and distort the situation and ignored, for example, the fact that the only provincewide crop failure was in 1937. In that sense, the 1930s themselves grew to mythic proportions.

In this kind of a political climate, the 1930s became a dividing line where issues changed from those of immigration and economic expansion, to economic dislocation and social deprivation. Much of the political debate in the first 25 years was focused on issues related directly to that of a rapidly growing immigrant society. Such tensions had coalesced and been played out in the 1929 provincial election, when an undercurrent of racial and religious intolerance helped elect J.T. Anderson and a Conservative government.

During the latter 1920s the Ku Klux Klan developed a strong presence in the province as a reaction against the close connections between Jimmy Gardiner's Liberal government and the Roman Catholic church, as well as the Liberals' strong support for increased immigration from central and eastern Europe. The farm movement itself, namely the Saskatchewan Grain Growers' Association and later the United Farmers of Canada (Saskatchewan Section) were dominated by British-Canadians who sought a restriction on immigration, particularly those of a non-Anglo background.[19]

While the Jimmy Gardiner Liberals presented a more tolerant approach to immigration, racial issues were clearly fundamental to the politics of pre-Depression Saskatchewan. Indeed, former Liberal premier Charles Dunning in 1923 made it clear that only certain kinds of people were welcome in Saskatchewan:

We want no cesspools in this country. We want to see people of sound healthy bodies, active and intelligent and industrious brought into the country; people who can be absorbed into an enlightened citizenship. We want to see people who will not change our institutions, but maintain and foster them.[20]

In political terms, one major effect of the Depression on Saskatchewan was eventually to change the focus of public debate from such racially based concerns of a rapidly growing immigrant society, to economic issues. While racist attitudes often intensify in troubled economic times, as in the case of 1930s' Saskatchewan, plummeting levels of immigration helped to defuse what was an ugly climate. The inability of the Conservative J.T.M. Anderson government to adequately cope with the Depression opened the door for the creation of the Farmer-Labor Party, which eventually became the CCF. Initially, the Anderson goverment believed the drought was temporary and did not begin to take action until August 1931, when the premier announced the establishment of a provincial relief commission. Later, the Anderson government launched a program that encouraged people from the drought-stricken southwest to resettle in northern reaches of the grainbelt.

But to suggest Saskatchewan farmers, traumatized by the Dirty Thirties, eagerly embraced the CCF would be untrue. In fact the CCF's radical social-ist message, which called for the public ownership of the means of produc-tion, did not resonate with farmers. They sought reform, not the overthrow of the system as some of the more radical members of the CCF espoused. Even with the suffering created by drought, farmers had developed a deep emotional attachment to the land. They did not seek revolution and feared they could lose ownership of their land as part of a socialist economic system called for by the CCF. What they finally relinquished was a "naive optimism of the settlement period."[21] What remained unshaken by the Dirty Thirties was the essentially conservative impulse of Saskatchewan people. Thus, one flaw in the original CCF platform, that reflected its internal contradictions, was its policy on land tenure. The CCF applied a Marxist/socialist strategy of protecting the farmers' means of production, not their ownership of the land. As such, a CCF government would guarantee farmers a job, if not title to their land, by replacing their right to ownership with a right to a use-hold title.[22]

Until it recognized the conservative reality of Saskatchewan voters and, in particular, adjusted its policies to recognize the importance of private farm ownership, the CCF had little success at the polls. In the 1934 provincial election, with the province in the depths of drought and depression, the Farmer-Labor Party won only five seats and got fewer votes than even Anderson and the Conservatives. Instead, Saskatchewan people returned to the Liberal fold, embracing Gardiner's promise of progressive, non-socialist reform in the form of higher prices for farm commodities, more relief and protection from farm foreclosures. Just how the Gardiner government was going to produce higher prices for farm commodities was not clear. But, as is the nature of politics, what matters the most is instilling hope.

A year later in 1935, now running under the CCF banner in a federal election, the party fared no better. It won only two of 21 seats, and one of the victories was in a constituency where the CCF candidate had been endorsed by the Social Credit Party. In both elections the Social Credit, which had burst on the scene in Alberta and won power in that province in 1935, had been a force that cut into CCF support. Like the CCF in Saskatchewan, the Social Credit emerged as a populist, rural reaction to the Depression. But unlike the CCF, Social Credit did not seek to replace the capitalist system with socialism. It sought monetary reform, arguing the economic problems were a result of people not having sufficient purchasing power to buy the abundant goods produced by a capitalist economy. The party advocated the distribution of money through a system of "social credit" to maintain demand in the economy[23]

The rise of Social Credit and the results of the 1934 and 1935 elections had a sobering and, more significantly, a moderating effect on the CCF. It realized that a radical socialist message would not sell with Saskatchewan people, who by nature were pragmatic and intensely committed to the notion of private property, which was clearly the economic foundation of an immigrant, family-farm economy.

Although it maintained that it was a "movement" rather than a political party in the traditional sense, the CCF succumbed to the imperatives of politics. In its 1936 provincial convention, the CCF embraced a new program that expunged the word "socialism" from its text. More significantly it dropped a contentious policy that called for the nationalization of farmland, which had made the CCF an easy target for Liberals and Conservatives who claimed the party was, at its core, communist.

By the 1938 Saskatchewan election, the CCF had moved much closer to the political mainstream. Seymour Martin Lipset, the American academic whose PhD dissertation studied the origins and policies of the CCF, says a more moderate CCF laid the foundation for ultimate political success:

> The whole purpose and program of the CCF had therefore changed. It could no longer carry on a systematic attack on capitalism and all its institutions. The party had become a farmers' pressure group seeking to win agrarian reforms.[24]

This move towards moderation by the CCF in the last half of the 1930s was undoubtedly a key political turning point in the province's history. What it did was reflect the conservative reality of a province with people whose economic destiny, indeed whose lives, were tied to the land and, more specifically, private property. Saskatchewan existed because of a belief in the land, and even though many who came to the province felt betrayed by the land, especially during the Dirty Thirties, they clung to their belief in it. To give up ownership of their land as part of a socialist plan would be to deny the very reason hundreds of thousands had come to the province.

When you appreciate the conservative nature of Saskatchewan people, the CCF's rejection of radical socialist ideals in the latter 1930s and its eventual rise to power can be seen as closely attached cause-and-effect events. As support for the CCF grew, much of it came from people who had traditionally been Conservative supporters. One simplistic, but still telling, explanation of where the CCF drew its support is to think of the 1930s as a dividing line in Saskatchewan politics. In the first 25 years of the province's existence the political cleavage was between the ruling Liberals on one side and the Conservatives (under various names, such as the Provincial Rights Party) on the other. By 1938 the division was between the Liberals and the CCF, so it's not difficult to see what party the CCF replaced.[25]

To argue there is more similarity than differences between the CCF and Conservatives might sound illogical to some, particularly socialists who see Conservatives as wanting to preserve an economic system they wish to radically change. But by the 1938 election, the CCF and Conservatives were openly courting each other and seeking to build an electoral alliance. In the midst of the campaign, the CCF party's paper *New Era*, defended the idea of an alliance with Conservatives:

> The western Conservatives who are opposed to a farmers' wheat board and a marketing act are very scarce ... The Conservatives who would sooner see our present reactionary government retain power than the election of one of a more progressive nature, are non-existent. Our Liberal government has become a reactionary Tory organization and most of the Conservatives have gone far to the left.[26]

Moreover, Conservative leader and former premier Anderson even explicitly appealed for CCF support in seats where it was not running candidates:

> Every plank in the CCF platform is ours and there is no reason why the members of the party cannot conscientiously support us in this effort to rid the province of a discredited administration.[27]

The Conservative platform was itself filled with policies that were designed to win left-wing support. For example, the Conservatives called for government to establish new industry if the private sector would not absorb the unemployed, state medicine "made available to all," expansion of social services and education opportunities, as well as the "development of our natural resources in the interests of the province rather than the interests of a few favored individuals."[28]

The idea that conservatives and socialists have much in common is rooted in the recognition that both seek to limit freedom for what they identify as the general good of society. Restraint, rather than the classical liberal idea of individual liberty, is a value that is common to socialism and conservatism. This shared value between the two was identified by the late conservative political scientist George Grant:

> [W]hat is socialism, if it is not the use of the government to restrain freedom in the name of social good? In actual practice, socialism has always had to advocate inhibition in this respect. In doing so, was it not appealing to the conservative idea of social order against the liberal idea of freedom.[29]

© M. WEST, REGINA, WEST'S STUDIO
T.C. Douglas, premier of Saskatchewan, 1944–61.

If ever there was a practical political example that demonstrated the intimate philosophical unity of socialism and conservatism, it was Saskatchewan in the final years of the Dirty Thirties. Their dreams shattered, people still clung to the hope that had brought them to the province. What they wanted and needed was someone who could make them believe their hope was not in vain. Someone who could motivate them. Someone who could renew the myth. Someone like Tommy Douglas.

Eight   Suffering and Redemption

"We have come to see that the Kingdom of God is in our midst if we have the vision
to build it. The rising generation will tend to build a heaven on earth rather than live
in misery in the hope of gaining some uncertain reward in the dim distant future."
                                                                        (T.C. Douglas)

Denied the dream of its immigrants, and with its economy on its knees,
by the last years of the 1930s what Saskatchewan needed was someone
who could redeem the province by restoring faith in itself and the myth upon
which it was founded.

As we have seen, for 30 years Saskatchewan had been sustained, in no
small measure, by a combination of factors—which included rapid immigration that spawned artificial, unsustainable growth—coupled with the sheer
dedication, gritty determination and worth ethic of the people who had come
to the province. They were pioneers, willing to build a new life often in the
face of tremendous adversity. It took a special kind of people to leave their
roots, their families, their communities and their homelands to start over on
the harsh, unforgiving and windswept prairies. Many came from other conti-
nents, eager to embrace their new country in the belief that a better life awaited. More than anything, what Saskatchewan gave them was a sense of hope
that they could make better lives for themselves than the ones they left had
behind. Indeed, faith was a core ingredient to the pioneer character.

Clearly then, by definition, the people who came to the province had a
great deal of personal fortitude. They were industrious and determined to
succeed. Indeed, to fail was not an option, because for many it was not realistic to go back to the homeland they had left for Saskatchewan. The enormous strength and resilience of the people themselves became the driving
force and the lifeblood that coursed through the veins of the province.
Saskatchewan was populated by individuals who not only didn't fear hard
work, they actually thrived on it. They recognized the importance of their
own labour in achieving the economic security they sought for themselves
and their families.

But with the economic setback of the 1930s came the realization that
Saskatchewan was a land that offered equal doses of hardship with each
dream of opportunity. Too often, hard work, dedication, fortitude and

personal courage would not necessarily be enough to overcome the economic odds that seemed stacked against the people. This sobering reality of the Dirty Thirties became a turning point in the political psychology of the province.

To that point, politics in Saskatchewan had been a fairly sterile exercise, at least in terms of mobilizing people towards a collective vision for the type of society they wanted to create. It was a process that concerned itself with the mechanics of governing and the necessities of prairie life. There was a certain sameness in the political discourse of the province, a kind of pedestrian quality that was reflected in the leaders themselves—Scott, Martin, Dunning, Gardiner and Anderson. While Jimmy Gardiner certainly was a powerful figure, whose influence spanned provincial and federal politics, he too was more a political tactician and strategist than a political visionary. The real strength of the Liberals, and the key to their long political hegemony throughout most of the first 40 years of the province's history, was their pragmatism. The Liberals were able to reflect the shifting interests and issues in the province in such a way that they appeared to be a dynamic, ever-changing party. The Liberals dealt with the political opposition through political opportunism. They simply co-opted the views of others, particularly those involved in farm organizations such as the Saskatchewan Grain Growers' Association, by bringing them into the party and government.

That is not to say there was not a consistent ideological current to Saskatchewan politics prior to the trauma of the 1930s. A specific, identifiable political culture had grown and taken root in those years. The challenges of creating a pioneer society had quickly fused the population and created a sense of community. It was reflected in the values absorbed from the American Mid-West, in the institutions of the province, from grain marketing co-ops, to a vast expanse of roads and rural schools, and in the collective values of trying to work together. Farmers who operated independently had quickly discovered that protection of their interests in an international grain economy rested in banding together. Individually they had no market power. The notion of government enterprise for collective economic and social goals was central to Saskatchewan's character, predating even the province itself.[1] Together, whether through co-ops or government, people believed they could have some influence on their economic destiny. The 1930s shattered much of the confidence and stability that had been created by those cornerstone institutions and values. The decade raised doubts whether the myth could be achieved by adapting Saskatchewan to the economic system, or whether the system itself had to be changed. The deep emotional scars created by the Dirty Thirties also produced fertile ground for someone who could express the frustrated aspirations of people and give hope to the belief their expectations of a better life on the prairies were not in vain.

It was into this political vacuum that Tommy Douglas appeared. For a province that had its confidence shaken to the core, he became the politician

Annie Buller addressing a crowd two days before the Estevan coal strike, which began September 7, 1931. The strike, and its attendant violence, which resulted in the deaths of three miners, deeply affected T.C. Douglas, who was a preacher in Weyburn at the time.

who provided the vision of a future much better than the present. He became a merchant of hope, a dream maker in a province that wanted desperately to believe in the myth that had become part of its identity. Douglas was a visionary who offered a roadmap to the promised land.

A Baptist preacher, Douglas became an exponent of the social gospel. He followed in the political-religious tradition of CCF founder J.S. Woodsworth, and Salem Bland, a Methodist minister who helped form the Ontario CCF in the mid-1930s. The social gospel was a movement that sought to apply Christian principles to the social and economic problems confronting an industrializing society. Central to the social gospel was the belief that involvement in public processes to improve the collective welfare was an expression of religious morality and the equivalent of doing God's work in society. Rather than a revolutionary attack on capitalism, the social gospel sought to reform the system from within. It recognized that Christianity—through the gospel—had profound ethical obligations to help build a better society.[2]

In many respects, the rise of the social gospel movement on the prairies flowed naturally from the years of agrarian revolt. The church played a central role in the pioneer settlement of Saskatchewan, as people sought the emotional comfort provided by religion as they struggled to establish themselves on the great, often lonely expanse of the prairies. One definition of religion is what a person does with his or her solitude. If that is the case, then the solitude that came with the settlement of Saskatchewan made issues of faith and religion central to the lives of the people who knew intimately the meaning and emotional effect of being alone with nature.

But to fully appreciate the rise of the social gospel, and why it became such a powerful force, it is important to place it within the context of the Great Depression. More specifically, the rise of the social gospel as a political expression was very much an outgrowth of the religious notion of suffering and redemption. The concept shared by most of the world's religions—that there is redemptive power in unearned suffering—was a crucial factor in allowing the social gospel to transform the Saskatchewan political discourse during and after the 1930s. It is through suffering that our perspective and values change. Suffering makes us more human. It not only tests one's faith, but strengthens it. In the case of Saskatchewan, the unearned suffering of the Dirty Thirties had the redemptive power of raising politics to a higher moral plane, one that drew its inspiration from the Christian gospel. From it flowed a greater sense of community, a commitment to collective welfare and an even stronger faith in the attainment of a better future that was embedded in the Saskatchewan myth.

There was no escaping the importance of religion to life in the province. It was an undercurrent to the moralism of the Progressive movement, which sought to raise politics to a higher ethical level. Norman Lambert, secretary of the Canadian Council of Agriculture, made the link between religion and farm politics explicit. He said "hand in hand with the organized farmers movement on the prairies has gone religion and social work."[3] The Saskatchewan Grain Growers' Association was described as a "religious, social, educational, political and commercial organization all in one" by the Regina *Leader*.[4]

This symbiosis between religion and agrarian politics was natural. Historian Richard Allen notes that ideas and movements that have economic beginnings also contain aspirations that cannot necessarily be reduced to either economics or politics:

> Patterns of behaviour, individually and collectively, emerge which sometimes owe more to religious concerns of alienation and reconciliation, of guilt, justification, redemption, and ultimate hope than to the cold rationalities of economic interest. The two impulses meet in a framework of ideas, or an ideology, combining self-interest and ultimate aspirations by which a group, class, section or nation, explains to itself and to the world, what its problems are, how it is approaching them, where it is going and why. To a remarkable degree, the social gospel and the ideology of the agrarian revolt coincided.[5]

The CCF and Douglas believed that socialism and Christianity "are but secular and sacred visions of the same philosophy." There was a religious and moralistic emphasis in the CCF that was similar to British socialism, founded on the belief that capitalism and Christianty were not compatible.[6]

Inherent, then, to the social gospel and the CCF was a current of moral supe-riority that was embedded in partisan politics. This self-righteousness gave the CCF a kind of evangelical fervour that combined the moral supremacy of religion with the passion of politics. It was a heady brew.

The idealism central to the social gospel of Woodsworth and Douglas was rooted in the 19th century Fabian Society of Britain, which led to the forma-tion of the British Labour Party. In his doctoral dissertation on the early years of the Douglas governnment, Albert Johnson notes the philosophy of Woodsworth reflected the ideas of 19th century idealists such as T.H. Green and Bernard Bosanquet:

> In the words of Adam Ulam, their philosophy was "character-ized by the search for a formula to define the moral task of the state and to set a single standard of value which would guide men in their public and private actions."[7]

By the mid-1930s, all the factors were in place for a political figure to emerge who would capture the spirit of the time. A skilled orator like Douglas, preaching the political and economic morality of the social gospel, became a compelling figure in an era of economic deprivation, when public debate was both the primary means of communication and the social lifeblood of communities. Douglas recognized the spoken word as the most important weapon at a politician's disposal. In a 1979 book of Douglas's speeches, which he edited, L.D. Lovick observed:

> He [Douglas] believes that people can be converted, correct-ed and inspired by effective speech-making. He believes that hostile or indifferent listeners can be neutralized and even swayed by the power of words. And he believes that fools, charlatans and evildoers will be exposed in open debate. The power of speech is an article of faith for Tommy Douglas.[8]

This fusion of religious and political values is best explained by Douglas himself, who outlined his ideas in popular radio broadcasts after he became Saskatchewan CCF leader:

> A new economic system is only a means to an end and not an end in itself... We're desirous of building a more just and secure economy; but we are conscious of the fact that when we have improved the economic lot of mankind, we have only begun the much greater task of building a new society ... After all, "a man's life consisteth not in the abundance of things which he possesses"; life at its best consists of spiritu-al values such as a regard for truth, a love of beauty and a seeking after righteousness.

As a young preacher in Weyburn during the early years of the Depression, Douglas came to the conclusion that much of the economic misery was man-made and, therefore, could have been avoided. He merged religion and politics, arguing that socialism offered by the CCF was based in the morality of Christianity:

> We believe that socialism is the teachings of Christ applied in our economic, social and national life. A fair appraisal of the CCF policies will reveal that instead of being the antithesis of religion, the CCF is an endeavour to Christianize a pagan economic and social order. The program of the CCF is therefore an honest endeavour to apply the social message of Christianity to life. It is complimentary, rather than in opposition to the work of the church. For while the church is seeking to establish the right relationships between man and God, the CCF is endeavouring to bring about a brotherly relationship between man and man. We must recognize this cannot be done under the present competitive system.[9]

His political beliefs were sharpened by two events in 1931. In the summer of that year he travelled to Chicago where he went to register for a university sociology program that he never completed. While there, Douglas ventured into the slums of America's second-largest city and saw the human fallout from the Depression. During his time in Chicago, Douglas met with leading "thinkers" in the US socialist movement, but was unimpressed with their fanciful theoretical discussions while people suffered. Moved to act, a few months later back in Weyburn, he formed the Weyburn Independent Labour Association and helped organize a truckload of food for striking miners in Estevan.

From that small-scale beginning, Douglas steadily grew to be an important figure in the Farmer-Labor Party and later the CCF. Although he played a minor role in the creation of the party, and attended only the last day of the three-day 1933 convention that produced the Regina Manifesto, Douglas was nominated as the Farmer-Labor candidate for Weyburn in the 1934 election. Douglas lost to the Liberal candidate and the Farmer-Labor Party won only five seats to Jimmy Gardiner and the Liberals' 50.

But a year later Douglas was back. This time he won as the CCF candidate for Weyburn in the federal election. The turning point in that campaign was thought to be a public debate between Douglas and Liberal incumbent E.J. Young. An overflow crowd of about 7,000 packed the local hockey rink for the debate that Douglas clearly won. But electoral succcess for Douglas also brought with it controversy and internal dissension.

Fearful that the rise of Social Credit to power in Alberta could spill over into the federal election in Saskatchewan, Douglas created an alliance with

Social Credit supporters in his area. In fact, when Alberta Social Credit premier William Aberhart heard the Liberals had put up a token Social Credit candidate in a bid to stop Douglas, Aberhart publicly endorsed Douglas. It was not entirely a marriage of convenience. Like Alberta MP William Irvine, who was a major force in creating the CCF and someone he greatly admired, Douglas had embraced some Socred economic policies, such as creation of a provincial bank and the issuing of local currency for use in the province. The link Douglas had to Social Credit made many in the CCF uneasy, not the least of whom was provincial leader George Williams. For a time, Williams wanted Douglas kicked out of the CCF, but the issue died after Douglas became an MP, although the rivalry between the two continued for years.

Another curious association Douglas had was with a man named Don Grant, who acted as his "driver-adviser" in the 1935 campaign. At one time Grant had been an organizer for the Ku Klux Klan, before getting a job with the Anderson government running its labour and employment bureau in Weyburn.[10] It was Grant who travelled to Alberta to get Aberhart's written endorsation of Douglas that was used to win Socred supporters over to the CCF.

During this period, Douglas was also a strong advocate of eugenics, which called for genetic engineering as a means to rid society of those with low intelligence or unacceptable moral standards. In 1933, Douglas wrote his thesis for an MA in sociology from McMaster University on the benefits of eugenics. Entitled "The Problems of the Subnormal Family," the thesis studied "twelve immoral or non-moral women" and their offspring in Weyburn.[11] Douglas states his premise at the outset when he says "the subnormal family presents the most appalling of all family problems." The pattern of "immoral" behaviour and offspring of lower intelligence, that Douglas traces from the 12 women he considered, led him to a series of conclusions that include sterilization of those with lower intelligence.

Douglas's rather chilling views are expressed in these unequivocal terms:

> Some have objected to sterilization on the grounds that it is depriving human beings of an inalienable right. But medical science declares that it is possible to be sterilized and yet have sexual intercourse. In the main this is all the defective asks. Among them the parental instinct is not paramount, but is entirely subordinated to the sex urge. Thus, sterilization would deprive them of nothing that they value very highly, and would make it impossible for them to reproduce those whose presence could contribute little to the general well-being of society.[12]

But, at the time, such ideas were not far out of the psychological and sociological mainstream. Eugenics had been a growing movement since the

1920s, when the popular sociological notion emerged that the number of "deviants and morons" was increasing so rapidly that they would eventually be the statistically dominant group if efforts were not taken to curb their growth.[13] The origins of eugenics can be traced to the rise of capitalism and the Industrial Revolution and the views of people such as Robert Malthus, whose theories on population growth emphasized the need to curtail the growth in numbers of those with lower intelligence who become a burden for society. "When a poor man persists in marrying and having children, and then hard times deprive him of the opportunity to work and he turns to society for relief, he becomes, in Mathus' view, an enemy of society," says Allan Chase.[14] Of course, at the time Douglas was flirting with theories on eugenics, nowhere was the idea stronger than in Adolf Hitler's Nazi Germany, where it became state policy.

At one level, the fact Douglas would subscribe to the notion of eugenics was not surprising. Such social engineering was consistent with his belief that the state needed to take an active role in planning the economic and social framework of society. Certainly he saw it as neither malicious nor an unacceptable intrusion on individual rights. To Douglas, the collectivist goal of a better society—even though it might come at the expense of individual freedom for some—was apparently a greater good than the loss of individual liberty for the mentally handicapped was a social negative.

It was during this period, after he was elected a CCF MP for Weyburn in 1935, that Douglas travelled as part of a parliamentary delegation to Nazi Germany. At the time Douglas was a member of a group that called itself the League Against War and Fascism. It was dominated by Canadian communists that pressured the federal government to take a stronger stance against the rise of Fascism in Europe, and what is believed was a right-wing influence in domestic Canadian politics.

When Douglas returned he went on a speaking tour around the province, warning about the rise of Nazi Germany. He predicted that war with Germany appeared inevitable given Hitler's belligerence and the size of the German military. The criticism of Hitler did not go down well with some members of the German community in the province, particularly those who were members of the pro-Nazi *Deutscher Bund* in Saskatchewan. As Douglas observed:

> The warnings from the Deutscher people said I had better stop talking like I was or I would be in trouble. In my own constituency I had some fairly strong German communities who were very incensed at what I said about Hitler.[15]

But not everything Douglas had to say about Germany under Hitler was negative. Douglas admitted that the economic role of the Nazi socialist state had demonstrated how government in some ways could be used as an instrument for economic progress.

Still, the exposure to what was happening in Germany changed many of his pacifist views. While in Germany he met with labour leaders who were being persecuted and suppressed by the Nazis. Many had been thrown in prison for their views. "I recognized then that if you came to a choice between losing your freedom of speech, religion, association, thought … and resorting to force, you'd use force," Douglas said after his visit to Germany.[16] It was at that point when Douglas openly split with the Canadian communists, who went from publicly opposing Hitler, to being against a war with Germany.

As an MP, Douglas steadily raised his profile. His regular columns on federal affairs in the CCF party paper *The New Era*, which later became *The Commonwealth*, made Douglas a popular and well-known figure in the CCF. When provincial leader George Williams enlisted for the Second World War and went to Europe, it became clear the party had to find a new leader. Douglas was an obvious choice. Lured from the federal to provincial political arena, Douglas defeated John Brockelbank to win the leadership in 1942.

Ironically, it was Canada's war effort that became the final crucial factor that tended to validate the CCF's economic views in the public mind. As a party that called for a planned economy as the means to ensure economic growth and stability, the CCF maintained that if the federal government could seize control of the economy for the greater good of the war effort, the same could be done for other social and economic goals.

During the war years of the early 1940s, the dominant political issue became what would be done with the returning veterans when the war ended. Would they return to the prospects of unemployment, or could the economic output change from producing the necessities of war to the necessities of peace—the social needs of food, clothing, shelter, health care and education? Douglas and the CCF argued the benefits of state planning had been demonstrated during the war and the same approach, where government would play a central co-ordinating role in the economy, should continue. It was an argument that resonated with Saskatchewan people. The war effort had brought the economy out of depression and by 1944, when Douglas and the CCF won power in Saskatchewan, the economic picture in the province had brightened considerably.

The idea of state intervention in the economy had gained enormous political legitimacy throughout the United Kingdom and in North America. The ideas of John Maynard Keynes, the British economist and bureaucrat contained in his 1936 *General Theory of Employment, Interest and Money*, had become widely accepted. Keynes attacked classical economic thinking, arguing the economy could reach either high levels of unemployment or inflation and remain locked in that position. Instead of brief periods when the economy goes into recession, Keynes said long-term depressions are inevitable because the free-market economy is not self-correcting. Of course, free market purists dismiss that argument. They maintain that the ups and downs of an economy are not inevitable at all. They are made inevitable because of rigidities built into an economy by government intervention that does not allow it to operate as a true free market. If such a true free market existed, it would, by definition, be constantly adjusting to market signals. In such a world, the business cycle would not exist.

There were two central elements to Keynes's argument. One is that saving and investment decisions are not always synchronized. In other words, if people are saving more, Keynes argued that does not mean business will invest more. Saving, he argued, means less consumption which means less reason for business investment. The second key point for Keynes was that prices and wages are downwardly inflexible, which makes it difficult for the economy to be self-correcting. With the rise of labour monopolies in the form of unions to offset business monopolies, the economy has a limited capacity to correct itself easily or quickly.

What Keynes proposed was for government fiscal policy to play a greater role during periods of high savings/low consumption and stagnant investment. In effect, the highs and lows of the business cycle could be moderated by the fiscal policy of government. By spending more during recessionary times, government could stimulate the economy, raise demand and help spur business investment. In that way, Keynes argued the economic calamity of the Great Depression could have been averted.[17]

One of the primary adherents of Keynes was US president Franklin Delano Roosevelt. Elected president in 1933 in the depth of the Great Depression, Roosevelt promised a "new deal" for American people. Upon taking office, Roosevelt launched a 100-day program of government intervention to stimulate the economy. The initiative included an Agriculture Adjustment Act which paid farmers to reduce production so grain inventories could be reduced; this would then, theoretically, raise wheat prices. The US government also started a huge public works program as part of a National Recovery Act that included laws to protect labour. The National Labour Relations Act, more commonly known as the Wagner Act, guaranteed employees the right to form a union and bargain collectively. The government also created the Tennessee Valley Authority to take control of hydroelectric dams and other industrial plants built during the First World War, as well as provide electricity to a wide region of the southeastern US. For farmers and labour, Roosevelt's 100-day program and his longer term New Deal policies, where government spent more to bring the economy out of depression, were seen as the nation's economic salvation.[18]

The rise of Keynesian economics as a response to the Depression, coupled with the political success of Roosevelt, gave credibility to the idea of state intervention as a means to level out the boom-and-bust cycles of the economy. But the effectiveness of Roosevelt's economic policies, in terms of having any measurable effect on ending the Depression, is debatable. In 1939, after six years of Keynesian intervention into the stagnant American economy, the unemployment rate in the US remained at 17%. What ended the Depression was not Roosevelt's New Deal, it was the Second World War.

But that is not to say an activist role for government did not have an effect on public attitudes. American journalist Robert Samuelson says the greater role of government that flowed from the Depression and then the Second World War created a welfare state that raised public expectations as people began to believe in the inevitability of economic and social progress:

> The wartime boom ended the Depression and, in so doing, created an economic and political model that seemed to work. Afterward, government and business could collaborate, as they had during the war, to engineer prosperity and progress.[19]

Similarly in Canada, the idea of interventionist government became part of the political mainstream, as answers were sought to overcome the economic problems created by the Depression. The advent of the Second World War proved to be the economic stimulus that Canada needed to get the economy moving again. But equally important was the economic lesson contained in the war effort.

At the start of the war, unemployment remained high with 529,000 out of work. But as the nation mobilized for war, the economy quickly improved and in a matter of months more than one million jobs were created in industries involved in the war effort. By 1941, the Canadian economy was operating at full capacity and unemployment had fallen to 1% and some industries even faced labour shortages.[20] Using powers under the War Measures Act in 1941, the federal government seized control of the economy and used wage and income controls to prevent inflation from spiralling out of control. The Saskatchewan farm economy was also directly affected by governnment intervention when Ottawa closed the Winnipeg Grain Exchange and turned the Canadian Wheat Board—which up to that point had been a voluntary marketing agency for farmers' grain—into a monopoly. The reason the Board was given monopoly status was to allow the government to keep the price of wheat down as part of its war effort to help feed the allied nations. All of this raised an obvious question: If it was possible for government to mobilize the economy into a military imperative with positive economic results, why couldn't government play an equally strong economic role in peacetime?

During the war years, the Department of Finance in Ottawa was filled with disciples of Keynsianism. Several economists and senior civil servants are credited with bringing Keynesianism to Canada. They included Robert Bryce a former student of Keynes at Cambridge who went on to Harvard University, before joining the federal finance department in 1938. Also in the group was W.A Mackintosh, the political economist from Queen's University who had worked for the Rowell-Sirois Commission and joined the federal government as an adviser in finance and post-war economic reconstruction. In 1945, Mackintosh did a white paper on employment and income which set out a Keynesian plan where consumption would be supported by government initiatives such as unemployment insurance, family allowances, old-age pensions and price-support measures.[21]

Before the Mackintosh white paper, a committee headed by McGill University principal Cyril James had been formed to advise the government on post-war measures for reconstruction. The research director for the committee was Leonard Marsh, who had worked as a research assistant in Britain on the 1942 Beveridge Report, which was heavily influenced by Keynesian economic analysis. In February 1943, Marsh presented his *Report on Social Security for Canada*. It mirrored much of what the Beveridge study had recommended, such as a comprehensive social security system for Canada and a full-employment policy.

Historian Desmond Morton calls the Marsh report a "blueprint" for a post-war welfare state:

> Financed by revenues from a fully-employed work force and, in turn, helping full employment through education, job training and stimulation of purchasing power, Marsh offered Canada an escape from the business-cycle nightmare of boom and bust. His report argued for a national health insurance, universal contributory pension plans for the elderly and "an unequivocal place in social security policy" for the needs of children. At the heart of Marsh's policy were family allowances of up to $7.50 per child per month. The total bill for Marsh's plans would be $900 million a year or 60% more than all federal spending in 1939.[22]

While the Mackenzie King government ignored much of what Marsh proposed, his ideas clearly had a significant influence on public policy. In 1944 a universal family allowance system was inaugurated, and a wartime housing construction program and government-supported, low-interest mortgages for returning soldiers—later renamed the Central Mortgage and Housing Corporation—were established. The government policies built into the economy the kind of structural spending that many believed would reduce, if not eliminate, the chances of returning to the Depression of the 1930s.

As Mackintosh himself explained, by the early 1940s this idea of activist government was considered neither radical nor novel:

> They put in careful context a consensus which already had been substantially reached. It had been reached less by the winning of hot verbal disputes than by the experience of the war. It had already been confirmed to a large extent as government policy by the legislation already on the books.[23]

In effect the federal government ran a command-and-control economy during the war years, intervening in the marketplace to the extent it believed was necessary to achieve its social or economic goals. The central figure in Canada's wartime economy was C.D. Howe, the minister of munitions and supply who put private business at the disposal of the state. "Howe and most of the other war organizers thought their achievements were magnificent," says University of Toronto historian Michael Bliss. "In six years they had transformed Canada from a depressed, agricultural society, they believed, into an industrial powerhouse." No other event validated state intervention more than the Second World War, which left a political legacy that lasted decades. Says Bliss:

> The state would never shrink to anything like its prewar role. If Ottawa could spend without restraint to make war against Nazis, if it could compel citizens to work for a greater good, if it could supersede the marketplace in the national interest, why couldn't it be just as vigorous in waging war against poverty, inequalities and ill health after the war?[24]

So clearly, while Douglas and the CCF were depicted as radical socialists by many of their political opponents, including prime minister Mackenzie King himself, the fact was the CCF's ideas of activist government were not out of step with the prevailing political and economic wisdom. Certainly, the Second World War provided a major political opening for Douglas to argue that much could be done to alleviate the social and economic problems in Saskatchewan through government action. All he had to do was point to the war effort and the stimulating, job-creating effect it had on the economy to validate the CCF argument that government could play a positive and stabilizing role in the provincial economy.

The emotional power of the argument for government marshalling the economy for the purposes of satisfying the human needs of society during the war was undeniable. In a 1943 speech, and with typical eloquence, Douglas put the political emotion into words:

> Surely if we can produce in such abundance in order to destroy our enemies, we can produce in equal abundance in order to provide food, clothing and shelter for our children. If we can keep people employed for the purpose of destroying human life, surely we can keep them employed for the purpose of enriching and enhancing human life.[25]

In the folklore and myth of Saskatchewan politics, particularly among those devoted to both the traditions of the CCF and Douglas himself, there exists the notion that the party was in the vanguard of economic and political change in Canada during the post-war years. While there is some truth to that belief, especially in the early years of the Depression, the CCF was as much in the mainstream as it was pushing the envelope of public policy by the end of the Second World War. Another of those who witnessed the process of Keynesian, welfare-state policy development from the inside of the federal government, beginning in the early 1940s, was Mitchell Sharp, who was recruited to the Finance Department and eventually became a Liberal cabinet minister. He says that the CCF got too much credit for improvements to the social security system in Canada in the decade following the Second World War and suggests the process would have happened without the CCF's presence on the political scene: "Looked at from an insider's point of view, the CCF was pushing against an open door."[26]

Indeed, the idea of government, whether provincial or federal, playing a central role in economic reconstruction had become an article of faith well before the CCF took power in 1944. In 1943, the Liberal government of William Patterson passed the Saskatchewan Reconstruction Council Act, with a mandate to make plans for how returning veterans could be absorbed back into the provincial economy when the war ended. Two months before the election that brought Douglas and the CCF to power, Patterson presented a brief to the federal government's committee on reconstruction that promised both work and a level of social services in Saskatchewan that would create a "standard of living such as our resources reasonably warrant."[27] With a provincial election on the immediate horizon, the brief was as much a campaign document as a statement of government policy. It talked about the more than 70,000 Saskatchewan men and women who would be leaving military service, which created a pool of labour "available for a period of expansion and development in Saskatchewan."[28] The Patterson government said it would launch an aggressive $10 million program of public works, which included major construction at the University of Saskatchewan, as well as highway and school construction. Another $30 million was expected to be spent on public works by municipal governments.

Such notions of activist government also extended into social policy. While the provincial Liberal government had a fiscally conservative nature, it saw government as playing an important social and economic role. Clearly, some of this was a result of the political pressure coming from the CCF, but it was not out of step with the political traditions of the province. Toward the end of their term, the Liberals introduced expanded health measures to give people better assured access to health care. For example, the Cancer Control Act of 1944 gave anyone who had lived in the province for at least six months free cancer treatment. In its final days, the Patterson government also brought in health insurance legislation that expanded health coverage and established health regions. The Liberals also passed labour legislation that provided the right of labour to organize and bargain collectively, although it upheld the federal government's wartime power to prevent wage increases, unless specifically approved by the War Labour Board.[29]

But much of the Liberals' economic and social program in the early 1940s was an expression of intent for government initiatives once it had the financial resources. Patterson had earned the reputation of being fiscally cautious during his years as provincial treasurer in the Jimmy Gardiner government. In that sense, Patterson lacked the visionary quality, the ability to create a sense that Saskatchewan could rise above its economic uncertainty by taking control of its destiny, which was what Douglas brought to Saskatchewan politics.

Indeed, the decision by Gardiner to step down as premier in 1935 to become federal agriculture minister deprived the provincial Liberals of their strongest voice, and created a personality vacuum at the level of political leadership. Patterson had been Gardiner's hand-picked choice as his successor, but as a political figure he proved vulnerable to the passions stirred by the likes of Douglas. Political scientist David Smith points out that with the departure of Gardiner, the end of the Liberals' hold on power became inevitable:

> With his [Gardiner's[removal to federal politics, the Liberals were deprived of their creative, vigorous force... Firm convictions—even prejudices—and a determination to act upon them, had been characteristic of Liberal leaders. These traits were less evident in Patterson and his ministers whose views and opinions, some of which may have been strongly held, tended to be derivative and unoriginal.[30]

So a combination of factors came together in May 1944 that brought about a turning point in Saskatchewan's economic and political history when Douglas and the CCF took power. On the economic front was the impact of the Second World War and its effect on economic thought in the immediate wake of the Great Depression. The stimulative effects of government intervention in the economy as part of the war effort, coupled with the emergence of Keynesian economic beliefs in the mainstream of government fiscal policy, added tremendous credibility to the CCF argument that government should be a far more important tool in economic and social development. Although it was never envisioned that government would continue to play such a large role in the economy once the war was over, neither did anyone want a return to the pre-war years when depression gripped the economy. The memory of the 1930s was fresh in people's minds, and the war years had demonstrated that full employment was possible and that the economy could be managed by the government.[31]

Then there was the political landscape of Saskatchewan itself. The Liberals had become a spent force. With the loss of Gardiner to federal politics, the Patterson government was seen as part of a past that everyone wanted to forget, namely the last half of the Dirty Thirties. As the Second World

War wound towards a close, there was a clear sense a new era was emerging in the life of Saskatchewan. The war had dragged the world economy, and the province, out of the Depression, bringing with it new hope and a feeling of pride that came with the successful war effort.

The time had come to turn the page in Saskatchewan, to not only leave the 1930s behind, but find a way to make sure those dark days never returned. Tommy Douglas tapped into that sense of hope which had been at the core of Saskatchewan life from its very beginning. Politics would again renew our faith in the Saskatchewan myth.

Nine   The New Saskatchewan Myth

"The remedy to these deficiencies of capitalism—its competitive ethic and its economic performance—lay in social ownership. Here indeed was the magic of nationalization—it solved simultaneously a problem in ethics and a problem in economics."
(Albert Johnson)

By the mid-1940s and the end of the Second World War, there was a kind of naïve, but clear simplicity to the solutions that politics offered as a way to overcome Saskatchewan's deeply rooted, structural economic problems. As Albert Johnson says in his doctoral dissertation on the Saskatchewan CCF government, the cure was for the capitalist system to be transformed by "social ownership," whereby the collective goals of government would replace the profit-driven, private interests of capitalism. Just as with the National Policy, politics would be supreme over economics. The difference this time was it would be done for the "right" social and economic reasons.

In effect, the idea was to use government as a means to not only seize greater control of the Saskatchewan economy, but to transform the economic values of its society to those approximating the principles of the social gospel. At the core of the CCF doctrine was the belief that capitalism was morally wrong. It promoted values such as competition, individual success and greed, which were inconsistent with a moral code that said, because we live in a society, our interests are intertwined and we must put the interests of the group ahead of those of the individual. The political-economic extension of this moral code was the notion of a planned economy, where the crucial factor was not the making of profit, but the supply of human need.

Such idealism is surely a worthy goal, even if it failed to recognize how the profit motive is itself inherently linked to the satisfaction of need. This free market, argue liberal-minded economists, is the most efficient and effective model to meet individual and collective needs. "Everybody acts on his own behalf; but everybody's actions aim at the satisfaction of other people's needs as well as the satisfaction of his own need," asserts Ludwig von Mises. "Everybody in acting serves his fellow citizens. Everybody, on the other hand, is serving his fellow citizens."[1] But in the decade following the destitution and economic dislocation wrought by the Depression and drought in Saskatchewan, the collectivist mentality was never stronger. The idea that

Saskatchewan people were a community, with intimately entwined interests, had been fused into its political and economic conscience. In a very real way, the Depression had strengthened the egalitarian ethic in politics because, in an agrarian society with few class distinctions, very few in Saskatchewan had been spared the economic and social consequences of that period. The individual vulnerability each person felt created fertile ground for the belief in shared social and economic interests. What Douglas did was to use politics to raise this ethic to a higher moral level, one that spoke to the Christian morality that links the welfare of people to each other.

This collectivist impulse and the notion that government had to play a greater role in the economy—that we were not powerless to shape our economic and social destiny—certainly wasn't unique to Saskatchewan. As already noted, it was very much part of the political orthodoxy that emerged from the 1930s. It was reflected in the rise of Keynesian political economy and the economic results that flowed from government involvement in mobilizing the state into the war effort. The stimulative effect that government spending had on the economy, coupled with the sense of community created by the Great Depression, opened the door in Saskatchewan for the political notion that government could give us what we had been denied by capitalist economics. This became the new myth at the centre of public life in Saskatchewan, one rooted in the belief that we could define ourselves economically and socially through our own political institutions. It replaced what the Great Depression and drought of the 1930s had destroyed—the image and identity of Saskatchewan created, and externally imposed on the province, by the National Policy.

Moreover, by the mid-1940s there had been a fundamental change in public attitudes. Not only had the Depression been ended by the war, but the military success of the war itself, and the prospect of peace and economic prosperity, created an optimism that had been lacking for more than 15 years. The returning soldiers came home to a much different place than what they had left behind in 1939 and 1940. As Saskatchewan historian John Archer noted, the land looked prosperous and hope swelled in the hearts of people:

> The countryside was green in the summer of 1945. The rains had come and the memory of the duststorms of the 1930s were fading. Farmers were more prosperous. Business was good.[2]

At the time of the election that brought Douglas and the CCF to power in the spring of 1944, Saskatchewan was well on the road to recovery from the economic collapse of the 1930s. The timing could not have been more fortuitous for the CCF. It was a time of contrasts. The province enjoyed virtual full employment and farmers were more affluent than they had been in years, yet war rationing had created shortages of most commodities. In his study of this period in Saskatchewan life, Raymond Sherdahl depicts the time as a combination of frustration and hope:

> There was a general weariness with the regulations, depriva-
> tions and anxieties created by the war; yet there was a feeling
> of hope and optimism arising from the widely held view that,
> when the war was over, a new order would ensue in which the
> sufferings of the old could be put away and forgotten.[3]

Indeed, an economic turning point in Saskatchewan's history occurred in April 1945, less than a year after the CCF had taken power. The province's first oil well went into production that month, producing 1,019 barrels of crude oil in its first month.[4] Coincidental with the production of oil was the accidental discovery of Saskatchewan's vast reserves of potash in 1946. Although commercial production of potash in Saskatchewan did not begin until 1958, by the last half of the 1940s the province's natural resource base had been drastically expanded by discovery of oil and potash, opening new and potential sources of revenue for government.

This attitude of a new start for the province fit perfectly into the mood for political change. The decades-old stranglehold the Liberals held on government in the province came to an end as the CCF message, that prosperity and social equity through government was attainable, took root in the political consciousness. The war had shown that if government mobilized its resources, economic prosperity would follow. At the same time, it greatly undermined the argument used against the CCF that its calls for greater spending would bankrupt government and make economic problems worse, not better. As Douglas noted:

> The war had demonstrated the validity of many of the argu-
> ments the CCF had tried to advance before the war... With
> a million people taken out of production and put in to the
> service, we were still able to feed and clothe the entire nation
> better than it had been fed and clothed in peacetime, take
> care of a million people in the service, and fight a war. To a
> lot of people, this exploded the old myth that there was no
> money to implement the programmes of the CCF... The old
> reactionary cries that the CCF would bankrupt the nation
> didn't have the same terror for people in 1944 as they had in
> 1934.[5]

There was also optimism and hope flowing from the war itself. The Allied D-Day invasion at Normandy, which signalled the final major push to victory, came on June 6, 1944, while the provincial election campaign was on in

Saskatchewan. So throughout much of the campaign for the June 15 vote, the news was filled with hopeful reports from the war in Europe. Front page headlines in the Toronto *Globe and Mail* and Regina *Leader-Post* in the days leading to the election resonated with the clear message that the tide had turned in the war and victory was within sight. On the day that the banner headline in the *Globe and Mail* read "CCF Sweeps Saskatchewan," other headlines on the front page included "Allies Push 54 Miles Above Rome"; "Canadian, British Stop German Armor"; and, "U.S. Lands on Saipan; New Planes Hit Japan."

If, as many claim, that in politics circumstance is everything, circumstances could hardly have been better for Douglas and the CCF when they came to power. The idea of activist government was on the ascendancy across Canada and, throughout much of the industrialized world, the economy was booming and optimism flooded the land in the wake of the successful war effort.

What happened was that all these forces were harnessed by the CCF into a political belief that the Saskatchewan myth was still very much attainable. The end remained valid, only the means to achieve it had changed. It had not died with the Depression and the Dirty Thirties, but merely had been politically refashioned. Just as the politics of the National Policy had created the original founding myth of Saskatchewan, the politics of the CCF and Tommy Douglas re-energized the myth that Saskatchewan could still become the promised land sought by its immigrants. All it would take was for government to reflect the moral code upon which a caring, sharing society is based.

Others did not share such a magnanimous attitude to the political and economic era that unfolded in 1944 with the election of the CCF. They did not see the arrival of Canada's first socialist government as evidence that people had embraced socialist ideology as something they preferred to the free-enterprise capitalist system. The *Globe and Mail* said the election of the CCF was more a repudiation of the "machine politics" practised in Saskatchewan by federal Liberal agriculture minister Jimmy Gardiner than an endorsation of what the CCF believed:

> The explanation is … not in an evangelical conversion of Canadians to socialism. The sweeping support given the CCF was a protest, one in which the voters of all political faiths unquestionably joined.[6]

This view that people voted against the former Liberal government rather than for Douglas and the CCF was common among editorialists and others in what was a media hostile to the CCF. In a speech to the Sudbury, Ontario Rotary Club in October 1945, Regina *Leader-Post* editor D.B. Rogers reiterated the notion of the CCF win as a protest vote:

I do not think I would be wrong in suggesting to you that for every person in Saskatchewan who voted CCF because they sincerely believed in the state socialist doctrines of that party, there were at least two who voted CCF soley to protest against one thing or another. It was not so much a vote for as it was a vote against. The CCF campaign represented the shrewdest exploitation of war weariness, economic disgruntlement and political unrest I have ever seen.[7]

But the criticism of the CCF was not always so measured. Some saw the rise of the CCF as nothing less than a threat to freedom and democracy. In a world gripped by the Second World War and dealing with the two scourges of Nazism and Communism, the rise of a socialist party in Saskatchewan brought with it a strong reaction. Often the language was extreme, with an editorial in the Moose Jaw *Times-Herald* using the kind of highly inflammatory, irresponsible and irrational language that reflected the almost virulent hostility the CCF often faced:

The youth of Germany was socialized, the state claimed the child as its property, and made the school its propaganda centre to socialize the mind of the child. In a short 25 years, National Socialism in Germany produced a nation of Nazi-minded, might is right, fighting fiends who know not the meaning of freedom. They did it democratically.

Of course, this could never happen in Canada, not at least, on the German plan. But it could happen "democratically" under a Canadian plan if parents voted for it. The power in the hands of parents through the ballot is not fully appreciated,—it can be used for evil as well as good ... the CCFers would "Goebbelize" the schools of Saskatchewan; it's the inherent nature of National Socialism.[8]

Undoubtedly voter protest was a factor in the CCF's landslide election win. But no party can rout an incumbent government like the CCF did, winning 47 seats to only five for the Liberals, on the basis merely of a protest vote. What Douglas tapped into was both an unhappiness with what had been, and a sense of optimism and hope for what could be. He gave people, who had been emotionally battered by the Depression and then the war, reason to believe a better and more secure future was possible. There were contrasting moods at work in the province that produced a potent political well for the CCF to exploit. As Sherdahl points out:

There was a rarely expressed apprehension about the future, alongside of a deep determination that the events of the past 15 years would never again be allowed to recur.[9]

So, what Douglas did was create a vision of the future by harking back to a recent past that no one wanted to see repeated. On the election trail he reminded people of what they had been through as a means to create a determination to make sure it never happened again. In fact, the Depression was a regular theme in Douglas's campaign speeches:

> Stop and remember what you went through under this system for 10 years to the war. Do you think we have forgotten when our young people finished school and rode the freight trains or went to Bennett's relief camp at Dundurn for 20¢ a day, the same as we were paying our prisoners of war? Or under Mr. Gardiner our young men could go on a farm and be nurse maid to a cow for $3 a month.[10]

It became a powerful message that helped forge a consensus that if people dedicated themselves collectively to the task of building a better, more secure and sustainable economic future, the Saskatchewan they sought was possible.

This idea that government, through economic planning and social ownership, could unlock the potential of Saskatchewan that had been denied to its people, was central to CCF philosophy and the early years of the Douglas government. Upon taking power, the CCF quickly embarked on a massive program of economic and social reform that was designed by the party in the years leading to the 1944 election. Within months of winning government, Douglas called the legislature into session to implement an ambitious program that, within two years, was largely in place. Within 18 months, 146 pieces of legislation had been passed, four new departments created, 11 Crown corporations established and at least six Royal Commissions and special committees had reported to the government.[11]

Among the initiatives launched was farm security legislation that protected farmers from mortgage foreclosure on the home quarter, a trade union act that protected those seeking to form a union, higher pensions and free health care for seniors, free cancer treatment, free medical treatment and hospitalization for the mentally ill, creation of larger school districts, higher resource royalties, and legislation that allowed for government enterprise in resource and industrial development. The underlying theme to the Douglas agenda was that government could give Saskatchewan a more dynamic and stable economy, which would then pay for the social goods that would improve the quality of life for everyone. In other words, the people of Saskatchewan were entitled to a better life and could achieve it through activist government.

The economic and social philosophy was spelled out by finance minister Clarence Fines in his 1945 provincial budget, the first delivered by the CCF. It explained how government was the crucial instrument that would solve the problems that had afflicted Saskatchewan:

> We are convinced that government must provide not only the necessary social services on a generous scale and as a fundamental right of all the people, but also the overall direction and planning of economic development. Government must become the nation's or the province's nerve-centre as planner and sponsor of public development.[12]

There was no mistaking the direct economic role for government in creating a diversified and dynamic economic base that had been denied the province by the private sector, according to Fines:

> We realize that, except in times of war, private enterprise fails to provide enough jobs for all those willing and able to work. Hence, the state must assume direct responsibility for the citizens' economic welfare.[13]

But, for the state to play such an activist role, the issue of public debt overhanging the province as a result of the 1930s had to be addressed. In other words, a strange paradox existed. Before the government could have the financial latitude it needed to create economic opportunity and expand social entitlements, it first had to deal with the debt government created by trying to do the very same thing during the drought and depression. The most pressing debt issue facing the province was $20 million that Saskatchewan farmers had received from the federal government so they could buy seed following the total crop failure of 1937. The debt had been guaranteed by the provincial government and by 1944 the federal government was demanding the province make good on the debt. This created an immediate political problem for Douglas, who had held out an inducement to farmers during the election campaign that he would forgive them the seed grain debt.

Upon taking power, the new government was immediately served with the demand from federal finance minister James Isley that it pay a $16 million cash settlement, which represented half the total annual budget for the province. When the province was unable to pay, Isley withheld a $582,000 federal subsidy payment to the province that was due on January 31, 1946. The issue was brought to a head when two subsequent federal payments were also withheld and a tribunal ruled that Ottawa was within its rights to act the way it did. Eventually the province agreed to collect 50% of the money owing from the farmers who had received it and the remainder—about $8 million—the province paid by issuing 44 non-interest-bearing treasury bills that matured quarterly through to July 1956. The annual interest-free cost to the province was $700,000.[14] The settlement of the seed grain debt was symbolic of the new government's determination to deal with its debt obligations so that it could have the financial flexibility to pursue its state-led economic development agenda. In its first two years, the Douglas government reduced the net debt of the province by more than $18 million, from the almost $204 million it inherited, to $185.6 million by the end of 1946.[15]

As the first avowedly socialist government elected in North America, it was not surprising that Saskatchewan attracted a great deal of interest among those who subscribed to socialist beliefs. The province was seen as something of an economic and social laboratory, where ideas that had been abstractly debated mostly in academic circles—whether it was Canada's League for Social Reconstruction or Britain's Fabian Society—could now be tested in the real world. In some ways, the interest in Saskatchewan and public policy under a socialist government was greatest among left-wing adherents in the United States.

While the left-wing American influence on the Douglas government was not altogether obvious, it was undeniable. Indeed, Douglas himself was very much affected by American politics, politicians and political theorists. While studying at the University of Chicago, Douglas recognized and embraced the positivism of American-brand social science and he studied the theological writings of Walter Rauschenbusch and Harry Emerson Fosdick to expand his appreciation and comprehension of the social gospel. As well, US president Franklin Delano Roosevelt, whose New Deal politics were designed to lift the US out of the Depression, was someone Douglas saw as a political role model.[16] Indeed, in March 1949, Eleanor Roosevelt, widow of the former president, stopped in Regina as part of a United Nations tour and addressed the provincial legislature. In his introductory remarks, Douglas referred to "the revered and beloved Franklin Delano Roosevelt" and described Mrs. Roosevelt as "the wife of one of the greatest presidents of the United States."[17]

Very early on, a key American figure in the public life of the province arrived on the scene. He was Dr. Henry Sigerist, a professor of medical history at Johns Hopkins University in Baltimore. Remembering Sigerist from an appearance before a House of Commons committee, and recognizing him as a renowned expert in public health and socialized medicine, Douglas phoned Sigerist and asked him to head a study into the Saskatchewan health system. Although the government offered only to pay Sigerist's expenses, he agreed to take on the job and arrived in the province in early September 1944, less than three months after the CCF had won the election.

In 1932, when he was teaching at the University of Zurich, Sigerist had been asked by President Roosevelt to do a survey of public health throughout the US. Like many socialists, Sigerist had been influenced by time he had spent in 1935, and again in 1936, studying the health care system in the Soviet Union. Based on his time there, he wrote a book entitled *Socialized Medicine in the Soviet Union* that was a comprehensive and detailed account of how health care was brought within the financial reach of all Soviet citizens.

The Sigerist commission was the first major social policy initiative of the government and was acting on the CCF's election promise "to set up a complete system of socialized health services ... so that everybody in the province will receive adequate medical, surgical, dental, nursing and hospital care without charge."[18] The Sigerist commission held less than a month of hearings and submitted its report to the minister of health on October 4, 1944. It proposed the creation of a Saskatchewan Health Services Planning Commission that would divide the province into health districts, creating a decentralization of activities that would "greatly increase the efficiency of public health and medical services, while the principle of centralized direction will be maintained." The commission also proposed a widely dispersed system of hospitals to serve a rural population:

> The policy should not be to build many new large hospitals in
> the cities, or to add considerable extensions to existing ones,
> but rather to erect a larger number of small hospitals in rural
> districts. Fifty rural health centres of 10 beds each would
> provide 500 additional hospital beds and relieve the larger
> hospitals of thousands of patients.[19]

Another—rather shocking—recommendation was for the health system to practice eugenics, which of course was an idea Douglas believed had merit. It said the sterilization of "mental defectives should be given careful consideration" and suggested "one should not be deterred by the fact that Nazi Germany has practised sterilization in a brutal and wholesale manner."[20]

The report was quickly embraced by the government. The Saskatchewan Health Services Planning Commission, as recommended by Sigerist, was established, headed by the husband and wife team of Drs. Cecil and Mindel Sheps, committed socialists who came from Manitoba. Two other key figures that emerged in the health planning field were Americans Dr. Fred Mott, who held several health positions for the US government and eventually became Saskatchewan's deputy health minister, and Dr. Len Rosenfeld, who Mott brought to the province. Another American who played a role in the development of Saskatchewan health policy was Dr. Paul Dodd, an economist from the University of California. He was enlisted to carry out a study and make recommendations on a compulsory health insurance system for the cities that Sigerist had recommended.[21]

In retrospect, the recommendations of the Sigerist commission and the health policy followed by Douglas were symptomatic of the false expectations central to the Saskatchewan identity. The roots of the growing challenge—some say crisis—in health care that afflicted the province in the 1990s, and continues to this day, can be traced directly to Sigerist and the public policy path followed by government down through the past five decades. The belief instilled by Sigerist, and accepted by government, was that a sustainable health system could be created that would be patterned on the widely dispersed demographic reality of the province. While the Dirty Thirties might have sown the seeds of doubt whether the Saskatchewan farm economy and the socio-economic structure it created were sustainable, the same doubt was not applied to the issue of government creating social programs, particularly a public health structure, to support that same system. When put into its political context, this is probably not surprising. The re-energized myth that politics had spawned by the mid-1940s stated that activist, interventionist government would solve many, if not most, of Saskatchewan's economic and social problems.

In that sense, the notion of constructing a decentralized health system, where government would take health care to the people by building, equipping and staffing hospitals in small towns, fit with the emerging new political identity. It was possible because, through collective action in government, the economy was going to be broadened and diversified from its boom-and-bust, one-crop agricultural base. Saskatchewan was going to regain its position as an economic powerhouse and reclaim the hope that had been lost in the turmoil and tumult of the 1930s.

The political desire to escape the economic uncertainties inherent in Saskatchewan's agricultural economy was certainly understandable. No one wanted to relive the distress of the1930s. The problem was how to overcome the structural problems within the farm economy that existed because of unplanned and unwise settlement of many areas that were not economically sustainable. Deputy agriculture minister Maurice Hartnett talked about the need "to come to grips with some of the province's fundamental agricultural problems."[22] One example of an attempt by government to overcome the problem of uneconomic farmland was known as the Mortlach Project. But efforts to turn marginal land into productive farm enterprises failed. "These soils are actually non-arable types, although attempts have been made to cultivate them. Such attempts not only resulted in bankruptcy to the farmer, but also resulted in a serious soil erosion problem," the agriculture department reported.[23]

All this presented a dilemma for the Douglas government. It promised expanded social entitlements and a growing economy, both to be engineered by government. As Clarence Fines had said, there needed to be a wealth-generating economy to pay for social programs that people deserved. The challenge was to demonstrate that economic diversification in Saskatchewan could be achieved through the CCF's notion of social ownership. It was an alluring idea for many.

According to Allan Blakeney, who was attracted to Saskatchewan's socialist experiment from his home in Nova Scotia in the early 1950s to work for the Douglas government,

> In 1945, Saskatchewan was in many ways still a frontier province with services at a level the Douglas government was

determined to improve. Secondary industry was needed...
The Douglas government believed that Saskatchewan needed
to diversify. [It] wanted to see new industries, but unlike some
of our private enterprise friends, they did not believe that this
could be done only by people coming in from outside
Saskatchewan and Western Canada and showing us how.[24]

Thus, the path to economic security in Saskatchewan would be through
government planning. Government was seen as the primary instrument to
development and all it would take was the concerted effort to achieve specific goals. As the focal point for economic and social planning, says historian Jerry Granatstein, the Saskatchewan civil service became a place where
innovation was expected:

It was a government that believed in planning, one that
refused to accept the idea that politics had limits. As a direct
result, the provincial civil service attracted able, innovative
officials... The process was open and fresh, motivated by
Douglas' social gospel idea that government was an instrument for positive change and social good.[25]

Aside from the Americans attracted to the economic and social experi-
mentation going on in Saskatchewan, another who came to Canada to be part
of the pursuit of the new Saskatchewan myth during the early Douglas years
was noted British socialist George Cadbury. A member of the wealthy
Cadbury family that had made its fortune in the chocolate business, Cadbury
was recruited by Douglas in 1946 to sort out the organizational mess and economic misadventures that had struck the government in its early years. He
had first met Douglas while passing through Regina in 1945, when the two
discussed the government's organizational problems. A year later Cadbury
returned as the premier's key economic adviser and held the official position
as chairman of the Economic Advisory and Planning Board.

The initial challenge Cadbury tackled was the chaos produced by a cabinet that lacked coordination and proper accountability. The primary example
of the problem were the efforts by Joe Phelps, minister responsible for
industrial development, who aggressively got the government involved in various industrial projects, ranging from a box factory, to a leather tannery, to a
woollen mill. Many turned into outright failures. Ultimately the government-
owned shoe factory, woollen mill, box factory and, to a lesser extent, a brick
plant, all became economically and financially unsustainable. By the end of
its first term, the Douglas government had invested $6.5 million into com-
petitive commercial Crown enterprises and received a return of only 3.1%.[26]

A 1949 report by the planning board harshly condemned what turned out
to be foolish and ill-conceived investments that had been based on a lack of

due diligence and faulty feasibility studies. The estimated capital cost of the woollen mill had been $125,000; it turned out to be $425,000. The shoe factory was forecast to produce 800 pairs of shoes a day and during its first seven months produced only 130 pairs daily. "The original investment was in second-rate equipment and ... there is every evidence that those who laid out these two plants had little knowledge of modern techniques," the planning board said of the ill-fated shoe factory and tannery in Regina. Its assessment of the woollen mill in Moose Jaw was no less critical:

SASKATCHEWAN NDP PHOTO ARCHIVES
Joe Phelps, minister responsible for industrial development in the first CCF government, 1944–48.

We know now that we made a very poor start. Our buildings and machinery were the best we could get but were inadequate, and there has had to be a great deal of costly replacement to bring the mill anywhere near to a reasonable cost basis.[27]

In retrospect, Phelps merely applied to government policy the conclusions of the CCF's natural resource and industrial development committee that had prepared a report prior to the 1944 election. The report, issued in January 1944, maintained that natural resource development should be done by government, not the private sector. The report stated:

The CCF provincial government [should] plan for the eventual and complete socialization under provincial administration of all natural resources now controlled by the province.[28]

Although such social ownership was advocated for natural resources, Phelps extended the economic argument to other competitive industries where there was no clear need for public ownership, nor any comparative advantage or economies of scale that justified the investment of taxpayers' dollars. The naïve belief appeared to be that through import substitution, the very economic-development theory that tariffs were based on as part of the National Policy, would also work in a small market like Saskatchewan. Thus, if Saskatchewan people needed shoes, why not have a Crown corporation make them instead of importing them from Ontario?

Missing from the equation was any hard-headed economic analysis that comes with private commercial enterprise, which is based on the need for a profit margin that makes the investment worthwhile. In its place was a kind of well-motivated, but simple-minded, notion that if the private sector found a specific investment worthwhile, then there was no reason why it shouldn't also be the same for the government. There was no apparent calculation of the higher marginal costs that result from a small market with weak economies of scale. The point is made well by John Richards and Larry Pratt, political economists who studied public enterprise, and specifically the failed Douglas government enterprises:

> If the problems had been solely the quality of initial planning and management they could presumably have been resolved. But there existed fundamental cost disadvantages to these secondary manufacturing ventures, disadvantages quite independent of the form of ownership or the competence of initial planning. The low quality of local wool and the breakage of threads aggravated by the dry prairie climate were, for example, continuing impediments to the competitive potential of the mill. The shoe factory, even with a much larger share of the Saskatchewan market, would still have suffered from too small a market to permit exploitation of scale economies.[29]

But perhaps where the idea of social ownership as a means to economic development was the most misguided was when government believed it could seize economic opportunity that the private sector failed to exploit. In the case of the woollen mill, Phelps justified the public investment in December 1944 with the rather remarkable argument: "The opportunity for a woolen mill has been ready in Saskatchewan for 40 years, but private enterprise has not seized it." Quite rightly, the Saskatoon *StarPhoenix* editorialists came to a rather different conclusion:

> The fact that the opportunity has existed and that no one has taken advantage of it should prompt Mr. Phelps to be somewhat cautious about committing the province to an undisclosed investment in a potential liability.[30]

Essentially there were three arguments used by the CCF, and eventually the Douglas government, why social ownership was necessary for economic development in Saskatchewan. The first was that private companies would produce to meet the needs of the public only if they received "unreasonably" high returns. Often that led to the formation of monopolies, and the only way to counter the economic muscle of monopolies was through social ownership. The second argument was that the market-price mechanism be eliminated for essential social goods such as housing, health and education. Third was essentially the Keynesian argument that excessive profits reduce purchasing power and lead to under-consumption and recessions.

While these proved to be useful arguments as political rhetoric, there is reason to question how valid they were as the basis for economic policy in government then, or now. In his thesis, Johnson dismisses the argument that greed and high profits were harming the Saskatchewan economy as neither closely reasoned nor well documented:

> For that matter there were in the 1930s scarcely any statisti-cal data which would show objectively what profits the capi-talists were demanding. It was all the easier, therefore, to attribute the nation's economic woes to greed. Moreover, it probably seemed unnecessary under the circumstances to state what a reasonable rate of return might be—certainly the CCF never did.[31]

These kinds of economic notions, that were produced by the internal processes of the CCF, were often applied to government without any serious analysis of their practicability. Not that it mattered. When one is fervently convinced of the righteousness of one's ideas—as members of the CCF gov-ernment were in their early days—adequate due diligence is at times not a factor. Firmly convinced by its ideology, the CCF government saw social ownership as the key to Saskatchewan's economic and social ills. Collective control of the crucial economic levers by government would ensure that maximum profits went to the people of the province and would eliminate monopoly control by private industry. While, in the abstract, there was some logic to the concept, social ownership also brought with it serious economic flaws.

For example, while on one hand the government wanted to take control of the economy by selectively squeezing out private companies and investors, it would have to depend on the financial community for the capital necessary to achieve the social ownership it sought. There were also inherent questions about how to attract the skilled managerial class necessary to run government enterprises, and the issue of finding markets. The fact remained that the Douglas government was seen as hostile to private business and while the case might have been overstated by the political opposition and the business establishment itself, it put government enterprise at a disadvantage when it sought to operate in the business world. Still, the idea of social ownership was attractive at several levels. It held out the promise of taking control of the province's economic future and, in the process, developing an indigenous managerial class through government enterprise. The belief was that if eco-nomic development was left to the private sector, much of it would not hap-pen in Saskatchewan.

The idea of central planning as the key to unlocking Saskatchewan's economic potential produced processes in government that were attempts to apply Fabian socialist methods to the economy. As head of the EAPB, Cadbury's mandate to bring a sense of order and strategy to economic planning in Saskatchewan translated into three roles for the body he headed. First, to demand that cabinet keep better records of its deliberations; second, to use the planning board as a mechanism that linked democratic will expressed through politics with the expertise of technocrats in the civil service; and third, to oversee the operation of government enterprise in Crown corporations through the creation of the Government Finance Office. Robert McLaren, a professor of business administration who has studied Cadbury's role in Saskatchewan economic planning during the early years of the Douglas government, says that bureaucratic process within government was seen as crucial to successful development of the economy:

> The characteristics of this solution rose from the Fabian focus on planning, coordination, technocratic efficiency and an organizational form appropriate to a particular problem: there should be a place for everything and everything should be in its proper place.[32]

The political influence of the CCF party on the Douglas government should not be underestimated during this period. The more committed party adherents saw themselves as part of a crusade to transform Saskatchewan economically and politically. Thus, the Douglas administration was not just another government, but the vanguard of a political movement with no shortage of self-righteous fervour. As such, Douglas would meet weekly, if not more often, with CCF party president Carlyle King to discuss the government's agenda. The party also had a legislative advisory committee that included the party president and others members of the party executive who, remarkably, were allowed to attend government caucus meetings. In one letter that King sent to Douglas in 1946, the party president called for greater input by CCF members into the decisions of government. The letter called for each cabinet minister to map out a schedule for the main projects he proposed during a three-to-four month period and then call together the party's legislative committee to consider the proposals. The letter went on to propose that a full legislative caucus should be called at similar three-to-four month intervals to discuss the plans of all departments as modified after suggestions from the committees.[33]

This idea of central planning by government and direct intervention in the economy as the way to economic diversification in Saskatchewan resulted in the creation of six provincial Crown corporations by October 1945. Barely 15 months after taking power, Saskatchewan Clay Products, Saskatchewan Wool Products, Saskatchewan Leather Products, Saskatchewan Fish

SAB R-A10954-2
A Saskatchewan Fur Marketing Services employee sewing pelts, 1948.

Products, the Saskatchewan Timber Board and the Saskatchewan Fur Marketing Service had all been established. Each was a creation of the provincial Department of Natural Resources Industrial Development Branch, which had responsibility for advancing ideas of government-led economic development.

The concept of government planning and social ownership was explained in the rather stilted and rigid language of the natural resources department annual report of 1945–46. It explained that the chief function of the Industrial Development Branch was to investigate potential "industrial" projects. Should preliminary study be encouraging and the project lend itself to "public participation through social ownership," then more information would be gathered. Once the idea reached the "blueprint stage," the EAPB would take over and determine if the project should go forward.[34]

In effect, then, the belief was that economic analysis of investment opportunities in Saskatchewan done by government bureaucrats was somehow superior—at least in terms of the best collective interests of people in the province—to similar investment decisions made by the private sector. While the private economy was motivated by profit and an acceptable return on investment, government would have other motivations that went beyond the profit motive. For example, would such investment create other social

SAB R-PS5837705

A bi-plane ready to fly out products from the Saskatchewan Fish
Marketing Services plant, 1958.

benefits such as additional employment, a more diversified and therefore more stable economy, a broader tax base, add expertise in the economy by creating a new managerial class, and attract new investment to service the manufacturing industry that had emerged? The answer is obviously yes, assuming that the public investment was economically feasible, sustainable and profitable, which are the same key factors that also determine if private commercial investment will be successful.

Ultimately, whether or not social ownership and central planning by government was successful in Saskatchewan goes to the heart of the province's continuing political debate. There is little doubt that in the immediate wake of the Second World War, the Saskatchewan economy gathered strength. But how much, if anything, that had to do with the political landscape—whether positive or negative—is difficult to measure. In fact, the Douglas government quickly backed away from its aggressive, interventionist economic approach during its first few years in power.

For one thing, to compare the situation with the pre-war period of the 1930s is hardly legitimate. The world economy was in depression throughout much of that decade and the agricultural sector in Saskatchewan bore the brunt of falling demand, depressed prices and a long, recurring period of drought.

Moreover, when the political tides turned in Saskatchewan and the CCF took power to end the Liberal hegemony, the economy was already on the rebound. The massive economic mobilization as part of the war effort ended the Depression and then, very quickly, the war's devastation of agriculture in Europe created new demands for Saskatchewan wheat. At the same time, mechanization created by the war effort brought new efficiencies to farming, while exploration for natural resources helped to open up new economic horizons for the province.

This was also the period in world history when the importance of trade liberalization and freer trade was recognized. In the aftermath of the war, there was a determination in the world community not to regress into the pattern of trade protectionism that most recognized as the critical reason that plunged the world economy into depression. International structures were created, such as the General Agreement on Tariffs and Trade and the International Monetary Fund, which sought to reduce trade barriers and create a more liberal world-trading environment, as well as promote sound fiscal and monetary policy by governments.

The result was a period of post-war economic growth unparalleled in world history. From the late 1940s through to the mid-1970s the economy of the western world grew at a phenomenal pace. Swept along by those events was Saskatchewan, a province that believed it was finally going to achieve the promise of greatness upon which it was founded.

How much success and prosperity Saskatchewan enjoyed during those years relative to other provinces, and what role politics played in the province's fate, remain matters for debate and questions of perspective. As with most things in Saskatchewan, it has to do with the myth that is so central to the province's character and identity. We see ourselves as victims, somehow denied the success we believe is rightfully ours.

Ten   **The Bittersweet Years**

"There can be no doubt that the activities of the provincial government, both direct and indirect … have met with success. However, it is impossible to make any estimate of the proportion of the impressive industrial growth of the 1950s which has been a direct or indirect result of these efforts."
(Stanford Research Institute study of Saskatchewan, 1959)

Of the decades in the 20th century, the 1950s remain perhaps the least understood, and most overlooked, in trying to understand the Saskatchewan psyche. Yet the modern and most enduring identity of Saskatchewan emerged in the years that stretched through the 1950s into the early 1960s. It was a period when the province finally, and grudgingly, came to terms, if only partially and temporarily, with its limited economic potential and concentrated on achieving social stability.

There are specific political events that can be used as bookends to define this era. While in rough terms it is encompassed by the 1950s, the period extends from 1948 to 1964. Each of those years marks a provincial election. The first was the re-election of the CCF to a second term, but with a significantly reduced majority and a smaller popular vote. It was a result that tended to moderate many of the Douglas government's views on social ownership as the critical solution to economic development. The second was the defeat of the CCF after 20 uninterrupted years in power and the election of a vigorously free-enterprise, anti-socialist government under Liberal premier Ross Thatcher.

As an era unto itself, the years add up to a paradox. On one hand the province seemingly made great strides to overcome its economic dependency on a rural, agricultural economy by diversifying into new resource sectors such as oil, uranium and potash. Yet, at the same time, the province failed to keep economic pace with the rest of western Canada. The notion of Saskatchewan as a burgeoning economic power in the West that was shaken to its foundations in the 1930s was finally laid to rest in the 1950s. The province's image changed from one of great potential—a vestige of the National Policy—to that of a province unable to match the promise or economic dynamism of its neighbours, particularly Alberta and British Columbia. So, while in absolute terms the 1950s were a coming of age for the modern Saskatchewan of the 20th century, in relative terms it was an era when the province fell behind economically with the rest of the prairie region that it once had dominated.

What happened in the 1950s was the realization that the Douglas government could not deliver on its promise of an economic revolution through socialism. There was to be no political solution to the reality of economic underdevelopment. The economic hope inspired by politics and the sense of renewal that came with the end of the Second World War dissipated somewhat in the 1950s as Saskatchewan settled into a period of more modest expectations. But simultaneously, for the first time since it became a province, in the decade of the 1950s Saskatchewan became more comfortable with itself and its status.

In some ways, government itself led this transformation of public attitudes. The spirit of economic innovation that marked the last half of the 1940s, when the Douglas government pursued its economic development agenda of social ownership, was replaced by more modest, and realistic, goals. Instead of chasing an ideology based on economic hope that—through a mixture of social ownership of resources, government enterprise, co-operative development and private enterprise—Saskatchewan could escape the insecurity of a farm-based economy imposed by the National Policy, the new public attitude was one that sought consolidation and stability. It was not that the desire for economic growth and diversification disappeared, but rather that the limits of government, as an instrument for development and diversification beyond traditional natural and raw resources, became obvious.

In the months following the CCF's re-election in 1948, provincial treasurer Clarence Fines outlined how economic growth and the path to a robust, dynamic provincial economy rested with a vibrant private sector. Nowhere was there a mention of the development of resources through social ownership. It was quite a stunning reversal of both earlier rhetoric and policy. Promising to press on with a program of industrial development, Fines said:

> To this end, we propose to encourage private capital to come to Saskatchewan and to co-operate with us in the development of industries based on our natural resources. All of these developments involve tremendous capital investments, far greater in amount than any provincial government dare venture from the limited sources of revenue they presently possess. So we propose to extend an earnest and sincere invitation to private capital to join us in this great task. We are prepared to participate with them in a joint program.[1]

The CCF had come to power as an economic and social reform movement that promised to protect people from the trauma and dislocation that had occurred in the 1930s. As it turned out, the Douglas government's first term was as much a chastening economic and political experience as it was an uplifting time for the province. The 1948 election left Douglas with a greatly reduced majority as the number of CCF seats fell to 31 from 47 and the Liberals climbed to 19 from 5. At the same time, the CCF's popular vote fell from an outright majority of 53% in 1944 to 47% four years later.[2] Editorial opinion reflected a sense the CCF has been tarnished during its first term and that it had failed to deliver its promise of economic growth and social stability through public ownership.

In the election's wake the Toronto *Globe and Mail*'s editorial, headlined "The CCF Loses Ground," said the personal popularity of Douglas and the remaining radical sentiment in the province "were enough to offset rumblings of discontent with the socialist experiments which began in 1944." The same editorial went on to detect signs the CCF in Saskatchewan, as was the case in Ontario, was becoming an urban-based party, noting the CCF swept all the urban Saskatchewan seats.[3] In its report on the election results, the *Globe* stated:

> This setback of the socialist forces in Saskatchewan, while not sufficiently decisive to be reassuring in the national picture, is a significant sign of the way sentiment in the farming areas has swung away from the CCF.[4]

The same anti-CCF, pro-Liberal bias was expressed by the Winnipeg *Free Press* editorial position:

> Although denied victory, Mr. [Liberal leader Walter] Tucker emerges from the election with enhanced prestige. His policies, which might be better called principles, gained strength for the Liberal party in Saskatchewan—a fact not lacking in wider significance.[5]

By the end of the 1940s, the Douglas government's agenda of economic diversification through social ownership had lost much of its early naïveté. It was well intentioned, but misguided, and attempts at the creation of secondary industry through government enterprise had proved less than successful. In his 1949 budget speech, Fines talked about how the government recognized the need to diversify Saskatchewan's economy and had tried to use Crown corporations as instruments of industrialization. He conceded that some of the state ventures had failed and would be abandoned:

> It is this responsibility which motivated the government to establish, as Crown corporations, enterprises which would help to diversify Saskatchewan's economy. A large number of them had never been tried here by private concerns, with the

> result that this government was admittedly experimenting in the diversification of Saskatchewan's agriculture and industrial economy… There are certain Crown corporations which have not demonstrated an ability to compete for markets and at the same time make a profit. I should like to inform honorable members that it will not be the policy of this government to continue uneconomic industries.

With those words, Fines was signaling a new attitude where less emphasis would be placed on government as a direct instrument of economic development. Instead, Saskatchewan entered an era when the focus was placed on the modernization of society through public investment in social and economic infrastructure that would indirectly help create a stronger and more diversified private-sector-driven economy.

A story that former Saskatchewan premier Roy Romanow likes to tell about Tommy Douglas many years later illustrates how priorities changed after the initial enthusiasm of the CCF government for government ownership as a means to achieve economic diversification through the development of secondary industry. Romanow says that once, in the late 1960s, he was flying over Saskatchewan at night in a small airplane with Douglas, who by then had gone on to become federal leader of the New Democratic Party. Romanow asked Douglas what he believed was his greatest achievement during the 17 years he was premier. Peering out into the darkness on a clear moonlit night, Douglas pointed to the tiny lights glistening below like jewels on a black canvas, each one a farmhouse with electrical power. His most proud achievement, Douglas told Romanow, was rural electrification.

There is no denying the social and economic significance of developing a grid that brought electric power to 25,000 farms by 1954 and, by the end of 1950s, covered virtually all of rural Saskatchewan.[6] It added greatly to the quality of life for thousands of farm households and allowed farmers to become more efficient. But neither was there anything particularly unique in the achievement. The same scale of rural electrification was done sooner and more rapidly in neighbouring Alberta and Manitoba. In fact, by 1945 Manitoba had a program to bring electric power to 35,000 farms within seven years, a target that it had exceeded by 1953. "While Saskatchewan is often cited for its 'firsts,' it was last when it came to rural electrification," notes Joan Champ, who conducted a study of the issue for the Saskatchewan Western Development Museum.[7]

Moreover, across the border in the US, farming states adjacent to Saskatchewan, such as North Dakota and Montana, also developed similar rural electrification systems beginning in the 1930s, long before this occurred in Saskatchewan. If anything, the US Rural Electrification Administration, which was formed in 1935 to help finance the distribution of electricity to sparsely settled areas through low-interest government loans and support for locally owned electrical co-operatives, provided the impetus for what happened in Saskatchewan many years later.[8] So, rather than blazing a trail of innovation, the Douglas government was merely trying to keep pace, and in some cases playing catch-up, in terms of developing public infrastructure.

More importantly, what emerged during the 1950s was a Saskatchewan identity that has become a permanent image for the province. While Saskatchewan made significant strides in the post-war years of expanding economies and opportunities, it also became evident that it could not match the scale of economic growth happening in other parts of the region. In absolute terms the province went through a period of steady growth in the 1950s, but in relative terms it went into decline.

The clearest evidence of this is in terms of population statistics. In 1941, Saskatchewan's population of 895,992 made it the third-largest province in Canada, behind only Ontario and Quebec. For example, in that year the population of Alberta was 796,169, BC's population was 817,861, and Manitoba had 729,744 people. A decade later, in 1951, Saskatchewan's population had fallen significantly behind Alberta and BC.[9] While the province's population decline was halted in 1952, it's slow growth rate for the rest of the decade was far behind that of its neighbours. So the emerging Saskatchewan identity of this period was of a have-not province, overly dependent on the vagaries of agriculture, with a political culture somewhat hostile to private enterprise and an economy that did not produce the opportunity of its neighbours because of the socialist proclivities of its politics and government.

No one was more aggravated by this kind of depiction than Douglas. The premier argued that Saskatchewan kept economic pace and dismissed the notion that his government was somehow an impediment to development. It's not surprising Douglas would take exception to such opinion, given how his government originally came to power promising to broaden and diversify the province's economy. Said Douglas in 1958:

> We're still being told that Saskatchewan would get more industry if we had a better political climate in the province. I have two answers to that claim. First, in a province that has consistently had $600 million of public and private investment annually, a lower unemployment ratio than either Alberta or Manitoba and a higher per capita investment than the national average, it doesn't look like the political climate has kept anybody out. In the last decade we've had more industrial development than in any 10-year period in our history.[10]

True, but what Douglas didn't mention is that every province had record economic growth in the 10–15 years after the Second World War. These were the golden years of economic and social development. Whether trade liberalization under the GATT that led to expanding markets abroad, the post-war baby boom, or a revolution in technology ranging from jet travel to improved home appliances—all were either products of the new economy or factors that helped create it. The 1950s were a period of affluence and stable, steady, non-inflationary growth. While we tend to look on those years as quiet and uneventful, they were a seminal period because they shaped an entire generation's expectations. The notion that things will, or at least should, always keep getting better is an idea that grew out of the politics of the 1950s. So, when Douglas talked of the economic strides made by Saskatchewan during this period, it was less a compliment of his government's achievements and more a comment on the general economic times.

It was understandable that Douglas would deny that the political climate in Saskatchewan would have in any way retarded economic development. To do anything less would be a condemnation of his own administration. But to suggest that the CCF government's policies—whether legislation that gave it the power to expropriate existing industries, or labour laws opposed by business—had no effect on investment is obviously absurd. Whether the policies were right or wrong for the province is another issue, but there can be no doubt that business investors from outside the province were not ambivalent about the Douglas government. They viewed it with emotions ranging from skepticism to antipathy.

A primary voice of business in western Canada during this period was *Western Business and Industry Magazine*. It spoke directly to what business deemed to be an inhospitable political climate for investment. In his report on Saskatchewan in the December 1946 issue of the magazine, Victor Mackie wrote of how CCF policy was scaring off investment:

> Changes in provincial laws brought about by that government, particularly amendments to the Natural Resources Act, did not lend encouragement to private capital to enter the province. Under those amendments the government was empowered to enter the whole field of industrial development by constructing and operating its own industries or by expropriation of industries now in operation.[11]

Still, no one should diminish the economic strides, particularly in developing the province's resource sector, made during the 1950s. The discovery of oil and potash in 1945, and uranium a few years later, were critical developments in the province's economic history. By 1951 there was a strong sense that Saskatchewan had great natural resource development potential. In its first annual *Economic Review* issued in 1951, the government's Economic Advisory and Planning Board talked of how people outside the province saw Saskatchewan only as a wheat province:

> It might therefore come to him as a surprise to learn that the
> average citizen of Saskatchewan regards his province as stand-
> ing on the threshold of an era of important mineral develop-
> ment, and looks confidently to a future in which oil, natural
> gas, uranium, potash and other minerals will add volume and
> stability to an income now derived largely from agricultural
> pursuits.[12]

There was no denying the rich natural resource potential of the province.
The economic optimism it created for the province, which so desperately
wanted to reduce its dependence on the boom-and-bust income cycles of
agriculture, was to be expected. But ironically, it also helped to create the
firm conviction that a new era of development was at hand. In other words,
the politics of the 1950s helped spawn their own false expectations, not
unlike those based on agriculture, which became the economic cornerstone
for the province. The same 1951 *Economic Review* confidently predicted:

> As the mineral industry takes its place beside agriculture and
> the potential industry inherent in the province's not inconsid-
> erable forest wealth, Saskatchewan is moving into a new
> phase of growth that will equal or exceed that of the first 30
> years.[13]

The assertion that Saskatchewan in the 1950s could possibly expect the
same, or greater, growth than it experienced in the first three decades of the
20th century was fanciful, if not bizarre. But it was also in keeping with the
myth.

This idea of Saskatchewan as a burgeoning economy that was on the verge
of tapping into great natural resource wealth and, thus, breaking away from
the boom-and-bust cycles of an agricultural economy, was not without merit.
In many respects the 1950s ushered in a period of greater economic potential. For example, in terms of government income, resources became a major
source of revenue in the 1950s. In 1957, Clarence Fines said:

> Symbolic of the changing emphasis of our economy is the fact
> that today Saskatchewan has more oil and gas wells capable
> of production than it has grain elevators. And we've only
> begun to discover and develop the resources that lie under
> our wheat fields.[14]

Thus, by 1960, the nature of the Saskatchewan economy had changed
dramatically. For example, the value of total agricultural production typically varied wildly, depending on the uncertainties of weather and a volatile
world market. It ranged from $250 million in 1954 to $514 million the

following year, $625 million in 1956 before falling to $314 million in 1957, and then climbing to $496 million in 1960. However during the same period there was steady growth in the non-agriculture economy. Other than a slight dip in 1959, it grew from $334 million in 1954 to $507 million in 1960.[15] In percentage terms, in the 10-year period from 1948 to 1958, agriculture fell from 71% of the net value of production in the Saskatchewan economy to 37.4%. During the same period manufacturing almost doubled from 7.6% to 14.8 and mining went from 7.6% to 19.4%.[16] The labour forced reflected the shifting economy, with agriculture employment falling from 149,000 at the start of the 1950s to 122,000 at the end of the decade. Meanwhile, non-agriculture employment grew from 150,000 to 189,000 by 1960.

In its 1959 study of the Saskatchewan economy entitled *A Study of Resources and Industrial Opportunities for the Province of Saskatchewan*, the Stanford Research Institute talked in glowing and hopeful terms about the Saskatchewan economy. Given that the study was commissioned by the government's Economic Advisory and Planning Board, such a positive report was not unexpected. The study noted the "accelerating rate" of industrial and resource development during the 1950s and predicted an even brighter future:

> The province faces a future in which diverse types of industry will continue to bring new buoyancy and stability to the economy. The rich endowments of natural resources and, to a much lesser extent, the location of the province in the center of the Prairie market, are fundamental to continued economic growth and development.[17]

Casting their gaze into the future, authors Paul Lovewell and Charles Hamman saw steadily growing population that they predicted would range from 1,170,000 to 1,480,000 by 1981.[18] In fact, some 45 years later, Saskatchewan's population is nowhere near the Lovewell-Hamman prediction. Indeed, in 1981, Saskatchewan's population had yet to reach one million and although it finally broke the one-million barrier in the mid-1980s, it has again fallen back to just under one million.

Even by what it considered to be modest assumptions, given that less labour-intensive farming and larger farm units meant fewer people producing the same or more in agriculture, the government predicted strong population growth. Based on the rate of population increase between 1951 and 1955, the Douglas government suggested the province's population could grow to 1.25 to 1.3 million by 1981. As we learned, it was typically far too optimistic an assumption, another product of the false expectations created by politics.

The same kind of economic optimism was expressed by the provincial government itself, in its November 1955 brief to the federal government's Royal Commission on Canada's Economic Prospects, chaired by Walter

Gordon. The picture of Saskatchewan's economic landscape was painted in optimistic and colourful language:

> This potential is very broad in scope. It lies in the continuing ability of the farms, and of added farm lands, to produce in still greater abundance. It rests in the resources of lakes and forests, and particularly in the wide and varied range of mineral production undergoing such rapid development. It derives as well from the extensive supplies of cheap energy fuels, from the growth prospects of processing and manufacturing industries, and from the anticipations of rising productivity of a steadily growing population.[19]

While there was reason for optimism in the 1950s that Saskatchewan was gaining some relief from its dependency on agriculture, there was no escaping the truth that it remained locked in the trap of being a staples-based, raw-products economy dominated by agriculture. The entire Saskatchewan social and economic structure was built on the pattern of farm settlement that took place in the first three decades of the 20th century. As economic historian Harold Innis demonstrated in his staples analysis of the development of the Canadian economy, the nature of an economy will dictate the economic structures, which in the case of Saskatchewan meant a transportation system that supports a wheat economy and a widely dispersed population. Those kinds of fundamental structural underpinnings of an economy create rigidities that make any significant change or transformation in the nature of the economy extremely difficult, if not impossible.

Such has been the great dilemma in the endless political attempts in the post-Second World War era to diversify Saskatchewan's economy. How can you change the fundamentals of an economy when it is structured to support and sustain a family farm, wheat economy? Moreover, the political imperative is to protect the dominant economic class, which means the farm community, which depends on the very economic structures that lock the province into its one-dimensional economic character. The result is a province where political reality and economic truth have often been at odds.

By the 1950s, the future of rural Saskatchewan and the economic and social sustainability of the farm economy were very much on the public agenda. What happened was that the rapid mechanization created by the war effort changed the nature of farming. Farm labour was being replaced by machines, which meant that fewer people could farm larger farms and be far more productive than the days of labour-intensive farming. Thus, many young men who left the farm to fight in the Second World War, came home to discover that their labour was not needed on farms to the extent that it had been in the 1930s. As a result, the structural problems created by the settlement patterns of the province during the wave of immigration in the first 30 years of the century were aggravated as the rural farm economy began a steady trend of depopulation. As the provincial government's own report to the Gordon commission stated in 1955, there was much evidence to suggest the problems faced by Saskatchewan were a result of the province being settled too rapidly and too soon.[20]

For a province with an economic and social structure built upon the pattern of family farming, the technological changes that resulted in the wake of the Second World War were a destabilizing threat. Rural Saskatchewan underwent nothing short of a technological revolution from the end of the war to the mid-1950s. In the 10-year period from 1946 to 1956, the number of tractors on Saskatchewan farms increased from 71,596 to 121,388. During the same period the number of farm trucks almost tripled, going from 27,756 to 74,498, and combines went from 22,498 to 61,861.[21] With less need for farm labour and resulting larger farm units—the average farm size went from 473 acres in 1946 to 686 in 1961[22]—there was a steady migration from the land in search of other economic opportunities. From its peak of 564,012 in 1936, the total farm population had fallen to 304,672 by 1961, a decline of 46%.[23] By the 1950s, the central economic and social issue facing the province was how to maintain viable rural communities and the social system to support agrarian life.

The Douglas government recognized the economic and social revolution that was happening in the province as the small-farm, pioneer society was being forced to adapt to a period of rapid mechanization. The factors that had been the cornerstones to Saskatchewan's economy and way of life— quarter-section farms, crude farm implements, labour-intensive farm methods, towns eight to ten miles apart to accommodate farmers hauling their grain to elevators with horse-drawn wagons—became anachronistic in the new farm economy. In its report to the Gordon Commission, the Douglas government explained the forces at work in the province by the mid-1950s:

> No sooner had this pattern been established than the modern forces of a mechanized, commercialized and urbanized agriculture began to pull at the warp and woof of the early fabric. To these basic changes in agriculture there was added somewhat later an increasing industrial diversification of the non-farm segment of the economy. A mechanized and commercialized agriculture creates expansion in industry and commerce. Further impetus came from resource exploration and development. These forces have accelerated in the last decade and Saskatchewan is now in a period of transition of deep social and economic consequence. The earlier pattern is being challenged and reformed on a broad front.[24]

So, in a very real sense, government understood well that the problems confronting the Saskatchewan economy were rooted in settlement patterns, the creation of a farm economy and resulting rural society that was becoming less and less sustainable. The first and, arguably, to this day only serious attempt to come to grips with the issues facing rural Saskatchewan came in the midst of the 1950s when the Douglas government created a Royal Commission on Agriculture and Rural Life. The mandate of the commission was

> to investigate and make recommendations regarding the requirements for the maintenance of a sound farm economy and the improvement of social conditions and amenities in rural Saskatchewan.

Established in October 1952, the commission was supposed to tender its report by 1954, but was three years late and did not table its massive 12-volume report until 1957.

By the time the commission began its work, which included a long series of exhaustive public hearings, it was clear that 1950s rural Saskatchewan was at a turning point. As historian Paula Rein noted, the commission's work came after a long and traumatic period:

> the Royal commission appeared at a crucial period in the history of Saskatchewan. Its establishment was the culmination of a quarter century of turmoil.[25]

The tumult began in the 1930s with the drought and Great Depression, followed by the social and economic dislocation created by the Second World War. What the war did was tend to compel a diversification of the Saskatchewan farm economy due to the loss of western European markets to the advancing German army. Moreover, with government asserting greater control over the farm economy during the war years through price supports and the monopoly granted the Canadian Wheat Board, farm incomes began to rise. For example, in 1939 farm income was double that of 1932 and by 1942 farmers' income had doubled again, only to see levels in 1944 triple those of two years earlier. Moreover farm debt dropped from more than $500 million in 1937 to $310 million in 1943. By the end of the war, the Dominion Mortgage and Investments Association declared the farm debt problem of the 1930s had vanished. But disguised by the improving farm income situation was the reality that during this period, only in 1943–44 was Saskatchewan farm income higher, even in nominal dollars, than it had been in 1928.[26]

At the same time, growing mechanization changed the economic nature of farming itself. Gasoline and diesel power tractors, threshers, combines and trucks meant farmers had higher fixed costs as machines replaced labour. But while capital replacing labour might improve productivity, it reduced the ability of farmers to adjust to the effects of variable income. In the past, when farm income fell, farmers could reduce their costs by laying off farm labour. Not so when they had their money invested in capital equipment that had replaced the hired help. With mechanization, individual farmers could be far more productive, which led to a steady growth in farm size, displacing people off the land at the very time that many young men who had left the farm to join the military for the war, were coming home to find they were no longer needed on the family farm. According to Rein,

> By the end of the 1940s, Saskatchewan farmers were begin-
> ning to realize that post-war prosperity did not, for them at
> least, mean a post-war boom. As they looked around and saw
> the apparent prosperity of their urban neighbors they began
> to feel a growing discontent.[27]

It's worth noting that net farm income in Canada was consistently lower than the average non-farm income. For the period 1924–54, the income of farm people was on average 40% of non-farm income.

It was the recognition that the foundations of rural life were facing fun-damental structural change that prompted the Royal Commission to do its work. The root of the problem was to somehow reconcile the reality of the 1950s farm economy with the agricultural economy that had been created by the immigration and settlement priorities of the federal government in the first 25 years of Saskatchewan's existence. The Royal Commission zeroed in on the legacy of an unsustainable farm economy by noting that land tenure was the essential tool used to achieve rapid settlement. Promise people free land and they will come:

> Original settlement policy had the effect of placing too many
> settlers on holdings too small to support them. As mechaniza-
> tion progressed and as years of crop failure were experienced,
> the quarter-section homestead became acutely inadequate.[28]

But the settlement plan had a kind of built-in rigidity in that, by the time homesteaders made necessary improvements to their land and looked to expand into larger, more economic units, so too did others. The only solution was displacement of some people from the land.

The Royal Commission brought a clear ideological and partisan bias to its deliberations. It was chaired by University of Saskatchewan school of agricul-ture director W.B. Baker, who had a doctorate in rural sociology and social psychology. Other commission members were Harry Fowler, an activist in the co-operative movement for more than 25 years, Saskatchewan Co-oper-ative Producers Ltd. director Charles Gibbings, former cabinet minister and advocate of government intervention in the economy Joe Phelps, and farm wife and school teacher Nancy Adams. The lone business representative was T.H. Bourassa. A merchant from Lafleche who helped organize the local co-op, Bourassa was active in the credit union and was a last-minute addition to the commission. A Regina *Leader-Post* editorial of October 17, 1952, argued the commission could have been more representative, noting "it was heavily weighted with representation from farm organizations and the co-operatives to the virtual exclusion of other types of business and industry."

Ultimately, what the commission saw as a means to enhance the quality and stability of rural life was better planning and co-ordination between various levels of governments. Among its recommendations were better municipal roads, more rapid development of rural electrification, easier farm credit, a county system of local government to reduce the number of municipalities, crop insurance, and a centre for community studies at the University of Saskatchewan.

The Douglas government moved fairly quickly on some of the recommendations. It brought in a system of crop insurance to help stabilize farm income, roads were improved and the final push was made to complete the rural electrification grid. Although the entire system was not completed until 1966, the bulk of the rural electrification work was done by 1958. By that point, 51,027 farms had received electricity and 50,300 miles of rural lines installed with the total program costing $47.5 million. Charged an average hook-up cost of $500, farmers ended up paying more than $25 million of the cost of the program.[29]

But, as has been a constant throughout Saskatchewan's history, there were two solitudes to the social and economic progress of the 1950s. Isolated to the margins of mainstream Saskatchewan life were the province's Aboriginal people. They remained an underclass within Saskatchewan society, clustered on reserves or in low-income areas within the cities, primarily Regina, Saskatoon and Prince Albert. The barriers faced by Indian and Métis people—at the time the concept of First Nations had not entered the lexicon—were immense and reflected in the economic and social outcomes of poverty, exclusion and alienation from white society. The Douglas government's approach to Indian and Métis people was rooted in the concept of individual rights and liberty, as reflected in the civil rights movement of the United States. The objective was equality through integration of Aboriginal people into the mainstream of white society. As Douglas explicitly stated in 1959: "Reservations are becoming insufficient to hold the increasing Indian population. The solution is for Indians to integrate into white society."[30]

A paternalistic attitude, one where government knew best, imbued the Douglas government's Native policies. It was most evident in northern Saskatchewan, where the government saw its role to move Aboriginal people off their traditional livelihoods and lifestyles, into non-Aboriginal society. Inherent in the CCF approach was the belief that Euro-Canadian culture was superior to the Aboriginal culture of northern Saskatchewan. As a result, there was widely applied forced movement of Aboriginal people into communities of the north where they would learn the ways of white society and be assimilated. But, as David Quiring, who studied northern Aboriginal policies during the Douglas years, notes, it ended in failure:

> For most Aboriginals the move from the bush came to mean a life lived in semi-urban squalor, and the better world visualized by the CCF remained far away... While the CCF could soon see the growing problems, it did not admit responsibility for them. Nor did it develop effective solutions.[31]

The Douglas government believed that key to ending discrimination against Indian people was the elimination of their special status. That meant getting rid of the federal government's Indian Affairs Department and transferring responsibility for Indian people to the provincial government. Argues historian James Pitsula:

> Saskatchewan Indian policy from 1944 to 1964 reflected the liberal values of equality, individualism and freedom... The CCF's tendency to draw on liberal elements of its ideology when shaping Indian policy was reinforced by a strong desire to fight racial discrimination.[32]

This was considered, at the time, a progressive approach and one that was further reflected in the federal government's 1969 White Paper on Aboriginal people. It proposed equality and non-discrimination as the keys to solving the massive economic and social gap between Aboriginal people and mainstream white society. The Douglas government believed that integration of both Indian and Métis people into the broader Saskatchewan society and economy was the key to improving their lives. The CCF laid much of the blame for the conditions faced by Indian people at the doorstep of the federal government. It argued Indian people were victims of a federal Indian Affairs bureaucracy that was uncaring and oppressive. The solution, therefore, was to eliminate federal control and allow the province to take jurisdiction over both Indian and Métis people. In that way, all Aboriginal people could take advantage of programs offered by the provincial government.[33]

The Douglas government's policy was set out in a 1956 provincial report by a committee on Indian affairs. It had three specific proposals. First, to extend the provincial voting franchise to Indian people; second, to remove restrictions on the sale of alcohol to Indian people; and, third, to transfer responsibility for Indian Affairs from the federal to the provincial government.[34] The proposals, however, did not have consensus support from

Aboriginal people and organizations in the province, which feared the loss of treaty rights.

By the end of the CCF's two decades in power, there was little to indicate progress in the quality of life for Indian and Métis people in the province. In fact, if anything, racial tensions dividing Aboriginal and non-Aboriginal people seemed more rooted than ever. In 1963, Peter Gzowski of *Maclean's* magazine, wrote about Saskatchewan being "Canada's Alabama." Using the racial tensions of the southern US as context, Gzowski visited the small town of Glaslyn near North Battleford to write about the murder of an Indian man by six local white men. As he noted, the murderers were not "young toughs out for a brawl. Most were farmers and businessmen" who attacked the victim in a tent on the town's sports grounds. Gzowski went on to write:

> In the next few years, we may have there, on a lesser scale, what the U.S. has had in the past few years in the South... In some ways our problems may be worse. Whether the Southern Negro has the same language, the same religion and, in most respects, the same culture as his oppressor, many Canadian Indians still speak neither English nor French as their mother tongue, still practice a pagan religion and still follow a scale of moral and cultural values utterly different from ours.[35]

Chilling though the commentary might have been, the complex social and economic issues confronting the province's Aboriginal people and their relationship with white society, remained very much in the background and far removed from the mainstream political discourse. The fact was that most Indian people remained segregated on reserves as wards of the federal government. Birth rates in the post-war baby boom period of the 1950s among the white population remained high and the demographic shift resulting from falling fertility rates among non-Aboriginals and the urban migration of Aboriginal people had yet to begin.

So as the 1960s dawned, the face of Saskatchewan had changed dramatically from a decade earlier. A modern society and more diverse economy were beginning to emerge. The development of a natural resource sector had provided government with the revenues it needed to improve the economic and social infrastructure and brought greater stability to government revenues as oil, gas, uranium, potash, sodium sulphate, coal and timber expanded the province's economic base.

But in spite of a more modern society and maturing economy that unfolded in the 1950s, as the 1960s arrived there was no denying that Saskatchewan had become a province that was seen as lagging behind the others in terms of economic opportunity. For outsiders, the new identity attached to Saskatchewan was that of a province whose time had come, and gone. It was a province others saw with modest expectations, a place unable to escape the limitations of a farm economy and the society it had spawned.

There were others who still harboured the belief that Saskatchewan could be more than it was, that it was failing to achieve its potential. As always, the problem was seen as political. Alas, so was the solution.

Eleven   **The Myth and Medicare**

"The greatest single step toward the social welfare state, and the issue that ensured the continuing politicization of the Saskatchewan community, was the introduction of a universal compulsory prepaid medical care plan in 1961–62."

(Gerald Friesen, prairie historian)

As with most political events that, over time, tend to be seen as defining moments in the life of a community, the medicare period in Saskatchewan has grown to mythic proportions. Indeed, it has become an integral part of the modern-day Saskatchewan myth. It is deeply woven into the political culture of the province and stands out with the drought of the Great Depression as one of the two most critical periods in the province's history and the creation of its identity. To understand and appreciate Saskatchewan, one must understand and appreciate the myth of medicare.

In political and psychological terms, medicare was a kind of coming of age for Saskatchewan. In the wake of the 1950s, when the province lost economic ground to the rest of western Canada, medicare stood out as an achievement that in many ways transcended economics. It became a time when Saskatchewan demonstrated that progress could be measured in more ways than just population and economic growth. Progress also had a social dimension, and by providing North America's first publicly funded, universal system of medical insurance, the CCF-NDP government achieved a goal many believed was not only impossible, but utopian and unrealistic. How could a province with little more than 900,000 people possibly afford a system that would provide medical care to everyone in a widely dispersed rural society paid out of provincial tax funds and a small annual premium? With no financial assistance from the federal government, many believed the idea was fanciful, untenable and the government destined for financial ruin.

But not only did the province successfully implement and finance such a system of public health insurance, but in 1968, six years after medicare's introduction on July 1, 1962, the federal government ensured the extension of universally accessible, publicly funded health care throughout Canada by helping to pay for similar schemes in all the provinces. Over the years, medicare has become one of the cornerstones to the Canadian federation, a unifying force that is seen as a crucial component in the Canadian identity. Given that public health insurance roots are in Saskatchewan, it is little wonder medicare has become an essential ingredient to the Saskatchewan *zeitgeist* that exists to this day.

So any analysis of Saskatchewan's identity must include not only consideration of medicare, which is generally regarded as the politically intense and socially explosive 1961–62 period, but the much broader and longer-term issue of public health care in general. While we tend to focus on the stormy introduction of the medicare plan that was ushered in with a 23-day doctor strike in the summer of 1962, the fact is that this was only the last and logical chapter in a much longer process. The roots of public health insurance go back much further, long before the arrival of Douglas and the CCF in 1944, extending into Saskatchewan's glory years of the first two decades of the 20th century. As such, the delivery of health care and the development of a public system is central to Saskatchewan's character and the formation of its political identity.

To find the roots of a public health system and the belief that equal access to health care was considered a social right, you need to look back to the years of settlement in Saskatchewan, when simply surviving the social and economic environment was central to life on the prairies. The loneliness and hardships of early prairie life instilled the realization that co-operation was an essential practical tool to survival. And nothing was more important than developing a co-operative system of health care that could meet the needs of a rapidly growing pioneer society.

Rural municipal governments led the way in pioneering a public health system when, in 1916, the Union Hospitals Act authorized municipalities to establish hospitals that could serve the common public health need. Indeed, some argue that the real founder of a publicly funded health care system was not Tommy Douglas, nor his successor Woodrow Lloyd, but a man named D.G. Tuckwell, who was mayor of Lloydminster and the key figure behind the creation of the union hospital system. "It is not too great a stretch of the imagination to argue that medicare may have been born in Lloydminster and that the father of collective health care could be the town's mayor, D.G. Tuckwell, supported by his election councillors," say Fiona Colligan-Yano and Mervyn Norton in their history of municipal government in Saskatchewan entitled *The Urban Age*.[1] At the 1915 convention of the Union of Saskatchewan Municipalities, Tuckwell delivered a paper that called for co-operation among municipalities in the funding of health care. Up to that point, the municipality where a hospital was located, with the help of a small per patient grant from the provincial government, paid much of the hospital care costs for patients who often came from other municipal districts. Tuckwell called for all municipalities to pay for hospital care, which took financial pressure off the province and led to the 1916 legislation opening the door to municipal union hospitals. The union hospital system capital costs were financed through the sale of municipal debentures, while maintenance and operating costs were paid for through user fees and taxation.

During the same period, local government developed the municipal doctor plan, where the local government would pay the salary and expenses of a town's doctor, who all residents would see for their health needs. The need for municipalities to hire a doctor was the only way that people in rural areas could get the most basic of health care. According to one explanation of why the municipal doctor plan was started,

> Rural life in pioneer days was rugged, lonely and difficult. There were few social amenities. Whereas doctors could readily be attracted to the larger urban centres, it was not as easy to attract doctors to isolated villages. Why should a medical practitioner forego the advantages—clinical, social and financial—of a city practice for the doubtful advantages of small town practice unless some added inducements were offered? The idea of a municipal doctor plan was formulated to meet this problem.[2]

The first such municipal doctor was hired in 1914 in the municipality of Sarnia. Two years later the Rural Municipalities Act empowered municipalities to levy property taxes to pay for the salaried municipal doctor, which was soon extended to urban municipalities. The idea of public funding of health care was extended in 1939 with the Municipal and Medical Hospital Services Act that brought in an annual personal tax not to exceed $50 a family to help fund health care. By 1948 the municipal doctor system was well entrenched, with 107 municipalities, 59 villages and 14 towns employing 180 doctors on either a full- or part-time basis.

So, by the latter 1940s, public health care was already well established in the province. The system might have been incomplete and far from satisfactory, but the foundations of medicare were in place. This long history of public health care, as a key feature to Saskatchewan, is noted by J. Harvey Perry in his exhaustive and definitive work on government policy following the Second World War:

> It is recognized that despite serious shortcomings the Municipal Doctors system ensured that thousands of rural residents of Saskatchewan had access to rudimentary medical services that isolation and cash shortages would otherwise put beyond their reach. This background also explains Saskatchewan's implementation of provincial hospital insurance in 1947 and medical care insurance in 1962, both long before federal assistance became available.[3]

One other figure who deserves special recognition as an early proponent and, arguably, the true founder of medicare, was Mathew Anderson, a municipal reeve from the town of Bulyea who admired the public health care system of his native Norway. As early as the mid-1920s, Anderson proposed a comprehensive medical insurance scheme for his municipality paid for out of taxes. Although his municipal colleagues annually turned down the idea, because they feared raising taxes to pay for the scheme, the idea of a publicly funded system was widely held. In 1933, urban municipal councillors passed a resolution calling on the provincial government to "immediately institute a plan providing for state hospital treatment and state medical and allied services for the province."[4] Finally, in 1938, as the reeve for the municipality of McKillop, Anderson introduced a municipal health plan that became the model that other municipal plans became based upon.

The Anderson medicare model truly met the core tenets of today's modern public health care system. It was comprehensive, universally accessible and publicly funded. It provided unlimited access to care from a doctor who was hired, and salary paid, by the municipality, as well as 21 days of hospital care and prescription drugs. With residents of the municipality to be charged an annual health fee of $5 and municipalities not having the power to apply such a charge, Anderson successfully lobbied the provincial legislature to pass legislation in 1939 that allowed for the creation of health insurance districts based on his plan. Many years later, in 1998, the pioneering health care work of Anderson was recognized by then federal health minister Allan Rock in a speech to the Canadian Federation of Agriculture in Ottawa:

> Seeing for himself the suffering caused by the Great Depression, he [Anderson] convinced his small community through plebiscite that a health insurance plan was needed. His initiative then triggered a bill in the Saskatchewan Legislature, bringing the health plan to the whole province. Now this was in 1939. It was seven years before Tommy Douglas took the concept to all of Saskatchewan… Matt Anderson took such a small step in the rural municipality of McKillop. The simply human concern that he felt is now reflected in a national health system of which we are all proud.[5]

Clearly, the idea of publicly funded and accessible health care was very much in the mainstream of political thought in Saskatchewan long before the arrival of Douglas and the CCF. In fact, as one of its final acts before being defeated by the CCF in 1944, the Patterson Liberal government passed legislation to create a system of publicly funded health insurance that would be paid for by the provincial and federal governments. Of course, significant federal funding for health care was not to emerge until the 1960s, which was not enough to deter the Douglas government from going it alone with its hospitalization plan in 1947, and ultimately medicare in 1962.

The other building block to a provincewide system of medicare was the

Swift Current health region. Established in 1946 by the Douglas government, the region's health plan provided comprehensive health care that covered doctors bills, hospital care and even some dental services. It was unique in North America and eventually grew to include 75 municipalities with a total population of more than 53,000, with 44 doctors providing health care services. The system was funded by compulsory annual premiums, a property tax and a provincial grant.[6]

Another crucial component in place before the introduction of medicare in 1962 was the Saskatchewan Hospital Services Plan of 1947. It provided publicly financed—through individual premiums and taxation—universal coverage for hospital care and was the CCF government's first step towards a comprehensive system of medicare. Although it faced criticism as being too costly for government and an example of "regimentation" by its ideological opponents, it soon became very popular with the public.

Therefore, when put into its historical context, the introduction of a publicly funded, government-administered and universally accessible medicare scheme in Saskatchewan was far from a radical move. If anything, it was a natural and logical progression in a social policy and political continuum, consistent with the deeply rooted values of Saskatchewan society. Indeed, the move to create a public insurance system that would cover doctors' bills as well as hospital costs, was even politically validated in the 1960 provincial election. In his last campaign as leader of the CCF, which was about to merge with the Canadian Congress of Labour to form the New Democratic Party, Douglas campaigned specifically on the promise to create a provincial medicare system. It had been a long-standing promise from Douglas, dating back to his days in opposition prior to 1944, when he put the creation of a publicly funded health care system at the centre of the CCF agenda. The fourth point in the CCF's nine-point election program in 1944 was "medical, dental and hospital services irrespective of the ability of the individual to pay."[7] In its first term from 1944 to 1948, the CCF government introduced programs to provide publicly funded cancer treatment, coverage for the mentally ill and finally its hospital insurance plan. As Douglas said in 1958:

> we were now beginning to come to grips with the overall programme. We thought we should start with hospitalization. We didn't feel then, and I don't feel now, that you can set up a complete health insurance programme covering every aspect of health services all at once.[8]

There is no doubt that the personal commitment Douglas demonstrated to providing health care at public expense was central to his political motivation and a reflection of his Christian morality. He talked about health care "as an inalienable right of being a citizen of a Christian country."[9]

So why, then, did the introduction of medicare in 1962, which was really the last step in a long process of developing a publicly funded health system, create such controversy and public anxiety? Why was the province so deeply divided, some families emotionally torn apart, over the CCF-NDP government's move to bring in a system of government insurance to cover doctor's bills? The CCF-NDP government had campaigned on the medicare promise in 1960 and received a mandate to proceed, yet it faced opposition and an emotional backlash that for a brief, but intense, period seemed to threaten the social stability of the province.

The answer can be summed up in one word: doctors. The Medical Care Insurance Act, introduced as legislation in 1961 and passed during a stormy special session of the legislature in November, but not enacted until July 1, 1962, was instantly characterized as an assault on the medical profession. It was turned into an issue of fundamental freedom and an attack on the civil rights of doctors. The government initiative, which forced doctors to operate under medicare, was denounced by the medical profession in Saskatchewan as nothing short of communism. Doctors were being forced to work for government, and the state was going to intervene in the relationship between doctor and patient because it would be the state that would determine what medical service would be insured.

Among those who led the medical profession's lobby against medicare was Dr. Efstathios W. (Staff) Barootes, who was vice-president of the Saskatchewan College of Physicians and Surgeons at the time of the medicare crisis. In a 1960 televised debate with Douglas, Barootes expressed the doctors' vehement and unreserved opposition to a compulsory government insurance scheme that would cover doctors' medical bills to patients. As the medicare crisis reached a boiling point in the spring of 1962, Barootes told a mass rally of doctors that "never ... has there been such legislation reversing the civil rights or liberties of citizens."[10] It was this kind of rhetoric, which led to threats by doctors that they would leave the province or go on strike rather than work under the medicare scheme, that ignited public passions and made the final step in the creation of a publicly funded and comprehensive health system so treacherous. As Barootes observed many years later:

> At first people were apathetic, it was just another extension of health care services that Mr. Douglas had always preached about, until the doctors got into the game. We had never been in this game before. We were clumsy, awkward, we were highly rhetorical, we used all the antics of bad politicians: exaggeration, dire threats of what might happen. Our concern was that once the government took over physician care services ... we would become technicians or tradesmen being paid salaries by only one paymaster.[11]

For a time the doctors' scare tactics worked. The fact is that, because of

Premier T.C. Douglas (right) as a member of a television panel discussing the government's medicare program, March 20, 1960. Debating Douglas were Dr. E.W. Barootes (left) and Alex Jupp (centre).

the sometimes "life-and-death" role they play in peoples' lives, doctors have a special and powerful status in society. Their labour is unique in two ways: its consequences on the life of individuals, and the fact that it is often scarce. Thus, a strike by doctors carried powerful and disturbing implications for people and their sense of personal security. Frightened by the prospects of doctors leaving, or refusing to see their patients in protest to the government's legislation, the public began organizing Keep Our Doctors (KOD) committees across the province. Theoretically they were grassroots organizations, in many cases launched by housewives, that spontaneously emerged because of the fear that medical care would be jeopardized if the government forced the doctors to work under the medicare system. While, to a certain extent that was true, the KOD movement was also a partisan instrument used to focus and stir up discontent with the government over medicare, while at the same time becoming a lightening rod that attracted all forms of anger with the government.

An illustration of just how extreme emotions became were the antics of Father Athol Murray, a Roman Catholic priest and founder of Notre Dame College for boys in the town of Wilcox. Murray was a powerful, motivational speaker who was also passionately anti-socialist and strongly opposed to the CCF government. In one sense, Murray's anti-socialist instincts were paradoxical to his core religious views. As the founder of Notre Dame,

SAB R-A12109-4
The "Keep Our Doctors" rally outside the Legislative Building in Regina, July 11, 1962.

Murray was strongly attached to the philosophy of St. Augustine. And, according to Augustine, all attempts at political organization are destined to fail if they are not firmly rooted in the tenets and teachings of Christianity. He argued that justice was not possible without a Christian mandate, which echoed much of what the social gospel itself espoused.[12] Murray was deeply and passionately committed to individual liberty and responsibility, which made his personal beliefs inconsistent with socialist thought and doctrine. The importance of the individual, and the need to overcome adversity and succeed as both a secular and religious value, was at the core of Notre Dame's teaching. Indeed, the motto of the college was "Struggle and Emerge," a challenge given to students based on Augustine's words: "To him who does what in him lies, God will not deny His grace."

Murray joined the fight against medicare and used extreme language in speaking to crowds around the province as part of the KOD movement's attempt to block medicare in the midst of a 23-day strike by doctors in July 1962. In Prince Albert, Murray warned about bloodshed breaking out and was widely quoted as saying "and God help us if it doesn't." Later, Murray's speech to a crowd of about 500 in Saskatoon was carried live on a network of radio stations. "A wave of hatred is sweeping Saskatchewan. There has been death, there will be violence and there could be bloodshed," said Murray, at his inflammatory best. He then went on to talk about being able to smell "Reds" in the audience, warning about the communists who were behind the medicare scheme.[13]

In this kind of charged, borderline irrational atmosphere, the partisan political rhetoric also became intense, adding to the sense of crisis. Liberal opposition leader Ross Thatcher saw medicare as a means to depict the CCF government as heavy-handed and intent on using the power of the state to control people. As a former member of the CCF, Thatcher became a powerful and unrelenting critic of socialism. He used the introduction of medicare as a means to condemn the socialist government as being more concerned about controlling people and forcing its will on doctors, than creating a workable and sustainable system of medicare.

The sarcasm dripped from Thatcher's words during heated legislative debate over the medicare legislation in the fall of 1961:

> My honorable friends are always willing to socialize something that belongs to someone else. They are never so generous with their own property. In this case they want to socialize the doctors' services. They are being generous with something that doesn't belong to them.[14]

But Thatcher and the Liberals were also wise enough to realize that medicare was, on balance, a popular idea with the public. As such their criticism was carefully measured. The issue was not whether a publicly funded system of medical coverage was a good or bad idea, but how it was structured. During the debate on the medicare legislation, Thatcher stated:

> I say again that the Saskatchewan Liberal party, on many occasions, in this House and out of the House, has stated that we favoured prepaid medical insurance. I think members on this side, without exception, favour some kind of insurance that would protect all our people against major, against catastrophic, against crippling medical bills. But we are opposed to socialized medicine.[15]

The Liberals also argued that because the Douglas government received less than 50% of the popular vote in the 1960 election, it didn't have the mandate to proceed with such controversial legislation. In that election, when medicare was the primary issue before the voters, the CCF's share of the popular vote actually declined to 40.7% from 45.7% in the 1956 election. Moreover, the government also lost three consecutive byelections in 1961 and 1962, just before and after medicare was implemented.[16]

What radicalized the issue was the doctors' vow that they would not work under the Medical Care Insurance Act. As the July 1, 1962 deadline for the enactment of the legislation approached, the doctors repeated their promise to withdraw their services if the legislation came into force. They argued the government had not consulted them, as promised, when it drafted the legislation. In December 1959, when Douglas announced his intentions to go ahead with a medicare plan, he said "the program should be in a form which is acceptable to both those providing the service and to those receiving it."[17] The medical profession also maintained that the government—through its medical care insurance commission—would interfere in the doctor-patient relationship. Because the commission would pay for insured medical service, the doctors claimed it would have the power to determine what medical treatment would be allowed. As such, the professional integrity of doctors was being compromised and corrupted.

The threat of a withdrawal of all but emergency services naturally created huge concern with the public, especially amongst people across rural Saskatchewan, where reasonable access to health care was particularly crucial to their sense of security and well-being. While the same was true for those in the larger cities, at least they knew that nearby hospitals would still provide emergency care. As the College of Physicians and Surgeons kept repeating its claim that the vast majority of the province's almost 900 doctors would not work under the system, a near hysteria began to seep into the public mood. But the government refused to back down. At stake was a fundamental democratic principle. A duly elected government had passed legislation and could not be held hostage by a specific group, even one as influential and essential as doctors.

There were some, such as Otto Lang, the young dean of the College of Law at the University of Saskatchewan, who maintained the doctors had the perfect legal right to operate outside the act. But even if doctors did not practice under the medicare system, Lang argued they would be controlled by it:

> Any doctor practising outside the act would still be subject to control by the commission because the commission has discretion in regards to payment of bills. We beneficiaries are not given a legal right to claim against the commission for proper medical expenses. We are forced to trust the magnanimity of the commission. By turning its magnanimity on and off, the commission has great powers over all patients and doctors. This has been the basic defect in the Medical Care Insurance Act, and it remains such.[18]

Ironically, the doctors' ultimate weapon of a strike proved to be their undoing. What turned out to be a 23-day withdrawal of all but emergency services by physicians ended up being less traumatic than people had expected. The tide turned against the doctors as the public hysteria and fear subsided when people realized that emergency medical care was available.

Woodrow Lloyd, who had taken over as premier from Douglas and had to stare down the striking doctors, built a persuasive argument when he talked about the doctors defying the law as passed by a government that had campaigned on its medicare promise and won a comfortable majority:

> The issue is whether the people of Saskatchewan shall be governed by a democratically elected legislature or by a small, highly organized group. The people of Saskatchewan have been served notice by this organization. The notice is that until we repeal the Medical Care Insurance Act or unless the group is permitted to ignore this act by a duly constituted government, the people of the province will be punished by curtailment of medical services.[19]

Eventually, cooler heads prevailed and the College of Physicians and Surgeons reached a truce with the government. The Saskatoon Agreement, as it was called, allowed patients to continue using private, doctor-run medical insurance agencies, such as Medical Services Incorporated or Group Medical Services, that had provided coverage for doctors' bills. These private health agencies would become clearing houses for medicare payments. As such, doctors could still bill the private agencies, which would receive payment from the government's Medical Care Insurance Commission (MCIC) and pass the payment on to the doctor. The agreement also allowed doctors to bill patients directly, if they wished, with patients then being reimbursed by the medicare plan. Very few doctors opted for the direct billing method and instead worked fully in the medicare system by billing MCIC on a fee-for-service basis.

With the benefit of more than 40 years hindsight, and the detached perspective of viewing the battle over public medical insurance within the historical framework of public health policy development in Saskatchewan, the medicare crisis tends to lose some of its momentous significance. There is no denying that, as a political event, it was historic. The doctors' strike was an event that focused national and international media attention on the province. It was a showdown between a government backed by the legitimacy of the democratic process and a powerful interest group in society that believed its professional and civil rights were being extinguished. Given the absolutely critical role that doctors play in society, the public's sense of vulnerability in the face of the doctors' refusal to perform their duties turned the medicare dispute into an emotionally explosive public issue. With the media drawn to the sense of crisis, the showdown over medicare naturally attracted massive national—and even international—coverage, which added to the sense of historic significance to what was happening.

Yet, if you look back at what the media was saying at the time, and when the idea of a publicly funded medicare scheme was put into an historical perspective, the radical and even visionary nature of what the Saskatchewan government was doing is somewhat diminished. There was very little support for the doctors' action. For example, even the conservative-minded Toronto *Globe and Mail* editorials condemned the doctors for going on strike:

> The doctors of Saskatchewan have taken an action which is not open to any individual within a democracy. They have deliberately decided to disobey a law of that province.

The Brandon *Sun* castigated the doctors for their rigidity and said:

> this seems now to prove beyond any reasonable doubt that it is the doctors and not the government, as many have alleged, who are the diehard.[20]

The same was true of the Regina *Leader-Post*, which had been virulently anti-government in the months leading up to and during the medicare crisis. It sounded almost apologetic when the Saskatoon Agreement was signed and the strike ended:

> Now that calm has been restored, the hope is the compromise that has been reached will impress the fact on the part of the world which lies outside Saskatchewan that the controversy was not over the principle of prepaid medical care, or medical care insurance. The issue was the form of the medical care plan to be adopted. The compromise merely resulted in the changing of the form to assure its acceptability.[21]

The emotions surrounding the issue and the panic associated with the doctors' strike tended to magnify the medicare dispute and, with it, create a sense that this was a truly revolutionary move by the CCF government of the day. From that has evolved over time a political mythology around medicare as a watershed event because of its radical nature. The NDP still sees the medicare crisis as the most important event in its history, a kind of defining moment that sets it apart from other political parties.

To some extent that is not an unjustified point of view. Certainly the CCF government had to demonstrate the courage of its beliefs by not succumbing to the doctors by making major changes to the medicare act. Although Douglas became, and largely remains, the political icon of medicare, Woodrow Lloyd deserves much of the credit. Unfortunately, his role in the birth of medicare is often overlooked. Douglas resigned as premier and left Saskatchewan to become federal NDP leader before the medicare crisis peaked. It was up to his successor, Lloyd, to pilot the legislation into law and stare down the doctors. Still, such a medicare plan was not a radical initiative for the government to take. In the post-Second World War years, the idea of a growing role played by government in the economy and society at large was very much in the mainstream. Indeed, attempts to fashion some kind of a national medicare scheme were a central feature of the national political debate and an on-going policy initiative of federal and provincial governments.

As early as its Throne Speech in 1944, the federal government committed itself to a national health insurance scheme and the idea had been put forward by the Rowell-Sirois Commission's 1940 report on Dominion-Provincial Relations. The federal-provincial Reconstruction Conference of 1945 contained a specific two-part proposal where the federal government would assist the provinces, which had jurisdiction over health, with the creation of a national health-insurance scheme. Part one would cover general practitioner and hospital care;

SAB R-B12052

The "Fathers of Medicare" in Saskatchewan, Woodrow S. Lloyd (left) and T.C. Douglas (right), at the founding convention of the NDP in 1961. Lloyd succeeded Douglas as premer.

the second stage would be extended to cover specialists, drugs and dental care. The first phase was expected to cost $115 million a year, with Ottawa covering two-thirds of the cost. The total program was estimated at $250 million a year, again with the federal government picking up two-thirds of the total. But the jurisdictional issue over health, coupled with other tensions relating to taxation after the war, prevented any kind of federal-provincial agreement on a national health plan.[22]

So, many years before the medicare legislation was brought into force in Saskatchewan, amid the tension and near hysteria of a doctors' strike, the idea of just such a plan had been on the public agenda both federal and provincially. What made it momentous in Saskatchewan was the conflict it created with the medical establishment and the fear of a doctors' strike that rippled through the public.

In retrospect then, over time medicare as a political event has grown far beyond its true significance as a groundbreaking and far-sighted initiative. It has woven its way into the political fabric and consciousness of the province and become a symbol of what makes Saskatchewan and its people unique. As such a defining moment in the life of the province, medicare became the crowning achievement in what had been a decades-long struggle to try to create a sense of social stability in a province that constantly wrestled with the social and economic reality of its early years.

When seen from that context, medicare is an essential ingredient to the modern Saskatchewan myth. It is an event that sets the province and its people apart, while at the same time it acts as a critical development that helped the province overcome the insecurities of a society and economy that had been built on its original false expectations.

Twelve   The Potash Myth

"The leader of the socialist party tells us that the Crown corporations have done more than any single thing to stimulate Saskatchewan's industrial development. In my opinion, such a statement is nonsense... The threat of expropriation, the competition of government-owned industries paying no taxes, the impractical theories of socialist planners have discouraged private investors from coming into Saskatchewan and has retarded industrial development."

(Ross Thatcher, 1957)

No event better symbolized the clash of political and economic visions for Saskatchewan than what occurred on a rainy spring day in May 1957 in the small town of Mossbank. It was there that Premier Tommy Douglas debated Ross Thatcher, a former CCF member of Parliament who had deserted the party and was running as a Liberal in the federal election of that spring. The two met before an overflow, and intensely partisan, crowd in the town hall, with the debate carried live on a network of radio stations across the province.

The clash was a turning point in the political culture of Saskatchewan. The conflict of ideologies embodied in Douglas and Thatcher represented a dialectic that helped usher in a new political era in Saskatchewan, one that drew into stark focus the perceived economic weaknesses of the province. Its significance was not the socialism-versus-capitalism undercurrent of the debate. That had been part of the political discourse since the arrival of the CCF and its 1933 Regina Manifesto, that called for social ownership and declared that no CCF government would rest content until it "eradicated capitalism" and replaced it with the full program of socialized planning. What made this different was the force of Thatcher's personality. He brought to the political debate the passion of a convert from the CCF and the zeal of someone who was on a mission to build a new Saskatchewan, one worthy of its founding myth.

What might be termed the "modern era" of Saskatchewan politics began that day. But the debate's relevance was not in its immediate political effect. Indeed, Thatcher lost his federal election bid, even though, in the highly subjective terms of debate scoring, he was widely seen as more than holding his own against Douglas, who, by that point, had become a living icon in

SAB R-WS15163 © M. WEST, REGINA. WEST'S STUDIO COLLECTION
The Mossbank debate, May 20, 1957, where Ross Thatcher (podium) confronted premier T.C.
Douglas (right). Thatcher was a member of Parliament at the time, but would soon become
leader of the provincial Liberals, and eventually premier.

Saskatchewan politics. But by standing up to Douglas and, at worst, debating the CCF leader to a draw, Thatcher achieved two things. First, he demonstrated that Douglas was politically fallible. Second, he recast the political debate in terms of economic underdevelopment. By asserting that socialist interventionist government policies had prevented Saskatchewan from reaching its full economic potential, Thatcher was appealing to sentiment rooted in the Saskatchewan promised land myth. He was speaking directly to the core belief that Saskatchewan was failing to reach its true economic destiny that had been so promising a half-century earlier. In the years of rapid economic development in Canada following the Second World War, there was a growing sense Saskatchewan had lagged behind and lacked the investment to overcome its status as an agrarian economy. The psychological hangover from the Dirty Thirties persisted.

This modern era of Saskatchewan politics, that began with Thatcher and continues to this day, is a period when pursuit of the Saskatchewan myth has been defined more than ever by the province's relative position in the West. Since the 1960s, Saskatchewan's external identity, as a province unable economically to keep pace with the region, has also become deeply ingrained in the provincial psyche. There is a recognition that the great hope once embodied in Saskatchewan, the sense that it represented a land of opportunity, a place where dreams come true, has been relegated to an artifact of the province's history, rather than a statement of its future.

So, as has been the case throughout the province's history, Thatcher adapted the myth to meet his political objective of ultimately winning power and ending the 20-year reign of the CCF. What he did was explicitly to attach it to what he said was a failed model of economic development under the CCF government. He set out to convince people that the key to the province finally reaching its economic potential was through private sector investment, particularly in natural resource development. The symbol of success for Thatcher would be to turn the province's natural resource wealth—both renewable and non-renewable—into a source of jobs and growth for the economy and revenue for the province to support its public policy choices.

The critical component was exploitation of Saskatchewan's vast potash reserves. Thatcher positioned potash as the key that would finally allow Saskatchewan to achieve its true potential and become a worthy rival—in terms of economic dominance in the region—of Alberta. Indeed, the potash era that began with Thatcher continued through the following two decades. During that entire period potash became as much, or even more, of a political symbol as it was an economic development outcome. In fact, to understand the evolution of Saskatchewan's political economy through the 1960s, 1970s and 1980s, one need only follow the potash saga. That is not to suggest economic development policy during the period did not reach far beyond potash. The oil and gas sector was, and remains, a cornerstone of Saskatchewan's resource economy. As well, beginning with the Douglas government and extending to this day, resource development in the north—such a forestry and uranium mining—have been important elements of economic policy.

It is also not fair to suggest that resource development and the need to capture greater revenues from the province's natural resources was something that began with Thatcher. In fact, control of natural resources, or more precisely lack of control, was a long-running grievance for the province, dating back to 1905, when the federal government retained control of natural resources to use as an incentive to stimulate settlement of the province. In the years before Saskatchewan gained control of its natural resources in 1930, the federal government granted mineral rights to the CPR and its vast land holdings, as well as the CNR, Hudson's Bay Company and others, including some homesteaders. It's estimated that by 1930, 18 million acres of land had "alienated mineral rights," or ownership of the natural resources in private hands.[1]

The anger over the federal government's treatment of Saskatchewan's natural resources, and the importance of resource development to the provincial economy, was seized upon by the Douglas government when it took power in 1944. One of its first acts was to pass the Mineral Taxation Act, which levied a per acre tax on owners of mineral rights.[2] In its 1947–48 annual report, the Saskatchewan Department of Mineral Resources expressed the sense of grievance over the federal government's treatment of the province's resources:

> The policy of allowing mineral rights to become alienated from the Crown, as followed out by Dominion authority in the past, was wrong in principle, was not in the best interests of the people, and militated against the conservation of the country's natural resources. In many cases companies and individuals acquired valuable mineral rights under circumstances which practically amounted to a free gift of the minerals.[3]

But this "modern era" in Saskatchewan politics, that took root in the 1960s, was not limited to perceptions of economic development, or the province's lack of it. The 1960s were also a decade when people finally started to become aware of the reality of Aboriginal life in the province. It was Thatcher who, more than any Saskatchewan politician before or since, brought the economic and social plight of Aboriginal people into a sharp and often compelling public focus. He took a personal interest in the issue, talked about it in stark terms and tried to use government as an instrument to better the lives of Aboriginal people. Granted, his was a paternalistic approach that, by today's standards, seems misguided. But it was not inconsistent with the norms and attitudes of the time. What Thatcher did was to put it on the public agenda, warn about how a failure to address the issue would have dire consequences for the province and, in that sense, predict the reality Saskatchewan faces today.

At the time that Douglas and Thatcher met in Mossbank, the province—in both relative and absolute terms—had been effectively in a state of slowing economic growth, if not decline, for three decades. The high expectations, embodied in Saskatchewan during the heady years of rapid immigration and settlement, when the province was seen as the most dynamic and with the most potential of any in the nation, were a distant memory. The reality was that the province, in many ways, had become merely a shadow of what it had been and what many had expected it to become.

Certainly, some of the economic and demographic facts tend to support that view. By 1960 Saskatchewan had fallen well behind Alberta, and to a lesser extent Manitoba, in terms of growth. For example in 1960, the value of manufacturing in Alberta was $877 million and the sector employed almost 27,000 people. In Manitoba, for the same year, production was worth $713 million and 31,800 worked in the sector. By comparison, total value of manufacturing production in Saskatchewan in 1960 was slightly less than $330 million and fewer than 9,000 worked in the sector.[4]

On a national basis, Saskatchewan's nominal GDP growth during the decade 1953–63 lagged behind that of Canada. Saskatchewan's average annual economic growth over that 11-year period was 4.8%, compared to slightly more than 6% nationally. But at the same time, GDP per capita in Saskatchewan, which trailed the Canadian average in 1953—$1,677 versus $1,778—had grown to $2,597 by 1963, compared to the national per capita average of $2,519.[5] While on one level the growth in GDP per capita indicates higher productivity levels in Saskatchewan, it also reflected stagnant population growth compared to the national average. The other interesting outcome was the incredible year-over-year volatility of the GDP numbers. Four times in that period, year-to-year percentage change in GDP was negative.

The decline of Saskatchewan was mostly evident in its falling share of Canada's population. Less than three decades earlier, Saskatchewan had been the third most populous province in Canada, behind only Ontario and Quebec. But by 1961 it had fallen to fifth place, behind British Columbia and Alberta, only to slip another rung down the ladder when Manitoba's population surpassed it in 1966.

The notion that Saskatchewan was not keeping pace, and economically stagnating compared to its neighbours, has been the continuing theme of political debate in the province from the early 1960s. More than anyone else, Thatcher was able to create such a comparative economic focus in the public dialogue. He brought credibility to the political argument and clarity to the issue of economic underdevelopment. Credibility, because as a former member of the CCF-NDP, he could speak with the passion of a convert who believed he had seen the error of his ways. Clarity, in the sense that the focus became how to achieve a stronger and more diverse economic future for the province. The view that public enterprise was ultimately an impediment, rather than a stimulant to growth, as the central dividing line for the political debate in the province therefore took root in the 1960s, particularly when Thatcher became premier and the Liberals took power in 1964.

While such an ideological divide was evident in the political and economic discourse of the province in the 1940s and 1950s, it was not fully engaged until the arrival of Thatcher, who starkly framed the choice as free enterprise versus socialism. He was relentless and unequivocal in his characterization of the problem. Neither before, nor since Thatcher, has Saskatchewan seen a political figure who so dominated the political debate by the sheer force of his views, personality and style. The issue was arrested development, the cause was bureaucratic government involvement in the economy. Of course the issue was not so black-and-white. But partisan politics does not lend itself to nuance, certainly not when it involves someone with Thatcher's strong presence and views. The fact was that CCF governments under Tommy Douglas had followed a mixed-economy model. Rather than hostility to free enterprise, the focus during the Douglas period was on building a more modern social and economic infrastructure of the province.

But it was also true that, with the only socialist government in North

America, Saskatchewan became something of a social and economic labora-tory under Douglas and the CCF. It attracted people from across Canada, the US and England, who subscribed—or were at least sympathetic—to the model of socialism as an instrument for social and economic development. As already noted, Douglas actively recruited ideological soul mates from abroad. There can be little doubt that the socialist label during the Douglas period meant Saskatchewan had less than a positive image with the business com-munity, particularly in the United States. At the same time, next door in Alberta the political hegemony of successive Social Credit governments, which welcomed foreign investment, while espousing free enterprise and small government, contrasted sharpy with Saskatchewan. Indeed, it was dur-ing that period when Alberta's economy raced ahead of Saskatchewan, in large measure because of Alberta's massive light crude oil deposits.

Ironically, when put in a longer-term context, Thatcher's stark character-ization of underdevelopment in Saskatchewan as an outgrowth of govern-ment intervention in the economy and society, was inconsistent with the political history of the province. From the province's earliest days, when the sense of external control of the province's destiny took root, the need for a collectivist response was very much part of the Saskatchewan psychology. Whether farmer-owned co-operatives, government mortgage companies to compete with private banks to support farmers, orderly marketing through the Canadian Wheat Board, or a government-owned insurance company, the central motivating principle was the need for the province to take greater con-trol of its economy and future. The belief that outside interests—the railway monopoly, the international grain trade, tariff-protected central Canadian industry, a political system dominated by Ontario and Quebec interests—were dictating the province's future, generated a homegrown political econo-my that sought to give the province a greater control of its destiny.

There is no doubt that in absolute terms, from the post-war period under Douglas through to the early 1960s, Saskatchewan made significant social and economic progress. The most obvious was in the health field—publicly funded hospitalization and eventually universal medicare—but the CCF gov-ernment also made strides in terms of labour legislation, creating, for exam-ple a Department of Labour. But what mattered by the 1960s was the province's economic position relative to neighbouring provinces and, more broadly, in terms of its status in the rest of Canada. By such a relativist yard-stick, the story was far less encouraging.

In retrospect what was truly remarkable about the Thatcher period in Saskatchewan history—specifically the 1960s—is that it defied conventional thinking at the time. The arrival of a conservative like Thatcher, who spout-ed the mantra of less government, fear of overspending leading to debt stran-gling government's fiscal capacity, lower taxes, free enterprise, more foreign investment and individual initiative, was counter-intuitive to the mood of creeping anti-Americanism that reflected the times. In the context of those opinions Thatcher was a radical. And, in the context of today, with a much more global open market, freer capital flows and little concern about foreign investment, he was a visionary.

This was an era when the "left" was on the rise in Canadian politics. There was a growing mood of economic nationalism. It had evolved slowly, taking concrete shape with the 1957 Royal Commission on Canada's Economic Prospects, which raised concerns about the impact of post-Second World War investment by the US in the Canadian economy. The notion was that Canada's branch-plant economy meant that Canadian economic destiny was in the hands of American corporate interests. The report stated:

> We do not believe Canadians will cease to be concerned about this matter unless something is done to make Canadian voices more strongly and effectively heard in some vitally important sectors of our economy in which non-residents exercise a large measure of control.[6]

Walter Gordon, chief author of the commission report, later became finance minister in the federal Liberal government and, in his 1963 budget, sought to restrict foreign ownership of the Canadian economy.[7] The budget called for a minimum of 25% Canadian ownership of all foreign-owned companies operating in Canada, and also set out a 30% tax on foreign takeovers of Canadian-owned firms.[8]

Two subsequent federal studies into foreign ownership of the Canadian economy eventually led to the creation of the Foreign Investment Review Agency, which limited foreign investment in Canada. The most significant was the Watkins Report, named after University of Toronto economic historian Mel Watkins who headed the study. Although it acknowledged the interdependence of economies and that foreign investment brought economic benefits to Canada, the study also clearly called for a "new National Policy" where government would play a much larger role in shaping the economy and overseeing investment:

> The Canadian public interest would be directly served by new national policies which recognize the need for a stronger government presence to countervail the power of multinational firms and, on occasion, foreign government power exercised over these firms.[9]

Therefore, the 1960s were an era in Canada of growing unease with our nation's economic and political relationship with the US. Opposition to the war in Vietnam was growing on university campuses across Canada—and the US for that matter—and more and more opinion leaders in Canada were expressing anti-American sentiments. Indeed, one of the hotbeds of anti-

SAB R-A8359 © M. WEST, REGINA. WEST'S STUDIO COLLECTION
Official photograph of premier Ross Thatcher, c. 1965.

Americanism and opposition to the Vietnam War during the mid-to-late 1960s was the Regina Campus of the University of Saskatchewan. During this period, the "new campus" emerging on the southeast outskirts of the city focused its academic development on liberal arts. As a growing new institution, the Regina Campus attracted many US-born professors in political science, sociology and the other social sciences who came to Canada in part because they opposed the war in Vietnam. In fact, in the late 1960s, the campus went so far as to advertise for professors in *The New Statesman*, a left-wing magazine published in Britain. Very quickly, and not surprisingly, a kind of left-wing, branch-plant American academic mindset was inculcated into the university culture.

Given this kind of environment, and the province's collectivist political culture that for 20 years was institutionally entrenched by the CCF, the rise of free-enterprise Thatcherism in Saskatchewan is all the more remarkable. In fact, Thatcher's often passionate rhetoric in support of foreign investment is noteworthy in that it was so clearly running against the current of conventional wisdom of the political times. While others warned about the effects of US investment—loss of economic control, the further growth of a branch-plant economy—Thatcher had no such concerns. His commitment to foreign investment and resource development was made unequivocally clear many times, but never more so than in an October 1965 speech to the potash industry:

> Because we know socialism, not from text books but from hard, bitter experience, our government today is dedicated to the principles of private enterprise... We are convinced that it [private enterprise] is the best system yet devised for economic progress. Under that system, Canadians and Americans both enjoy the highest standards of living in the world... Therefore, I believe, as I have said before, that the only thing wrong with American investment from

Saskatchewan's viewpoint is that in the past we haven't been getting enough of it. I hope we will see a good deal more in the years ahead.[10]

But, on the surface, what might appear counter-intuitive to many was, in fact, quite logical when put in the context of the Saskatchewan myth. What Thatcher understood and tapped into was the deeply rooted belief that the province was failing to meet the public's expectations and its own potential. The province that 40 years earlier was the most dynamic and fastest-growing in Canada, the place that immigrants and their families were told would rival the economic opportunity of Ontario and Quebec, had turned into a laggard. Thatcher converted that economic fact into political reality. He was able to distill the public's sense of economic frustration into a political motivation by rekindling belief in the myth of Saskatchewan as a promised land. Speaking to the Saskatchewan legislature while still opposition leader, Thatcher stated:

> I am opposed to socialism and all that it stands for. Because I think, given time, socialism erodes and destroys man's initiative and independence. I believe that a greater investment of capital in Saskatchewan is the one vital step towards the achievement of virtually every economic and social goal, which we hold dear. I believe that you cannot make a nation or province strong, united or productive, by fomenting class hatred. I believe in the dignity of labour and I support its reasonable and legitimate aspirations, but I do not believe that government is helping the wage earner by trying to undermine the people who pay the wages.[11]

Clearly, then, the April 1964 election that brought Thatcher's party to power, ending two decades of rule by the CCF, was a pivotal political event. Still, the Thatcher period has been largely dismissed by historians and political scientists as not particularly relevant in any permanent political or economic sense. They see it as a kind of interregnum, a time when Thatcher's radicalism did not produce a significant political or economic legacy. As noted Saskatchewan historian John Archer argued, Thatcher's rise to power was "not a victory of private enterprise over socialism." Rather, Archer said, in the election of April 1964 "the more prosperous classes in the electorate had spoken for change even though the evident prosperity in the province had come under the 'socialists'."[12]

Political scientist David Smith echoes the view that the 1964–71 period carried little significance in the political and economic life of the province. Smith, who has written extensively on the role of the Saskatchewan Liberal party in the 20th century, argues that

> From the first the Thatcher government could lay claim to a
> unique place in Saskatchewan history. Part of the distinctive-
> ness arose from its commitment to private enterprise. But the
> tenets of that doctrine were no more a break with the tradi-
> tion of Saskatchewan governments than the reluctance they
> inspired amongst Liberals to use their new power to develop
> policies. No government in Saskatchewan did so little with its
> mandate.[13]

But its lasting significance was transformative not in the sense that
Saskatchewan's economy reached the potential that Thatcher predicted, or
that the period radically changed the role of government in Saskatchewan.
Rather, its relevance was as a psychological turning point for the province,
one that has shaped the context for the economic and political debate to this
day. The 1960s under Thatcher became a period when the judgment of
progress, more than ever, was hard-wired in the language and rhetoric of economic development and diversification. It was a time when Thatcher's political rhetoric convinced Saskatchewan people their province was not achieving its economic promise. Therefore, their expectations of a more prosperous, populous and faster-growing province, consistent with the Saskatchewan
myth, were valid. As a result, the lens through which to view Saskatchewan
in the mid-to-latter 1960s was in terms of natural resource development. It
was to turn the promise and myth of Saskatchewan into reality.

In retrospect, and to some degree, Thatcher was right. There was an unrealized potential in the province, primarily in the natural resource sector. The
evidence is the rapid development that happened under the encouragement
of Thatcher's paradigm of a business-friendly, free enterprise, smaller government that valued initiative and private investment. It was during the seven
years under Thatcher that largely private investment created the foundation
of the potash, oil, uranium and forestry sector that flourishes to this day in the
province. Clearly, not all of that development is the direct result of the change
in government and, indeed, private potash investment had begun under the
previous Douglas CCF government. As in all markets, the key drivers were
world prices, costs and projected return on investment. But political climate
is also a business determinant. Thus, the arrival of a plain-speaking, pro-
business, anti-socialist like Thatcher was undeniably welcomed by the business community in Canada and the US. For Thatcher, the key to development was attracting private investment, as he told the provincial legislature
in 1964:

> This government believes that a greater investment of private
> capital in Saskatchewan is the one step that is vital in the
> achievement of every economic and social goal we hold dear.
> We passionately believe that only private enterprise methods

will achieve this much needed investment. We are convinced that industrialists will establish in Saskatchewan for only one reason—because it is profitable for them to do so.

This government, therefore, will endeavour to nourish our investment climate; take care of our investment worthiness; and improve our methods of attracting new capital. In every field of commercial endeavour, we propose to explore and provide sound incentives for risk-taking and development.

We intend to keep the burden of taxes and regulations at their lowest possible level. By doing so, we think we can obtain new mines, new oil wells, new manufacturing plants, new businesses on a far more comprehensive scale... Moreover, with more industries and more people we shall broaden the basis of taxation, which will provide the revenues for expanding our educational, cultural, transportation, health and welfare services.[14]

A primary role of politics is to raise public expectations of a better future. And, like Douglas and the other provincial political leaders who preceded him, Thatcher offered the hope of a better future. The key to jobs and growth was economic development; the means was private investment. The courting of private enterprise as the solution to Saskatchewan's underdevelopment was incessant under Thatcher's government, with the premier leading the cheerleading chorus.

By September 1964, at the International Williston Basin Symposium in Regina, Thatcher was claiming that oil and gas revenues for the province were running $4 million ahead of budget estimates. "If the oil industry—or any other industry—is to flourish and expand, there must be a proper political and economic climate. Royalty rates must be competitive and taxes not too excessive," Thatcher said.[15] The implicit message was clear—under the previous CCF government Saskatchewan had stagnated because the political and economic climate was hostile to business. The next day, at the same oil and gas conference, that view was echoed by J.C. Sproule, a consulting geologist and former employee of Imperial Oil at the time of the Leduc oil field discovery. Sproule said policies of the former government, such as an expropriation clause introduced in 1945, convinced Imperial Oil to abandon its exploration activities in Saskatchewan and focus more on Alberta.[16] A year later the Leduc discovery was made and Alberta's oil sector began to grow rapidly.

For Thatcher, in terms of symbolism and economic development, nothing was more important during the mid-to-latter 1960s than exploiting Saskatchewan's natural resource base. The notion that Saskatchewan could tap into its non-renewable resources—specifically oil and gas, potash and uranium—held the prospect that the province could escape its economic dependence on agriculture. The susceptibility of the farming sector to the uncertainties of weather, the variables of the world wheat market, the powerful economic forces of the multinational grain trade and what was seen as an unfair transportation system, produced a perpetual sense of economic vulnerability. What added to the economic angst was the growing wealth of Alberta's energy sector, which by the 1960s was already luring Saskatchewan people west.

By the mid-1960s is was clear that Saskatchewan did not have Alberta's reserves of light crude oil or natural gas. But the province did have a significant natural resource advantage in one area—potash. For Thatcher, Saskatchewan's massive potash reserves became an important messaging device to cast Saskatchewan as a burgeoning Alberta, in terms of non-renewable resource extraction. The importance of resource development as a rhetorical device for Thatcher to position the province as a rival of Alberta became obvious. In the February 1965 budget speech, speaking in his dual role as premier and finance minister, Thatcher dedicated an entire section of his address to resource development. He reserved his most optimistic words for the future of the potash sector:

> The day is not far distant, Mr. Speaker, when this province will rank as the most important producer of potash in the world, and when potash may rank second only to wheat among Saskatchewan products. Production of this mineral began in Saskatchewan only a little more than two years ago—yet in 1964, value of production already had climbed to $30 million. Two mines are in operation, with a third about to resume production shortly. Three other companies have begun work on their deposits. The government is negotiating with at least five additional potash companies.[17]

In many ways, the promise of potash that Thatcher seized upon in the 1960s, and its role in the political and economic debate of the province during the following two decades, is a window on the pursuit of the Saskatchewan myth. For the purposes of assessing the 1960s and understanding Saskatchewan's search for a stronger economy and more secure society, potash plays an illuminating role. It came to symbolize the modern era of development, a means for the province to escape its dependence on the boom-bust cycles of agriculture by expanding into the natural resource wealth that had brought prosperity to Alberta. This was to be the *entrée* for big business into the Saskatchewan economy. Or so Thatcher, and others, thought.

Through to 1967, there seemed good reason for optimism. Investment in

SAB R-PS80188532
An elevator shaft built inside a potash mine. The Thatcher government
aggressively promoted the potash industry in Saskatchewan.

the potash sector boomed, in no small part due to the provincial government's welcoming attitude to foreign investment. International Minerals and Chemicals, a Chicago-based multinational, opened the first potash mine in 1962 and by 1970 nine more mines were operating in the province. Of the 10 mines, five were US owned, two were Canadian companies, one was a British-South African joint venture, and another was a French-German consortium.[18] But ironically, rather than an escape from the cyclical nature of farming, potash only further tied the province's economy to the fortunes of the agricultural economy. As a fertilizer, demand for potash tracked the world agricultural sector. Thus, the rapid expansion of potash production followed a period of strong world agricultural growth and collapsed when the agricultural sector dropped dramatically in the later years of the decade. So, rather than insulate the economy from the vagaries of farming, potash production amplified Saskatchewan's economic reliance on world agriculture.[19]

The rapid overexpansion of the potash industry—to the point that by 1970 total Saskatchewan production of 8.3 million tons was twice the total level of North American consumption—led to an inevitable price collapse and crisis for the industry, both in Saskatchewan and New Mexico, where virtually all of the US production came from older, higher-cost mines. But the situation was particularly urgent for Saskatchewan, with the US government about to levy anti-dumping tariffs against Saskatchewan potash. As a result, Thatcher and New Mexico governor David Cargo, with the complicity of the private potash companies, agreed to a system of pro-rationing in 1969. It established a floor price and production quotas for each mine. The effect of the price decline was evident in the 1969–70 annual report of the province's

Department of Natural Resources. It noted the volume of potash production had increased by 25%, but the value of production rose by only 5%:

> In order to prevent a dissipation of provincial resources at "give-away" prices, the government of Saskatchewan established a system of production licences which prorates market demand to producing companies and requires that such production be sold at, or above, a minimum price.[20]

So, what started with great promise and high expectations became a source of controversy and even more economic uncertainty for the province.

Finally, in terms of lasting impact, this was a period when the modern era of Saskatchewan became evident in a significant social sense as more and more Saskatchewan people were confronted with the uncomfortable reality of native life in the province. It was during the Thatcher period that Indian and Métis issues were introduced into the everyday vernacular of the public discourse. "I consider few problems facing the present government to be more urgently in need of solution," Thatcher said of the social and economic conditions facing Indian and Métis people during a speech to the Canadian Club in Regina shortly after he was elected premier.[21] Within a year, the government established an Indian and Métis Affairs branch in the Department of Natural Resources and Thatcher ordered the civil service to reflect the reality of Saskatchewan's population, which meant 7% of government workers be Indian or Métis. He also demanded that private companies getting any support from the province, particularly those in the north, hire Aboriginal people in their workforce. Meanwhile, government policy was to actively encourage the migration of Aboriginal people from reserves and smaller northern communities into the major cities in search of jobs and promote the adoption of Indian and Métis children into non-Aboriginal families.

For Thatcher, the solution to poverty and social exclusion faced by Indian and Métis people was employment. He believed that the first step in addressing the social ills of life on and off reserves for Aboriginal people in Saskatchewan was finding a job. As such, Thatcher had little time for ideas around community development and support. His government's measurement for progress in helping the Aboriginal population was framed almost exclusively in terms of employment, coupled with the training and education required to find work. By the end of his government's seven years in office, 8,000 job placements had been made of Aboriginal people and 5,100 had received academic upgrading or skills training.[22]

As part of its policy, the Thatcher government also encouraged the migration of Indian people off reserves and into urban areas where there were greater opportunities for employment. It was during the 1960s that the Aboriginal population in cities increased, particularly in Regina, Saskatoon and Prince Albert, as people came hoping for a job and a better life than in

SAB R-B7227
Premier Ross Thatcher with a group of Aboriginal children, 1966. Thatcher was passionately committed to improving the living conditions of Saskatchewan's Aboriginal peoples.

their communities on reserves. The policy was completely consistent with Thatcher's belief, and the federal government's 1969 White Paper position, that integration and, ultimately, assimilation of Aboriginal people into white society was and should be the public policy objective. As James Pitsula notes:

> It believed [in] assimilation, not group rights; provincial responsibility for Indian Affairs, not federal jurisdiction and equality of citizenship, not special status.

Clearly, from today's perspective, Thatcher's approach was one-dimensional and simplistic for what was a complex social, economic and cultural issue with deep historical roots. But in retrospect, Thatcher's achievement was more in terms of his ability to elevate public awareness of a social and economic issue that for far too long had never been front and centre on the public agenda. His rhetoric was always powerful and his personal commitment to addressing what he saw as an unconscionable travesty beyond question. In 1965 he told the provincial Legislature:

> the treatment that Saskatchewan gives her Indians is not much better than the people of Selma and Alabama today are giving their Negroes.

And four years later in March 1969, again in the Saskatchewan Legislature, during debate of legislation to create a provincial department of Indian and

Métis Affairs, the premier called the problems faced by Aboriginal people to be "a ticking time bomb ... [with every effort needed] to stem a rising tide that threatens to become a major social disaster."[23]

The consequence of these efforts was to make the 1960s a period when the social, economic and political dimensions of the Aboriginal issue changed fundamentally and permanently for Saskatchewan. The issues of poverty, unemployment, substance abuse and lack of hope left the anonymity of reserve and northern life and became part of the urban fabric, particularly in Regina, Saskatoon and Prince Albert. To this day, and to a far greater extent than the challenge seen by Thatcher almost 40 years ago, the Aboriginal underclass is the most important social and economic issue facing the province and its future.

Ultimately, the decade of the 1960s under Thatcher, that ended with his government's defeat and the election of Allan Blakeney and the New Democratic Party in 1971, must be judged by the standards Thatcher himself had set. This was a period when the talk was of a "new Saskatchewan," one that was breaking free from its wheat-based agrarian economy, to a province that was finally diversifying and realizing its full economic potential. Just as the yardstick had been Saskatchewan's relative position to other western provinces—particularly Alberta—the same yardstick needs to be applied to determine progress in the 1960s. By that measure, the Saskatchewan myth remained as distant and unattainable after Thatcher as before him.

In the 1964–71 period, annual GDP for Saskatchewan in nominal dollars climbed from almost $2.4 billion to $3.4 billion, a 42% increase. During the same period, Saskatchewan's economy lost ground to Alberta's, which grew by almost 95%, from $4 billion to almost $7.8 billion. Moreover, Saskatchewan's nominal GDP under the final eight years of the previous CCF government, from 1956–63, grew by 47.6%, or 2% higher than under Thatcher.[24]

Measured in terms of GDP per capita compared to the national average, the picture for Saskatchewan coming out of the 1960s was no more hopeful. While GDP per capita grew from $2,521 in 1964 to $3,705 in 1971, a 47% increase, GDP per capita nationwide grew by more than 64% from a base that was higher than the Saskatchewan average.[25] In terms of personal income, a 66% Saskatchewan increase during the same period lagged far behind a 108% increase in Alberta and 80% growth in Manitoba.

Finally, and most importantly in terms of the province's psychology, the population drain continued. After growing to 955,344 in 1966 from 925,181 five years earlier, by 1971 the province's population had fallen to 926,242, only slightly higher than it had been in 1931 and the advent of the Dirty Thirties.[26]

In other words, as a new decade dawned, the Saskatchewan myth remained as elusive, but as alluring, as ever.

Thirteen Big Ideas, Big Government, Big Debt

"The history of Saskatchewan's Crown corporations goes back to the earliest days of the province. When settlers came to these, at times, harsh prairies, they quickly learned that they needed to work together in order to prosper and sometimes even to survive… They used their governments—municipal, provincial and federal—to help them in their battles against the elements and against an economic system largely controlled outside Saskatchewan and outside Western Canada."

(Allan Blakeney)

"There's so much more we can be."

(Grant Devine)

It remains, to this day, a truly remarkable document; remarkable in its breadth, remarkable in its intent. But most remarkable, looking back fully 35 years later, in its unfailing devotion to government intervention as the solution to virtually all the perceived problems and challenges facing Saskatchewan.

The election platform of the New Democratic Party in the spring of 1971—entitled New Deal For People (NDFP)—was to be the key that would finally unlock the door to achieving Saskatchewan's true economic and social potential. It was a roadmap that would fulfill everyone's expectations. Nothing was unattainable. Everything was possible. The myth could be reality. All it would take was a wide sweep of action by government.

As a political document, there is no doubt that the NDFP was a masterstroke. In the dialectical world of politics, it was the perfect antithesis to seven "long, lean years" of Ross Thatcher's rugged, confrontational and often divisive free enterprise rhetoric. The simple facts were that the Thatcher Liberal experiment had not produced anything approaching the results Thatcher himself had predicted. After a brief increase, Saskatchewan's population was again declining, the farm community was suffering from low prices as a result of a glut of wheat on the world market, there was labour unrest, the potash industry was in chaos, and the dream of Alberta-like resource riches was still a dream. But Thatcher's legacy was not just one of unfulfilled promise. What Thatcher also had done was establish the belief that Saskatchewan was failing to meet its economic potential, a theme Allan Blakeney and the NDP eagerly seized upon. The objective didn't change. The goal was to realize the myth, to achieve the ambition of a stronger

SAB R-A 21,674-1

Allan Blakeney (podium) addressing the audience at an election rally, June 19, 1971. Four days later, Blakeney's NDP defeated Ross Thatcher and the governing Liberals.

Saskatchewan that would regain its original role in Canada as a place of hope, of opportunity and a magnet attracting others.

What was needed was a new dream—a new dream for people, a vision of the way Saskatchewan could and should be, if only the right steps were taken by government. A dream that in tone, intent and application would be more consistent with Saskatchewan's social democratic traditions. Thus, the problem wasn't the myth as an objective, it was the process of attaining it.

Seizing the opportunity, Blakeney and the New Democrats took liberties with US president Franklin Roosevelt's depression-era New Deal to fashion their own new deal election platform. So encompassing was its scope, so, at times, glib and superficial its treatment of issues, one can only imagine the construction and drafting of this document—policy strategists sitting around a table and dutifully reciting social and economic wrongs and the solutions to each. In the retrospective reality of 2006, it's difficult not to think the New Deal was drafted in an intellectual closet, either with no sense of consequences, or a belief that government could simply act and achieve its predetermined outcome. If ever there was a chicken in every pot, this was it. It covered 17 policy areas, recited a litany of issues to be addressed and the proposed remedy by government, or some form of collective action, that would simply and neatly change reality, achieving the intended outcome. "We believe it represents a realistic, yet imaginative blueprint for the 1970s designed to put Saskatchewan once more in the forefront of social and economic progress," the New Deal For People stated in its preamble.[1]

But criticism today also comes from the perspective of a much different world than that of 1971. The world is a much different place. The Soviet Union no longer exists, Communism has been recognized as one of the greatest human and economic tragedies of the 20th century, government's role has been diminished by the forces of liberal economics—freer trade, more open markets, individual liberty and democracy. In short, Adam Smith ended up winning the great ideological debate of the 20th century. That is not to say there isn't a critical role for government in the economy and society, or that government and public policy are not forces for good, or the free market is always the best means to achieve the greatest good for the greatest number. But clearly, there is a consensus that trade liberalization, with open markets, social policy supports and labour laws to protect the rights of working people, is the best road to the creation, and a more equitable distribution, of wealth. In other words, the idea of "embedded liberalism"—where societies and government learn to integrate the efficiency of the market with broader community and social values that are, in fact, required to sustain the social stability necessary for the functioning of markets.[2] In essence, Roosevelt's New Deal was the manifestation of embedded liberalism, the compromise between state and market.

But the drafters of the New Deal For People in 1971 went a step further. For them, it was clear that socialism was not only an option, it was on the ascendancy and the preferred objective. The document itself was a reflection of the more radical left elements within the NDP that had formed into the so-called "Waffle" and had found a supportive voice in Woodrow Lloyd, who Blakeney replaced as leader in 1970.[3] If a modern, socialist economy was the destination, the New Deal For People was the roadmap. According to Eleanor Glor, who has studied and written extensively on Saskatchewan public policy,

> This platform sustained the government through three terms in office... This platform became the policy and program guide for the government.

As Tommy Douglas used to say, you don't need to drink a whole pot of soup to get its flavour. The same is true for the NDFP. A sampling is sufficient to get a sense of the document as a policy foundation for what turned out to be the next decade in Saskatchewan.

Two areas of the NDFP that were the most relevant in terms of the province's sense of self and the economic and political debate during the next two decades were agriculture and resource development. Both represented crucial dimensions of the Saskatchewan economy, and both were to become the defining issues of the 1970s and 1980s in Saskatchewan. In one sense, then, the skill of the document was that it set out a plan that linked the province's heritage—farming—with its greater economic future—resource development. It was at once both conservative and progressive. The NDP government would save and defend the family farm as a core economic and social pillar of Saskatchewan and unlock the riches of the province's resource sector by ensuring that the people of the province got the economic rent they deserved from development of natural resources.

In terms of agriculture, the NDFP promised to restrict corporate ownership to family farms and keep farm ownership in Canadian hands. In other words, foreigners were not welcome, a strangely xenophobic and regressive attitude for a province settled by immigrants. Moreover, it also defied a fundamental truth about Saskatchewan's rural psychology and a cornerstone of its heritage—the original rights of private property, homestead and 160 acres of free land that lured people from around the world to start a new life on the prairies. It proposed a Land Bank Commission where government would buy land from farmers and rent it back, with an option to purchase, thereby striking at the very foundation of the privately owned family farm. The concept of government as landowner and farmers as tenants was, of course, framed as a means to defend the family farm by creating a government-ordained market whereby farmers could access their farm equity, if they wished. But it was a kind of collectivism that was counter-intuitive to a founding truth to the province.

The platform also talked vaguely of "controlling unnecessary duplication of farm services and improve their quality," it promised low-cost credit and loan forgiveness for farmers and a farmers' bill of rights that, among other things, would provide a debt moratorium and guarantee electric power and other "essential services" for farmers unable to pay their bills because of "circumstances beyond their control." It did not, apparently, contemplate—or at least must have discounted—the negative effects such a debt moratorium would inevitably have on the availability of capital for farmers. It also called on the federal government to put in place "guaranteed price supports for farm products" and, in what was classic command-and-control economics, called on Ottawa to "establish meaningful farm production guides with guaranteed prices for agreed levels of production."

The other section of the policy blueprint that foreshadowed a fundamental policy debate and shift, related to the resource sector. Thatcher's use of foreign investment to develop and rapidly expand the potash sector was characterized as a sellout to corporate interests. Not only did the NDFP "oppose any further sellout of our resources," it stated that government ownership of resource development would be the preferred model:

> With respect to new development, the NDP will give first priority to public ownership through Crown corporations. Co-operative ownership will be encouraged… Limits will be established with respect to foreign equity capital, and every effort will be made to limit foreign investment in resource development to non-equity capital.

The NDFP went on to say that, "Where feasible, we will reclaim ownership and control of foreign-owned resources."

Just as potash had been the symbol of development under the Thatcher Liberals, for Blakeney and the New Democrats the lack of significant revenue to the provincial treasury from potash became the rationale for government intervention. Just as private enterprise and foreign investment were the keys to develop Saskatchewan's vast potash reserves, public ownership under Blakeney was to be the means to get a fair return from natural resources for the people of the province.

In fact, control of natural resources, particularly non-renewable resources such as oil and gas and potash, became the centrepiece of Saskatchewan public policy in the 1970s. The battle for control raged on two fronts. One was private enterprise versus public ownership. The issue was ensuring what the NDP considered a "fair return" for the resources the public owned, which put the government on a collision course with private sector companies. The other was a constitutional battle between Saskatchewan and Alberta on one side and the federal government on the other over jurisdictional control of resources. The issue of development and control of resources—particularly potash and oil—as a means to an economically more powerful and secure Saskatchewan, is the dominant theme of both the 1970s, under the Blakeney government, and, to a lesser extent, through the 1980s when the Grant Devine Conservatives were in power. By following the development of public policy as it related to those two resources sectors in the 1970s and 1980s, particularly as it relates to potash, it's possible to better understand and appreciate the pursuit of the Saskatchewan myth.

It is, in many ways, a Byzantine and complex story; a web of conflicting political, ideological, corporate, legal and constitutional issues. For its part, the NDP government of the day says it was driven not by socialist ideology or a desire to assert public ownership of resource development, but by reality. In other words, it was simply being pragmatic, trying to get the greatest return from resources for the public purse by dealing with circumstances as they presented themselves. But whether fuelled by political ideology, corporate hubris, or some mixture of the two, the fight over control of resources in the 1970s was a pivotal period in the life of the province. This was a time when, for a few fleeting years, attaining the Saskatchewan myth of a much greater economic future was perhaps, finally, within reach. Or at least, so it seemed.

Clearly, by 1971, the rapid and massive potash development of the 1960s had not translated into significant benefits for the public purse. Royalties from potash extraction amounted to slightly more than $2.4 million by 1971, up from $664,000 in 1964, or almost a fourfold increase.[4] During that same period, the value of potash production had grown from $30.6 million in 1964–65 to more than $126 million in 1970–71.[5] But, there was no corresponding increase in corporate income tax (CIT) revenue for the province.

In 1964, total CIT was slightly less than $9.9 million and seven years later in 1971, after 10 new potash mines had come on stream, total CIT for the province had risen only marginally, to barely $13 million.[6] Actual income tax contributions from private potash companies to the provincial treasury most years, due to generous incentives and allowances, had been zero.[7]

Very quickly, opinion was building in government asserting the need to take greater public control of resources. An early step of the Blakeney government was to create a central planning board, an idea resurrected from the Douglas social ownership governing model, that would tackle key economic issues and provide policy advice on how the government could achieve the outcomes it sought. The planning board reported directly to Blakeney's office and filed an analysis in 1972 calling for a dramatic shift in its resource development policy:

> It should be noted that Saskatchewan faces a major decision as to the degree of uniqueness and isolation of its economic development approach. If Saskatchewan follows the traditional path of being only marginally and superficially distinctive, a path into which provinces are pressed by the federal government, its future is predictable and bleak. If, on the other hand, Saskatchewan is to take its own development into its own hands, in its own interest, it will have to be distinctive. It will have to deal differently with economic issues and relationships, and with the dictates of power centers and of technology, than the North American norms ... if we are to be other than a depopulated province, limited to the export of raw materials to more developed regions, we must strive to become a net exporter of various finished commodities... Clearly, if we wish to bring about these developments, we shouldn't be in the situation where large multi-national corporations can arbitrarily make decisions which make sense to them with respect to their own corporate interest, but which make little economic sense for Saskatchewan, and which, in fact, work harshly against the development of the province.[8]

With potash prices beginning to rise, the Blakeney government believed the public share of the economic rent—that is, the difference between the cost of production and the market value of the commodity—was insufficient. Faced with a royalty scheme established in 1962, which offered the incentive to potash companies that the royalty rate would remain unchanged on mines where construction was started by 1967, the challenge was to find other means to capture a greater portion of the resource rent for the public treasury. Ironically, one tool to raise revenues from potash had been handed to the Blakeney government by Thatcher—pro-rationing. Realizing that the pro-rationing system was working, the Blakeney government used it as a means to raise revenue in 1972 by imposing a pro-rationing fee.[9] The new levy of 60¢ per ton, which was raised to $1.20 a ton in October 1973, allowed the government to capture a greater share of economic rent from potash, which began growing as world potash prices stabilized and began escalating in 1973 as world demand for potash increased. As a result, the government's revenue from potash climbed to $6.1 million in 1973, up by almost 70% in one year.[10]

But, if the political promise of potash as a means to greater financial security and economic progress for the province were to be realized, it would take more than a new fee applied to production. The issue was that few of the distributed profits from potash production by large corporations—many of them foreign-owned and based—remained in the province. Moreover, prorationing itself came under attack in 1972 when Central Canada Potash challenged pro-rationing as unconstitutional, arguing it impinged on the federal powers of trade and commerce. With a captive market in the United States, Central Canada Potash had a ready market to sell more potash than the production quotas allowed by pro-rationing.

The strained relations between the government and the potash industry deteriorated further in 1973 with amendments to the potash conservation regulations, which required the filing of detailed financial information as a means to develop tax policy that would capture more of the profits from potash development. The industry refused to comply. Individual companies argued they were being forced to share sensitive information with competitors. In response, the government imposed a potash reserve tax in 1974, which, in effect, was a "static predictive profits tax."[11] Again, the industry refused to pay.

Clearly, the Blakeney government feared it would lose the jurisdictional challenge to prorationing and believed the potash reserve tax was a constitutionally valid way to realize greater revenues from the potash sector. Although the government saw the reserve tax as a property tax, the industry considered it as an excessive, confiscatory tax on profits and started a new legal challenge. It was ruled unconstitutional a year later.[12] Into this poisoned environment, the federal government added more tension in its 1974 budget by announcing it would no longer allow companies to deduct provincial royalties to determine federally taxable corporate income. In her analysis of the Blakeney government's potash development policy, Nancy Olewiler sets out the situation succinctly:

> The province's ability to use traditional regulatory instruments was being seriously eroded. In particular, the power to regulate output through a system of quotas and the ability to regulate and raise revenues through taxation were becoming

more constrained. The extremely hostile environment between the province and the private sector and the province and the federal government did not give the Blakeney government much confidence in being able to meet its objective of keeping potash rent in Saskatchewan.[13]

Concurrent to all this, and in an effort to take greater control and realize more revenue from resources, the Blakeney government had developed a mineral policy with four objectives: greater return from resource exploitation to the province; a fair return for private companies in proportion to risk taken; as much as possible secondary benefits retained in the province; and, a pace of exploration and development that met long-term needs of Saskatchewan.[14] While not explicit, the new policy signaled the government's intent to get more directly involved in the development, conservation and management of resources, perhaps at the level of ownership. In fact, from the outset, the potash industry saw the reserve tax as part of a broader strategy of nationalization of the industry. Their argument was that the Blakeney government knew full well the likely consequences of its actions and would use the outcome to legitimize its argument to takeover the industry. As Peter Jack, the vice-president of Canadian operations for the Potash Corporation of America said:

> Over the period of escalating taxes, the provincial government adopted parallel policies which, in total, can be seen as a preconceived plan for extensive government control over the potash mines of the province.

John Carpenter, executive vice-president of Hudson Bay Mining and Smelting, echoed the same view:

> Indeed, it is very difficult not to conclude that control through ownership has always been the government's real objective.[15]

Given the province's long history of Crown corporations as both monopoly utilities and commercial enterprises, the thought that government ownership would be a model used in the potash sector was hardly surprising, especially in the context of the profile potash had in terms of the province's economic future. Pragmatism aside, the Blakeney government's ideological commitment to state enterprise through Crown corporations was obvious during its first term in office. As the Government Finance Office, the holding company for Crown corporations, which later became the Crown Investments Corporation, boasted in its 1975 annual report, the Crown enterprises had a record of success:

> Over the last 10 years, the GFO and related corporations
> have earned approximately $25.3 million, which is the equiv-
> alent to a return on revenue on average equity of 13%.[16]

With the government's stated commitment to capture more of the
resource rent from potash mining and assert greater control generally over
resource development, using public ownership as a public policy instrument
was an obvious option. Moreover, with its taxation challenged legally by the
potash companies and the federal government, and Ottawa imposing tax
changes that further weakened the sector, some would argue that public
ownership was the only logical option. Thus, public enterprise through
nationalization was driven less by socialist ideology than it was by the need
to defend the public interest, which in this case was a fairer return on natural resources, which were owned by the people of the province. As Allan
Blakeney argued:

> There is no particular virtue in public ownership itself. But
> there is virtue in using public corporations if the alternative is
> absentee ownership by distant corporations who have no
> commitment to the Saskatchewan people or its welfare.[17]

The same pragmatic argument is made by others. For example, Roy Romanow,
who was deputy premier at the time, maintained the Blakeney government
had no choice but to change its natural resource strategy and use public ownership as the means to capturing more of the resource wealth for the public
treasury. Romanow argued that the refusal by the potash industry to pay new
taxes, an end to expansion plans and their rejection of demands to show their
financial records, compelled the provincial government to act:

> These circumstances forced the government to depart from its
> 1974 decision not to use its expropriation powers. In the
> Speech from the Throne in November 1975, the provincial
> government declared its intention to resolve the impasse by
> assuming at least 49% of the existing productive capacity of
> Saskatchewan potash by means of expropriation if necessary.[18]

The tipping point came following the 1975 provincial election. Blakeney
and others in his cabinet had thought the hardline position taken by the
industry was tactical. They believed the industry would concede nothing
until seeing the outcome of the election, in the event that the NDP was
defeated. The assumption was that, when the NDP government was
returned to office, the industry would stop posturing and begin to negotiate
to resolve the impasse with the government. When that didn't happen, and
instead new legal actions against the potash reserve tax were started days

after the election, the Blakeney government decided to form the Crown owned Potash Corporation of Saskatchewan (PCS). According to Blakeney,

> This policy had two objectives. The first was to protect production of provincially owned mines from federal taxation—an answer to the federal corporate taxation moves. The second was to secure revenues from the industry that the potash companies were unwilling to pay.[19]

The creation of PCS was seminal in the development of Saskatchewan's political economy on two levels. First it was an immense ideological statement. Setting aside debate over the policy motivations argued by Blakeney and Romanow, namely that PCS was the culmination of intransigence by the private sector and jurisdictional intrusions by a federal government, not the socialist proclivities of the NDP government, the optics were much different. The announcement by the government in its Throne Speech in late 1975 that it would use powers of expropriation if necessary to take over half the productive capacity of the industry was a radical and, to some, a shocking move. Aside from outrage among private potash companies and in American and Canadian corporate circles, the federal government weighed in by speculating it might have to revisit the policy of not taxing provincial Crown corporations.[20] Second, the creation of PCS undoubtedly gave the government a powerful instrument to retain much more of the profits from potash development and the spinoff benefits, such as head office jobs, in the province. Under the private sector model of development, only mining operations and a few branch office jobs were in the province. With the creation of PCS, which was to become the largest potash company in the world, Saskatoon was the home of the potash giant's head office. As well, dividends from a profitable PCS would be paid into the provincial treasury, rather than to shareholders, most of whom were living outside of Canada, let alone in Saskatchewan. So in that sense, PCS became the instrument that would claim the riches of potash that Thatcher once said would rival the oil wealth of Alberta.

Aside from the obvious economic tensions between the NDP government and the private sector, the federal-provincial political strains of this period were even more intense and potentially dangerous. The depth of the frustration and anger is vividly reflected in an October 1978 letter from Blakeney to Prime Minister Pierre Trudeau that was sent a week after the Supreme Court of Canada ruled the Saskatchewan pro-rationing policy to be beyond provincial powers. The pro-rationing decision had come less than a year after the same court ruled the provincial government's 1973 oil and gas conservation and development legislation, which imposed a new tax and royalty surcharge, was an indirect tax and therefore invalid. In response, the government applied a new oil well income tax that took effect in January 1978.[21]

The original tax, that was declared unconstitutional, had been enacted to capture some of the windfall profits from rapidly rising oil prices, which rose from $2.28 (US) a barrel in 1970 to more than $11 (US) a barrel February 1974 that came in the wake of the OPEC crisis of the early 1970s.[22]

Originally, the federal government agreed not to oppose the pro-rationing system put in place by Thatcher and then joined the constitutional challenge against the tax on the side of the private companies. It was a move that deeply angered Blakeney. In his letter to Trudeau, an outraged Blakeney called the move against the province "a complete about-face and betrayal on part of the federal government." He went on to say that federal intrusion into the provincial domain of natural resources was destabilizing to the nation:

> These actions seem to indicate a deliberate strategy to expand federal jurisdiction at the expense of provincial powers to manage and tax natural resources. In my view, the federal determination to further centralize power at the expense of the provinces is imposing very serious strains on our federal system... I must tell you frankly that the time has come for you and your government to begin to respond to the legitimate demands of the Western provinces. If you continue to ignore the West, you will imperil the very fabric of our nation.[23]

Running parallel to the battle over control of potash and the creation of PCS, were similar public ownership strategies on other fronts. The NDP government also created Saskoil to give the province an equity stake in the oil and gas business and also established the Saskatchewan Mining Development Corporation as a government-owned uranium mining company.

The result of the aggressive and interventionist stance in the resource field was an obvious growth in the public sector during the 1980s. But, more importantly, there was a growing sense that Saskatchewan was finally escaping its status as a have-not province tied to the uncertainties of agriculture and taking its place as a resource rich province that was beginning to rival Alberta. Finally, it seemed the myth was becoming reality.[24]

Judging by the rapid growth of the Potash Corporation, and the Crown corporations sector in general, there seemed reason for optimism. In its first meagre annual report in 1976, PCS showed total current assets of $684,385, including furniture worth $25,860 and "employee advances" of $3,000. By 1981, PCS was the biggest potash corporation in the world. It had 2,267 employees, sales of $371 million, net income of $142 million, paid taxes and royalties of $71 million, payroll and benefits of $62.6 million, all of it paid in Saskatchewan, and had also paid dividends of $50 million in each of 1980 and 1981 to the provincial consolidated fund.[25] More broadly speaking, the "family of Crown corporations," as they became known, were also showing healthy profits. On total provincial equity of $1.5 billion, in 1981 the Crown sector showed net earnings of $119 million, on revenues of $1.7 billion. In total, the Crowns paid taxes and royalties that year to the government's consolidated revenue fund of $131 million.[26]

The infatuation with the resource sector, government resource policy and the Crowns knew no bounds by the close of the 1970s. The unparalleled rapid growth in resource prices on the world market during the decade had not only swelled provincial coffers, but also heads. Consider the prose of Bob Moncur, the deputy minister of mineral resources, in his introduction to his department's 1979–80 and 1980–81 annual reports:

> The 80s are certain to be important years for Saskatchewan, especially in the resource field. And, while the 1970s may be remembered as the decade when the true importance of Saskatchewan's resource base was only beginning to unfold, the 80s will no doubt be recalled as some of the most prosperous and vibrant years to date within the realm of provincial resources… The resource industries are booming in Saskatchewan like never before—our province has a resource base which far exceeds that of many nations, and it will always be the goal of this department to assure that every person in the province receives the benefits from resources which surely belong to us all.[27]

The following year the same deputy's optimism was fuelled even further by a record year for drilling of new oil wells—1,498, surpassing the previous record of 1,458 in 1965, the first full year of the Thatcher government. Although the deputy did mention that the successes of the year were "tarnished by the insensitivity of the NEP [the federal government's National Energy Program]," Moncur concluded by saying: "I am looking forward to the next few years with the belief that in Saskatchewan, the best is yet to come."[28]

But just when it seemed like the Saskatchewan myth could finally become the new reality, the old reality interceded. Consider the same Mineral Resources department's annual report a year later. By the time it was issued not only the deputy minister had changed, but so had the government. The Blakeney New Democrats were routed by Grant Devine and the Tories in an April 1982 electoral landslide unlike anything the province had witnessed in decades. To understand one of the key reasons for the seismic political shift in the province you need only read the opening words of the new Mineral Resources deputy minister Don Moroz's introduction to the 1981–82 Mineral Resources annual report:

> For Saskatchewan Mineral Resources, the combined effects of federal energy policies, falling resource markets, and an

emerging world-wide recession were obvious over the course
of the 1981–82 fiscal year. Restrictive prices and burden-
some taxes translated into greatly reduced levels of industry
activity.[29]

Ultimately, the legacy of the 1970s for Saskatchewan was yet another
bout of failed expectations. But what made the fall particularly harsh was
that expectations had been raised so high during the decade and even before,
in the 1960s. People believed what they were told about the immense
resource wealth of Saskatchewan. In many ways, it seemed that
Saskatchewan had an even greater potential than oil-rich Alberta. Not only
did Saskatchewan people believe the province had the best farmland in
Canada, if not the world, it also had a more diverse renewable and non-
renewable natural resource base than Alberta, and far more than Manitoba.
Saskatchewan was home to significant deposits of conventional oil and natural gas, and the world's largest deposits of heavy oil, potash and uranium. And
it also had a plentiful and largely untapped northern forest and hard-rock
minerals in its far north. Moreover, throughout the 1970s, people had
watched as the NDP government used every tool in its arsenal to take control of the province's resources and kept hearing about success stories like
the Potash Corporation, SMDC and other members of the family of Crown
corporations. Certainly, if growth was any measurement, the public sector
flourished throughout the 1970s. By 1982, as a percentage of provincial
GDP, total expenditures by the Saskatchewan government had grown to
23.3%, up from 15.5% in 1971.[30] In 1982, total government expenditures
had reached $3.5 billion, up from $535 million in 1971, an increase of a staggering $2.958 billion, or 554% in nominal dollars. Over the same period, also
in nominal dollars, Saskatchewan economy had grown by 328%—slower than
the growth of government—going from $3.45 billion in 1972 to $14.76 billion in 1982.[31]

But this rapid growth in government during the 1970s was hardly unique
to Saskatchewan. Next door, in free enterprise Alberta, the same thing
occurred. From 1971–82, Alberta government expenditures grew by an
incredible 609% in nominal dollars, rising from $1.24 billion to $8.81 billion.
But, unlike Saskatchewan, over the same period Alberta's annual GDP
increased even faster, by more than $51 billion, or 655%, and therefore gov-
ernment expenditures as a share of GDP in Alberta in fact actually declined
from 15.9% in 1971 to 15.5% in 1982.[32]

In spite of government getting bigger and, by its own admission, becoming quite a successful business operator based on the record of its Crown corporations, there was a troubling disconnect. People were not feeling better
off. Runaway inflation of the early 1980s, a worldwide recession, rising
unemployment and mortgage interest rates that were hovering around an
unbelievable 20% were a potent recipe for discontent. Moreover, using the

SAB 84-1494-R16-12

Grant Devine and his wife, Chantal, campaigning during the 1982 provincial election. Devine's Progressive Conservatives won a landslide victory, and over the course of the subsequent nine years would attempt to undo much of the Crown corporation infracture set in place by the previous NDP administration.

yardstick of population growth, which for Saskatchewan's sense of self is always the most important measurement, prosperity remained elusive throughout the 1970s. By 1981, after declining for the first six years of the 1970s, the province's population had rebounded to 975,900, but was still well below the long-sought target of a million.[33]

It was time for a new figure. Someone to capture people's imagination and keep them focused on the hope and opportunity that Saskatchewan represented. Someone who could make people believe again in the Saskatchewan myth. Someone like Grant Devine.

No one before, or since, has articulated the Saskatchewan myth better, in a more rudimentary or more effective fashion, than did Grant Devine in the spring of 1982. He traveled the province in March and April of that year with a simple and powerful line during the provincial election campaign. "There's so much more we can be," Devine told Saskatchewan people, over and over. It was the Saskatchewan myth at its most basic. And people, who believed in the Saskatchewan myth, believed him.

In retrospect, it's hardly surprising. What the previous two decades had done in Saskatchewan was prepare people psychologically for Grant Devine's message of April 1982. The politics of underdevelopment, first introduced by Ross Thatcher, had taken root in the 1960s. People believed Thatcher, which obviously was a key reason why he was elected. And because they believed Thatcher, they elected Blakeney in 1971 after the promise of development under Thatcher never materialized and the NDP offered a different means to the same objective. The same scenario played itself out in 1982. The 1970s and the state enterprise of the Blakeney government were built upon the concept of developing a modern Saskatchewan economy that finally would break free of the constraints of agriculture and tap into the riches of natural resources. In the 1970s, Saskatchewan people kept hearing about the strength, importance and successes of the resource sector. They saw government grow more rapidly than at any point in the province's history. But what they didn't believe, in 1982, was that it had translated into better lives for themselves.

As a populist, what Devine articulated so well was a renewed faith in the Saskatchewan myth. He was able to get people to focus on the belief that Saskatchewan had the potential for greatness. It could attract back to Saskatchewan the "children" who had been lured west by the promise of opportunity in Alberta. He portrayed government under the NDP as impersonal and interested in its own successes, measured by the growth of Crown corporations, their profits and, in some cases, the obvious excesses of a new class of Crown corporation elite that had emerged in the province. One of the most powerful symbols of the 1982 election was the so-called "golden bathtub scandal." It was mentioned in a television election advertisement by the Tories and referred to money spent on a private bathroom—porcelain, not gold—for a senior Crown corporation executive. What the issue did was drive home the bitter realization that, while government and its enterprises accumulated wealth, average Saskatchewan people were losing their jobs and facing crushing interest rates.

By offering subsidized lower interest mortgage rates, a reduction in the provincial gas tax, an eventual phase-out of the provincial sales tax and lower income taxes, Devine was arguing that he would take the profits from the family of Crown corporations and return the money to "real Saskatchewan families." Devine's appeal was powerful and popular. The NDP, by contrast, seemed completely out of touch. It equated progress with Crown corporation profits and balanced budgets, even when family budgets were deep in debt, and sliding deeper. It thought it could win rural voters by loudly proclaiming its defence of the federally subsidized Crow rate for wheat shipments, but all the while was being denounced for the growth of government-owned land in the Land Bank, which as a concept was fundamentally at odds with the history and heritage of Saskatchewan farm life.[34]

Central to pursuit of the myth in the 1980s under Devine and his Progressive Conservative government, at least in a rhetorical sense, was free enterprise and smaller government. In that context, it was Ross Thatcher redux; deja-vu all over again. Borrowing a phrase from Thatcher, Devine proclaimed that Saskatchewan was "open for business." Among the first

SAB 82-2101-R4-5

Premier Grant Devine addressing the "Open For Business" conference, October 1982.

initiatives of his government in October 1982 was an "Open For Business Conference" in Regina that was co-sponsored by the *Financial Post* newspaper. The idea of the conference was to focus national and international business attention on the fact that the NDP had been defeated in Saskatchewan. In its place, a business-friendly government—one that would restrict the role and expansion of Crown corporations and encourage growth through private sector investment—was in charge. The conference came at a time when recession gripped the world economy. But Devine, in his uniquely glib fashion, told conference participants that Saskatchewan had decided not to participate in the recession.

Obviously, the role of Crown corporations, particularly those in the natural resource sector—PCS, Saskoil and SMDC—would have to be at least constrained, if not privatized, under the Devine Tories. Just as the Crowns were hugely important political and economic symbols of resource and economic development under the NDP in the 1970s, they carried similar symbolic importance for Devine in the 1980s. The resource Crowns were explicitly Blakeney's legacy. The political imperative for the Tory government was to find a way to deconstruct the NDP's legacy and construct a new one that reflected Devine's argument that big government was denying Saskatchewan its true potential. Therefore, the government appointed the Crown Investments Review Commission to study the record of government investments in Crown corporations and propose new objectives, structures and financial arrangements. In its late 1982 report, the commission recommended the Crowns be grouped based on lines of business—as departmental service units, competitive commercial businesses and non-competitive commercial businesses. More importantly, the commission argued that private sector standards be applied to determine the performance of the resource Crowns.[35]

Unable to use public enterprise, at least in the form of government-owned corporations, as an instrument for economic development, the challenge was to find other levers. Making it more problematic was a recession in 1981–82 and slow economic growth through to the mid-1980s. Knowing that anything short of radical and costly tax cuts have minimal effect on business choices, the Devine government quickly realized that deep cuts in taxes were not a fiscally or politically sustainable option. The decision to eliminate the 29¢ a gallon provincial gas tax, which cost the provincial treasury $110 million a year,[36] coupled with lagging economic growth was already putting fiscal pressure on the government. Still, Devine's unbridled optimism, coupled with what seemed a literal belief in his own rhetoric and the myth that there was so much more Saskatchewan could be, was enough to form the basis of government public policy strategy. As a result, what the 1980s became was an extension of the 1970s in terms of government growth. The key fiscal difference was that the exponential growth of the public sector during the 1970s was supported by balanced budgets and strong, if not equivalent, growth in the economy. During the 1980s, the expansion of government's role in the economy was financed in part by growing annual fiscal deficits. The result was that although Devine and the Conservatives came to power promising less government, more free enterprise and private investment, they presided over not only the creation of bigger government, but bigger government financed through borrowed money.

The dilemma was clear. The political process, driven by Devine's rhetoric, had raised expectations to new heights. If the myth were true, and there really was so much more that Saskatchewan could be, all it would take was to mobilize the will and spirit of the people to achieve it. Believe hard enough and it will happen. Build it and they will come. It was an attitude not unlike that of Clifford Sifton, who said 80 years earlier when he talked with enthusiasm about the settlement of the prairies: "we have turned dismal failure into a magnificent success."[37]

In fact, "build" became a common and value-laden word in the political lexicon of Saskatchewan in the 1980s. For Devine, it was the point of departure between his government and the previous NDP administration. "They buy and we build," was a favorite expression of Devine. He used it to advantage, particularly in the first term of his two-term government, but it remained a staple of his messaging throughout the 1980s. The word was heavy with ideological meaning. It positioned NDP economic development policy as little more than a zero-sum game, where public money was used to buy already established private sector companies and make them government-owned Crown corporations. By contrast, instead of buying existing assets developed by the private sector, Devine argued that his philosophy was to use public money to lever additional private investment to build new productive assets for the province. It was a mixture of those factors—Devine's ability to sell the myth, the resulting high expectations and the use of public money in pursuit of the myth—that fuelled government policy through the 1980s. At one level, the approach to economic development in the 1980s was perfectly consistent with the province's history, in that government and the public sector had long been an important means to achieve economic goals.

There is little doubt that, in terms of development and diversification of the Saskatchewan economy into more value-added processing, the 1980s were a decade of progress. What is also clear is that the broadening of the economic base was largely constructed artificially, based less on natural comparative advantage and more on massive amounts of public money being used as incentives to lure private companies into the province. In most cases, particularly relating to the large developments, the government took an equity interest as a minority and passive investor. In many cases, the government also assumed most of the risk.

One of the most egregious examples of the private sector profiting from the public purse in the 1980s was the NewGrade Heavy Oil Upgrader project in Regina. An oil upgrader carried special significance at two levels for the Devine administration. First, the previous NDP government had tried and failed to fashion a deal for an upgrader. Second, with Saskatchewan holding the world's largest heavy oil reserves, an upgrader would make more of the province's oil a marketable commodity. So an upgrader deal would be seen as both a political and economic coup for the Devine government.

What added even more symbolism to the upgrader deal was that the Tory government was doing it as a joint venture with Federated Co-Ops, which owned the Consumers Co-operative Refinery in Regina. By striking a deal with the co-op movement, the Devine government was becoming a business partner with an organization that had long and deep roots with the CCF-NDP in the province. But in its eagerness to build the upgrader, the government also agreed to financial terms that had the taxpayers assume virtually all the risk. The government agreed to 15% equity and Federated took only a 5% equity stake, with the other 80% coming from debt backed by provincial and federal loan guarantees. In effect, Federated put up no money, arguing it was bringing its existing asset of a gas refinery to the project. Its 5% equity came in a loan from the provincial government, with repayment on the principal due only when the upgrader began to produce dividends. Of the $700 million in start-up costs, the province put up $120 million and the rest was borrowed with the support of government guarantees.[38]

The Devine government's eagerness to use the public purse to lure the private sector to the province and prove Devine's words that there was "so

much more" Saskatchewan could be, produced other questionable investments of taxpayers' dollars. Although on much smaller scales, they all
reflected the same devotion to the Saskatchewan myth that the province had
a much greater unrealized potential. All it needed was the will to achieve it
by selling the province to others. A sampling of the government-backed ventures that went bad included investments in a plastic shopping cart manufacturer that was going to make Regina the "shopping cart" capital of the world.
Supercart International received $650,000 from the provincial government
and another $355,000 from Ottawa and produced only one prototype plas-
tic shopping cart before going out of business. The government also lost
money in a failed computer system that was supposed to be capable of trans-
lating English to French and gave $22 million to Edmonton entrepreneur
Peter Pocklington to build three bacon-processing plants that ultimately were
never constructed.[39]

But Devine's model of using government money to attract private investment from outside the province also had its financial successes. Among them
was a joint venture with US agriculture multinational Cargill to construct an
ammonia fertilizer plant and a partnership with Edmonton-based Millar
Western to develop a pulp mill at Meadow Lake. The government also was a
partner with Husky Oil and the federal government to construct the Bi-
Provincial Heavy Oil Upgrader at Lloydminster, and international paper giant
Weyerhaeuser agreed to build a paper mill near Prince Albert as part of a deal
to purchase the government-owned Prince Albert Pulp Mill.[40]

What the 1980s produced, therefore, was a variant on the model of government enterprise that had long been a theme in the public life of the
province. The difference was one of control. Instead of government having
complete ownership of commercial operations, the Devine government used
its Crown Investments Corporation, the holding company for the provincial
Crowns, as an investment vehicle in commercial ventures largely owned and
completely managed by the private sector. So while government continued
to play a major role in the economy, its equity stake in the economy declined.

This clash of views on economic development was played out in the
debate over privatization. During the last half of the decade, the Devine government came under the spell of the privatization model followed by the
Margaret Thatcher government in Britain. Two figures from the Adam Smith
Institute in London—Madsen Pirie and Oliver Letwin—became consultants
to the Devine government on privatization.[41] To support the privatization initiative, some members of the more senior business community created the
Institute for Saskatchewan Enterprise, a short-lived policy think-tank that
focused almost exclusively on privatization. Ultimately, the Devine government privatized the Potash Corporation, Saskoil and the Saskatchewan
Mining Development Corporation.

Not surprisingly, the political and economic debate over privatization as a
model for development coalesced around the move in 1989 to privatize the

PCS. Here was the perfect symbol for both sides of the ideological divide. The potash industry, which was rapidly developed through private investment in the 1960s, then nationalized by the Blakeney government in the 1970s, would be privatized at the end of the 1980s. The debate over Bill 20—The Potash Corporation of Saskatchewan Reorganization Act—unfolded in the provincial legislature in the spring of 1989. The second reading debate on the legislation provides a fascinating perspective on how both sides positioned potash privatization as consistent with the province's history.

Finance Minister Gary Lane launched second reading debate, arguing that potash privatization, or "public participation," as the government called it, was in keeping with the province's traditions. Aside from allowing the government to take proceeds from privatization and direct them to public priorities such as health care, education and agriculture, Lane said privatization was true to Saskatchewan's economic and social heritage:

> This public participation initiative can be seen from an historical perspective. Saskatchewan people have a history of working together to build and develop their province. And that kind of partnership brought about the credit unions and the co-ops, such as the Saskatchewan Wheat Pool. People got together and worked together and they worked with each other to build and diversify this province. This was not imposed by government.
>
> In the 1970s, this concept was changed to one of government ownership and government participation. And we want to reinstall in the people of this province a way of life where people themselves work together and, with the government, set economic priorities, to participate in our province's growth and to create the enterprises which meet the people's needs.[42]

As NDP opposition leader and, by coincidence, the minister in the Blakeney government who piloted the legislation to create the Potash Corporation of Saskatchewan in 1976, Roy Romanow led the response to the privatization bill. He distilled the argument down to the question of control over the province's economic destiny:

> What this legislation offers Saskatchewan people is a future of economic servitude to outside investors. It does not offer Saskatchewan people control of their own future, but a future controlled by others. This bill will long be remembered by the people of this province as an act which sold out the future of the province of Saskatchewan.

> This bill presents the people in this House and the people of Saskatchewan with a vital, critical choice, a choice which can be boiled down to a single question and that question I put to this legislature as follows: Should we, the people of the province of Saskatchewan manage, develop and sell our potash ourselves, for our own benefit and make those decisions for our own benefit, or should we let others do it for us, for their benefit? That's the key question. It's as simple and as complex as that.[43]

Beyond the polemics of politics, the ultimate question that privatization of PCS raised was whether the government investment in buying existing potash mines and creating a Crown-owned potash company was a good one. A study done on the potash investment by Arthur Andersen and Company in June 1989 for the Institute for Saskatchewan Enterprise, found that the total government investment of $1.1 billion in nominal dollars amounted to $1.95 billion in 1988 current dollar equivalents, which included the cost of funds on an annualized basis. Total dividends paid to the province from PCS had amounted to $228 million. Therefore, the report concluded that privatization would have to raise $1.95 billion for the government to break even on its investment in current dollar equivalents.[44] Ultimately, the privatization of PCS raised $820 million for the government.

So, just as the 1970s had opened with a passionate public debate about pro-rationing and taxation of the potash industry, the 1980s drew to a close with an even more passionate debate about control and ownership of the potash industry. The province had gone the full cycle, starting and ending with a potash sector in the private sector after experimenting with more than a decade of government ownership.

In the interim, not a great deal had changed. Devine's promise of a province that would escape the shadow of Alberta and take its place as an economic power and magnet for people never materialized. The province's population did finally break through the one million mark in 1983 and peaked at 1,032,800 in 1988, but began backsliding and by 1991 was in its fourth year of decline and at 1,002,700, verging on again falling below the million mark.[45] In the meantime, provincial government expenditures as a share of the province's economy had grown from 23.3% in 1982, to 29.2% in 1991. During that nine-year period, the provincial government had run an uninterrupted string of budget deficits, in the process piling up accumulated annual operating deficits totaling more than $4.12 billion.[46] Reasons for the deficits were many, including factors such as recession, bouts of low world prices for Saskatchewan commodities and successive years of drought that were all beyond the control of a provincial government. But with Saskatchewan mired deep in debt, its credit rating reduced to slightly above junk bond status by the early 1990s, the province wasn't merely a passive victim of external forces. It had made public policy choices that led to the growth of government and public spending that was not sustainable. The hope that began with a new deal for people in 1971 ended 20 years later with a debt crisis.

Yet again, the Saskatchewan myth seemed more elusive and distant than ever.

Fourteen The Reckoning

"Our economy can no longer support the public-sector infrastructure that we have built to serve the quality of life and the standard of living that we have come to expect. We need to review our expectations and to determine what we can realistically support with the income generated by Saskatchewan's economy and resources."

(Saskatchewan Financial Management Review Commission, 1992)

"Demographics is destiny."

(Thomas Malthus)

The adherence to myth is about more than believing in something that is not attainable. It's also about denial. Reality is denied and replaced by myth; fact is substituted by belief; the truth of today is exchanged for the promise of tomorrow. What matters is not what you know, it's what you believe. And so it has been with the pursuit of the Saskatchewan myth. It may not be true, but it's real.

Eventually, though, reality always overcomes the obstacles that are put in its way. Facts can be denied for a time, sometimes a very long time. But ultimately they cannot be avoided. For Saskatchewan, what happened in the last decade of the 20th century and the first few years of the 21st century was that the province had to confront much of the truth it had spent the better part of a century denying. It was a time when many of the mistakes, misgivings and false hopes of the past converged to create a dire sense of urgency.

In terms of the province's future, two factors today are absolutely critical and intimately entwined. Both relate to the sustainability of the province's economy, its standard of living, its social stability and its quality of life. Yet only one is ever discussed, debated and addressed in a focused manner. The other looms over the province like a threatening storm on the prairie horizon. In relation to its implications for the province, it is too often ignored, or, at best, gets scant and superficial attention. It is seldom discussed in polite company. The first issue, the one that is central to the political debate, is the financial sustainability of the province's rural society. The other issue, the one that is on everyone's minds but very few lips, is the growing underclass of Aboriginal people. Inherent in it are the implications for the province's social

CABINET SECRETARY'S OFFICE, GOVERNMENT OF SASKATCHEWAN
The first cabinet of newly elected premier Roy Romanow (seated, second from left). Throughout much of its tenure, the Romanow government would struggle with the fiscal burden inherited from the outgoing Progressive Conservative administration.

and economic future, and the depth of racism that is part of the province's unspoken reality.

In the early years of the 1990s a mentality of fear took root in the province. Politically, socially and economically it was expressed as a crisis of fiscal sustainability. Faced with a public sector debt burden that had reached $14.8 billion and annual budgetary deficits that had peaked at $1.2 billion and hovered near $1 billion for 1992–93, the province was facing annual interest payments on the debt of almost $800 million.[1] In other words, the annual interest payments on the debt were almost double the entire provincial budget of 20 years earlier. What made the truth particularly uncomfortable was that it raised serious questions about what people could, and should, realistically expect from their province.

As always, the debt issue in those days was cast in partisan political terms. Who was at fault became the accepted wisdom. Clearly, the blame rested squarely on the shoulders of the Grant Devine government that was in office from 1982–91. After all, it was because of the decade of the 1980s, when unsustainable government debt had grown to become such a heavy drag on the provincial treasury, that drastic action had to be taken. The dilemma was expressed in suitably grave terms by the Roy Romanow NDP government. As is the custom for new governments, less than two weeks after taking power in 1991, a news conference was held to announce that the deficit was actually far worse than the previous government had claimed in its budget.

According to then Finance Minister Ed Tchorzewski, the operating deficit for the 1991–92 fiscal year was $960.3 million, not the $265 million announced in the previous spring's budget: "I am sure that the people of Saskatchewan will be as shocked as I was to discover the extent of the deficit, and how badly they had been misled."[2]

In an effort to cast the problem in non-partisan terms, and thereby win partisan points by appearing to be objective, the government appointed the Saskatchewan Financial Management Review Commission to examine the province's books. Chaired by Don Gass, a former president of the Canadian Chartered Accountants Association, the commission delivered its verdict in February 1992 and handed the NDP government the ammunition it needed:

> Saskatchewan faces a difficult situation... Government spending has been at levels which cannot be maintained based on the province's revenue-generating potential. To re-estab-lish a more secure financial position, the government must bring its spending back under control.[3]

It went on further to say the province faced a looming debt crisis:

> A major area of concern is the current level of public debt, which at Oct. 31, 1991 was $12.04 billion. The critical issue is its impact on the government's ability to borrow addition-al funds in the future to finance additional deficits, as well as the associated annual budgetary expenditures to pay the prin-cipal and interest on that debt.[4]

Naturally, the dire financial talk coming out of Saskatchewan rang alarm bells with credit rating agencies. Two weeks after Tchorzewski announced that the annual deficit was approaching $1 billion, Standard and Poors downgraded Saskatchewan government debt to the lowest rung of its A category. If the province were to fall another level, it would be B category debt, which is the equivalent of junk bonds, and unable to raise capital in many bond markets that do not venture below A grade debt.[5]

Just to make sure everyone understood the gravity of the situation, Tchorzewski announced in his May 1992 budget speech that the deficit for the previous year was $841 million—it actually came in at $842.4 million[6]—and used the opportunity to drive home the idea that only one issue really mattered:

> Today, Saskatchewan faces a financial crisis of immense pro-portion... In 1981–82 government interest charges amounted to only $43 million. This year, taxpayers will spend $760 mil-lion on interest charges, more than $2 million a day.[7]

Clearly, the NDP government's commitment to fiscal responsibility was sincere. In fact, given the pressure being put on the province by capital markets to get its spending and revenues aligned, as former finance minister Janice MacKinnon makes clear in her book *Minding the Public Purse*, it had no choice. But the NDP's policy conversion to the principle was relatively recent. It had called the tax cuts proposed by the Devine Tories in the 1982 election as fiscally irresponsible, but did not suggest it would roll back the tax reductions if returned to power. Throughout much of the 1980s, at least until the final years of the decade, the NDP opposition's critique of the previous Devine government was that it should be spending more, particularly in social programs. For example, during the 1986 election, the NDP campaigned on a so-called "Seven Percent Solution," promising to subsidize mortgage interest rates down to 7%, for the first $70,000 of a mortgage, for seven years. Fiscal probity was not a subject that was being raised by the NDP opposition during the election campaign that resulted in the Tories re-election, even though the Devine government was already deeply mired in deficit budgeting. The only one calling for fiscal restraint and balanced budgets was then Liberal leader Ralph Goodale, a lonely voice whose party did not have a seat in the legislature.

But if rapid growth in government was common across all governments throughout the 1970s and 1980s, the 1990s were a decade of fiscal retrenchment and rectitude. For the newly elected Romanow government, elimination of the deficit and the government living within its financial means became the focus of fiscal policy and the filter through which all policy decisions had to be made. The political rhetoric was not unlike that of Douglas in the 1940s, when he argued that government had to manage its finances carefully and reduce its debt so that its future and ability to make choices was not limited by the money it owed to banks, many of them foreign, and other bondholders.

In many respects, the Romanow government had little policy latitude. Certainly in terms of fiscal policy it had no room to move. It faced the dire prospects of a possible financial crisis where it would have been effectively been shut out of capital markets. "We had a gun to our heads. We really didn't have a choice. As they say, when you're about to be hung it focuses the mind," admits Romanow.[8] The fiscal pressure was so great, and the choices so difficult, that Ed Tchorzewski stepped aside as Finance Minister due to stress and the position was given to MacKinnon.

The framework for this austere fiscal policy was the March 1993 budget. It forecast a deficit of $592 million for 1992–93, projected a deficit of $292 million in 1993–94 and set out a plan to balance the province's budget within three years. The budget raised taxes, such as the corporation capital tax resource surcharge, the fuel tax and the sales tax, while cutting operating expenses by 7%.[9]

If that budget was a moment of reckoning for the province, the most powerful symbol of that reality was reflected in the NDP government's health care policy. The growth in the cost of health care—which had risen from $286 million in 1974–75 to $1.62 billion in 1992–93—was deemed fiscally unsustainable.[10] A year earlier, the government had announced its intention to reorganize the health system as part of a strategy to change how people thought about health care and appropriate treatment. The so-called "wellness model" of health care had been unveiled in August 1992 by Health Minister Louise Simard. The core idea was that health care had to be thought of in different terms. Instead of the acute care, interventionist model, where people considered access to doctors and hospitals as essentially the complete health care context, the approach was to reorganize the system on a model of 30 health districts where there would be more local control and greater rationalization of service. As Simard said:

> The goal of locally controlled health districts is better co-ordination of a full range of health-related services all aimed at promoting wellness. The wellness approach recognizes that there is a lot more to being healthy than merely not being sick. Wellness is related to healthier lifestyles and safer, more healthy environment.[11]

Reform of health care launched by the Romanow government was positioned as actually being faithful to the original plan for the evolution of medicare set out by Douglas. In 1983 at the national NDP convention in Regina, Douglas spoke passionately about medicare and the next step in what he said was a two-stage process. The first stage was to ease the financial burden on patients who needed health care, which was what medicare originally delivered. The second phase was to reform and reorganize the system so that health care was delivered in a more seamless fashion that provided a continuum of care to the population.

The fiscal and political calculus of health reform for the NDP was obvious. First, the financial situation the province faced dictated that it could not support the province's unwieldy and far-flung health care infrastructure. For decades, health care policy had been driven by politics. Quite simply, building rural hospitals in small communities was good politics, but often bad health care policy. It mattered not that the rural population had been declining for decades. The political influence of the rural vote remained and was a key driver of health policy. But by the early 1990s, reality could no longer be denied. The health care system had to be reformed, made more efficient and cost effective.

In that sense, the infrastructure that made up the Saskatchewan health care system of the 1990s was an outcome of the myth, a by-product of the province's history and political economy. Nothing better represented the intersection of state and market than health care. The pattern of a rural, agricultural society in the province that was established in the National Policy years of the early 20th century was the reality that framed political and economic decisions for decades to come. The political commitment to universal, publicly funded health care drove the development of a dispersed health care system where Saskatchewan at one point had more hospitals than any province other than Ontario, which had more than 10 times Saskatchewan's population.[12]

As the party of medicare, health care reform was an issue only an NDP government could tackle. Like Nixon to China, an NDP premier such as Romanow could address the need to cut health care costs and attempt to change the system, while still remaining credible, claiming his support and commitment for publicly funded, universally accessible health care. So, with fiscal pressure demanding action, and politics allowing it, the Romanow government launched its health reform strategy in 1993, still early in its first term. The March 1993 budget announced a 3% reduction in funding for acute-care facilities, which was made up of a 5.5% cut for rural hospitals, 3% for large, base hospitals and 2% for regional hospitals. As well, the system was reorganized into health regions. Each of the 30 regions was handed responsibility for the organization of health care in its area, at the same time that its financing for acute care was being cut by an average of 2.8%.[13] As well, the government ended its universal prescription drug plan for everyone other than seniors and those on social assistance.[14]

The brunt of the on-the-ground impact of the reform was felt in rural areas. Ultimately, 52 rural hospitals were either closed as acute care facilities, or converted into "wellness centres" as part of what was to be an integrated approach to health that focused more attention on primary care in smaller communities, and less on hospital-based acute care. A total of 1,200 hospital beds were eliminated.[15] The reality was that many of the rural hospitals had been little more than long-term care facilities for what was a rapidly aging rural population. Although staffed with local doctors and nurses, the fact was that any significant acute care was being delivered in larger regional centres or the large acute care hospitals in Saskatoon and Regina.

In a very real sense, the need to reform the rural health system was a reflection of two core issues that confronted the province. Eliminating small town hospitals was a symptom of both the government's fiscal crisis and the province's history. The health care issue became a proxy for the question about the sustainability of rural life.

The fiscal impact of health reform was to briefly reduce and then slow the growth of health spending by the province. Total provincial spending declined from $1.66 billion in 1990–91 to $1.62 billion in 1992–93. It did not recover to exceed the levels of 1990–91 until 1997–98, when health spending reached $1.7 billion.[16] In the meantime, the Romanow government was able to balance its budget in 1994–95, fully a year ahead of its schedule laid out in 1993. "Saskatchewan people should be very pleased with the province's financial statements," MacKinnon said when she released the 1994–95 public accounts. "The hard work put into restoring the province's financial stability by all Saskatchewan residents is paying off and for the first time in a very long time, the mortgage is decreasing."[17]

The importance of getting the province's books in order was crucial at two levels. First, it was necessary psychologically for the province. The concern over the fiscal crisis afflicting the government had weakened public confidence in the province's future. Unless, and until, the situation was turned around there was little room for economic optimism, which would sap economic confidence, creating a vicious cycle that would undermine the economy. Second, it was important to signal investors that the government had its house in order and a sense of stability had been restored. With the budget balanced, the government could begin to focus on important macroeconomic policies, such as tax rates and public investments that are important to economic growth.

Romanow made that point explicitly to a business audience (the Canadian Society of New York) at the Plaza Hotel in New York City in June 1994, more than a year before the government announced it had balanced its budget:

> To encourage even more investment in Saskatchewan, we also have to provide a stable, predictable fiscal climate for business. And, I view Saskatchewan's fiscal turnaround as one of the big success stories of the 1990s. Saskatchewan now has the lowest per capita annual deficit in the country. Just three years ago, we had the highest. We've made a billion dollar turnaround in the deficit, in less than 1,000 days. We're on track to balance our budget by 1996. And, our efforts are being recognized in the financial community.[18]

The lasting significance of the Romanow period, particularly the 1991–95 years, is evident at two interconnected levels. Not only was Romanow able to maintain a commitment to fiscal responsibility, but he demonstrated deficits could be eliminated while preserving and reforming the public health care system. Romanow's commitment to medicare, even during difficult fiscal times, was a reflection of the medicare myth itself, which states that the public health care system is an expression of the Saskatchewan and Canadian identies. A decade later, in his 2002 Royal Commission Report on the Future of Health Care, Romanow expressed the essence of the medicare myth well:

> This year we celebrate the fortieth anniversary of medicare in Saskatchewan, a courageous initiative by visionary men and women that changed us as a nation and cemented our role as one of the world's compassionate societies.

In retrospect, the mid-1990s was a positive economic period for the province. From 1992 to 1997, Saskatchewan's economy averaged 4.3% real growth per year, compared with an average of 2.7% for the Canadian economy as a whole. The value of the province's key resources—oil, potash and uranium—all increased on the world market during the period. For example, the value of oil produced in Saskatchewan climbed from $1.2 billion in 1991 to $2.9 billion in 1997. During the same period the value of potash sales doubled, from $765 million to more than $1.5 billion and uranium went from $304 million to $580 million.[19]

The stronger economy was evident as well in other measurements. The population grew from 1.002 million in 1991 to 1.018 million in 1997 and the province's GDP per capita—the measurement of standard of living—also improved. It climbed from 86% of the national average in 1991 to 99%, or virtually equal to the Canadian average, by 1996, when GDP per capita in Saskatchewan was $27,427 compared to the national average of $27,646.[20]

Thus, the mid-1990s represented a period where the province appeared to get itself back on its feet, both in fiscal and economic terms. While it was not a time of huge growth, there was a sense that progress was being made and perhaps a modest sense of optimism could take root after the retrenchment of the 1991–94 period. In fact, the newly re-elected Romanow government set out in 1996 to establish a policy framework for the 21st century. It launched a provincewide series of public consultations, using town hall meetings, a 1–800 line and the Internet, to determine priorities and key pressure points facing the province. The exercise to engage citizens and plan for the new century is noteworthy on a number of levels. It helped to stimulate discussion and focus the public debate on what were seen as the challenges and opportunities facing the province. In that sense, it provided a window on the psyche of the province, on how Saskatchewan people saw themselves and their future. It might have been called a reality check, an opportunity to confront difficult questions and challenge long-held assumptions.

Romanow went on television to report on the findings. There were no surprises. Saskatchewan people wanted investments in health care, education, reform of social assistance through employment incentives for those on welfare, and cuts to government waste. In his televised address, the premier used emotive language that played to the province's history and sense of itself:

> Saskatchewan people are common sense pragmatists, who offer solutions to today's problems. But we are also visionaries, with a burning desire to build a better world.[21]

Part of the prescription for the new century was to address one of the crucial factors that rooted in the settlement of the province almost 100 years earlier. A central part to the agenda was to be the reform of the local government system that had remained virtually untouched throughout much of the

20th century. The result, as Romanow noted in his speech, was that Saskatchewan had more local governments than Ontario, which had more than 10 times Saskatchewan's population:

> On the one hand we have a declining rural population, yet on the other hand we have a huge system of local government that is getting harder and harder to maintain, and less and less relevant to today's real needs... In some of our smaller communities we have one elected official for every two or three families.

In the mid-1990s, the province had more than 800 municipal governments, or the highest municipal government to population ratio in Canada.[23] This structure of local government clearly bore little resemblance to the reality of life, either economically or socially, in the province. It existed, and continues to exist, as an artifact of National Policy, the remnant of a settlement pattern where communities were established 12–14 kilometres apart along railway lines to service a farm economy built on 160-acre homesteads.

The forces of change, particularly in the second half of the 20th century, slowly but constantly altered the face of rural Saskatchewan. The displacement of farm labour due to increased mechanization following the Second World War, economies of scale that forced ever-increasing farm size and the elimination of the Crow Rate—all were factors in the ongoing and inevitable remaking of rural Saskatchewan. Some, such as the University of Saskatchewan's Jack Stabler and Rose Olfert, who have extensively studied the changing face of rural Saskatchewan, maintain adjustment has been inevitable and inexorable, from the beginning:

> Even as the settlement of the Prairies was nearing completion, however, technological advances were being made that would render obsolete the system that was being built. Only the Depression of the 1930s and World War Two postponed the inevitable secular adjustment that would have otherwise begun just as the settlement phase ended.[23]

It might seem like a harsh judgment, but Olfert and Stabler conclude that the vast majority of Saskatchewan's small rural communities are not viable. Using methodology based on what they term "central place theory," the two studied the evolution of the province's communities, or trade centres, over a 40-year period. Their conclusion, in a 2002 study, was stark. The province has two cities—Regina and Saskatoon—that are economically strong and growing, as well as eight secondary cities that are either stable or growing, 14 rural towns that are "reasonably strong" and 72 towns struggling to remain stable or are declining.[24] That's the good news:

> At the other end of the spectrum, the 502 communities in
> the lowest category no longer play any meaningful role in the
> trade centre system. There is no single function of any type
> that is common to this set of communities. They will contin-
> ue as communities only as long as people are content to live
> in them and commute elsewhere to work, to shop and to
> obtain public services.[25]

By any logical standard, the reduction and rationalization of local government, to reflect the decline of rural Saskatchewan in economic and social
terms, was a worthy objective. Unfortunately, it never got beyond a stated
policy goal and, unlike attempted reform of the health care system, significant changes to the organization of local government have yet to happen in
the province.

But the most remarkable and telling aspect of what Romanow himself
called "a massive listening expedition" was less what was said, and more what
was not talked about. Nowhere in the report were questions asked, or comments reported, on the subject of the province's Aboriginal population. What
was then, and clearly remains today, the most important social and economic issue facing Saskatchewan, was not discussed, probed or studied in any significant manner. So, as the government and the public looked ahead to the
21st century and the province's 100th anniversary, it avoided confronting a
crucial piece of its reality. The continuing adherence to belief in a greater
future, to an unattained potential, to the Saskatchewan myth, did not permit
a frank discussion about the core challenge that faced the province.

Sadly, there was nothing surprising about that fact. The often grim social
and economic reality of Aboriginal people in Saskatchewan has never been on
the public or political agenda to the extent that it should be. The subject
remains marginalized by the potent dynamics of politics, political correctness
and racism. In the 1999 election that returned the Romanow NDP government to power, the issue of how to bring Aboriginal people into the mainstream of Saskatchewan's economy and society was not in any way central to
the election agenda. In fact, it lurked beneath the surface of the public
debate, in the coded language of a platform promise of "tax fairness" by the
conservative Saskatchewan Party, which meant extending taxation to the
Aboriginal population. When questioned in a private conversation about the
political failure to engage the Saskatchewan population in a dialogue and
debate about what needs to happen to improve conditions for Indian and
Métis people in the province, a political advisor to Romanow had a stark and
telling answer. "No one knows what to do and, if we raised it in the campaign, we were afraid of the racist attitudes it would bring to the surface," he
said.[26] Better to say nothing and pretend the issue doesn't exist, than attempt
to deal with it.

Such is the unspoken truth about the Saskatchewan of today. People know there is no more important social and economic issue confronting the province than how to address the issues faced by a large and growing Native underclass. It goes to the core challenge of the province's future. Specifically, how to avert a growing social and economic crisis that, unless addressed and dealt with, will make the years and decades ahead for the province more uncertain than ever. The challenge was expressed starkly in a study on Aboriginal people in the labour market by the Caledon Institute:

> The threat to the economic well-being is especially grave for the Prairies. There is probably no single more important issue for the economic future of the Prairies, particularly Manitoba and Saskatchewan, than the advancement of its Aboriginal human resources.[27]

To understand the depth and dimension of the issue, it is important to not only appreciate the reality of life faced by people of Aboriginal ancestry in the province, but to contextualize it with the general population. In 2001, as a percentage of census metropolitan areas, fully 29% of the population of Prince Albert was Aboriginal. In Saskatoon the Aboriginal population represented 9.1% and 8.3% in Regina. The only other western Canadian city with a similar ratio is Winnipeg, where 8.4% identified themselves as having Aboriginal ancestry.[28] For Saskatchewan, the absolute and percentage numbers of Aboriginal people as a proportion of the total population will grow at an increasing pace in the coming years.

Two factors will drive that demographic outcome. First, Saskatchewan's population is not anticipated to grow significantly, if at all, during the next 20 years. In fact, it is anticipated to probably decline, while the population of the other three western provinces grows rapidly, specifically in the case of BC and Alberta with projections of 34.8% and 19.3% respectively. Under a medium-growth scenario for the West, Saskatchewan's population is projected to decline by 1.1% by 2025, and by 3.9% in a high-growth scenario for the region.[29]

Second, during this same period, Aboriginal people will account for an increasing share of the working-age population. The reason relates to birth rates, age distribution and migration patterns: the Aboriginal population has a higher fertility rate than non-Aboriginals, on average is younger than the general population and is also less mobile interprovincially. So while Saskatchewan will continue to export its younger people to other provinces, primarily Alberta and BC, people of Aboriginal ancestry move less between provinces and rather migrate from reserves to urban areas within the same province. The important dimension of the issue is most evident in the under-15 age cohort, which made up 39.6% of the total Aboriginal population, compared to only 18.7% in the non-Aboriginal population.[30] It is projected that by 2016, the share of Aboriginal population in Saskatchewan will increase from current levels of 14% to 17%. During the next 15 years, Aboriginal youth are expected to account for one in four entrants to the labour force.[31]

Moreover, a 1997 study of Aboriginal population trends by the Federation of Saskatchewan Indian Nations (FSIN) forecasts a significantly higher number of Aboriginal people than the Statistics Canada projections. According to the FSIN, based on data from Stats Canada, a 1991 Aboriginal Peoples Survey and the Department of Indian Affairs and Northern Development— now Indian and Northern Affairs Canada—the Aboriginal population in Saskatchewan will climb to almost 204,000 by 2011 and 255,000 by 2021.[32]

In the abstract, those demographic projections mean little until they are put into the context of social reality. For example, based on 2001 census results, 49% of the Aboriginal population in Saskatchewan had less than a completed high school education, compared to 18% for the non-Aboriginal population.[33] Not surprisingly, the result is reflected in employment, where only 42% on reserve and 58% off reserve are employed in the province. For young Aboriginals, Saskatchewan had the lowest employment rate (35.2%) of the four western provinces.[34] Logically, income levels correspond with the education and employment outcomes, with the annual median income for Aboriginal people in Saskatchewan equalling $14,949, compared to $28,334 for the non-Aboriginal population. At the same time, fully 51% of Aboriginal children to the age of 14 live in low-income families off reserve, compared to 21% for non-Aboriginal children. As well, based on 2001 census data, in the large Saskatchewan cities, 59% of Aboriginal children do not live with two parents, compared to 19% for non-Aboriginal children.

These indicators translate into other social pathologies. The most stark and disturbing statistics relate to young offenders. In Saskatchewan, Aboriginal youth aged 12–17 make up 19% of the age cohort, but account for 80% of admissions to sentenced custody.[35] The issue of over-representation of Aboriginal people in crime statistics extends beyond the youth population. In its study of Aboriginal issues, the Canada West Foundation found Aboriginal people in all four western provinces grossly over-represented among offenders compared to their share of the population:

> The most extreme case is Saskatchewan, where Aboriginal people account for eight percent of the adult population but three-quarters of admissions to facilities and two-thirds admissions to probation.

At the same time, Aboriginal people are also victimized by crime at higher rates than others. An Aboriginal person is almost three times more likely to be the victim of crime than a member of the non-Aboriginal population.[36]

Add to this other issues, like alarmingly high rates of fetal alcohol syndrome in the Aboriginal population and an economy where education and knowledge are more and more the keys to employment and a decent life, and the scope of the social and economic problems facing Aboriginal people and Saskatchewan becomes apparent. Clearly, the key to better lives for Aboriginal people, as it is for all, is eduation. The United Nations Human Development Index is based on per-capita income, life expectancy, and measurement of education outcomes. Those who lag in terms of education are "condemned to low-paying occupations, even if the national economy prospers."[37]

As deeply troubling as the statistical profile is for Saskatchewan Aboriginal people, some progress has been made. Today, more than 60% of Aboriginal people in Saskatchewan live off reserves, about 47% of them in cities. The migration off reserve to the cities, where there are more opportunities, has produced better income levels. The median total income for Aboriginal people living off reserve in 2000 was $17,655, compared to $14,949 for those on reserve.[38] As well, the establishment of the First Nations University of Canada at the University of Regina is helping to open the door to a post-secondary education for Aboriginal students.

But that institution is also facing its own problems, as questions around its governance and management have deeply damaged its reputation. In fact, the very idea of a separate post-secondary Aboriginal institution itself raises questions about a "separate but equal" approach to education. As University of Saskatchewan president Peter MacKinnon has argued, the traditional notion of liberal education is that the university experience is about bringing together people of differing backgrounds in a rich, diverse and challenging learning environment:

> Postsecondary education is, in part, understanding the differences. It is counterproductive to develop institutions that do not accommodate the many peoples of local and global communities coming together. Separate institutions for a race or particular races are fundamentally at odds with a liberal education.[39]

There are also examples of provincial government initiatives to increase employment opportunities for Aboriginal people. For example, the Aboriginal Employment Development Program, started in 1992 and carried on by the current Lorne Calvert government, is geared to increase training and employment for Indian and Métis people. As well, the strategy for Métis and off-Reserve First Nations people, started in 2001, co-ordinates efforts across the provincial government. Its four objectives are to increase the number of Aboriginal people who complete high school and post-secondary education, prepare them to enter a more representative workforce, ensure their greater workforce participation in the province's economy, and improve their individual and community well-being.[40]

But it serves little purpose to pretend that modest progress has had any significant impact on changing the reality and the future the province faces. The dilemma was expressed aptly and pointedly in 2003 by Janice Stokes, a senior policy analyst with the Saskatchewan Institute of Public Policy:

> Recent census results and projected demographic trends for Saskatchewan are troubling. An aging non-Aboriginal population and a very young Aboriginal population are demographically polarizing the province, and related statistical trends indicate that Saskatchewan will experience arduous challenges as a result of its population features. Demographics in Saskatchewan are negatively affecting the condition of the workforce, health care system, education and race relations, threatening long-term socio-economic sustainability in the province. Less important in past years, demographics now have significant implications for Saskatchewan that require acute governmental action to avoid a crisis in the near future.[41]

Defining the dilemma by reciting the statistical reality faced by the Aboriginal population is easy. The challenge that the province, its people and its government face is confronting the issue and building the public will to find the solutions that will change reality for Indian and Métis people.

The first step is giving the issue the prominence on the public agenda that equals the urgency it represents for the province's future. For that to happen will require that credible Aboriginal and non-Aboriginal voices speak out frankly and forcefully about the issue. It means a coming together of people of good will to overcome the past, by a commitment to ensure a better future. It means non-Aboriginal society must acknowledge its failures in dealing with First Nations and accept its share of the responsibility. And, just as importantly, it also means that Aboriginal leaders get beyond the politics of victimization and admit that they too bear some responsibility for their condition and that Aboriginal people and their leaders have also, at times, failed their families and their communities. That is not to say that Aboriginal people must shoulder the blame for their situation. Clearly, government policies dating back to the National Policy period and earlier, as well as systemic racism in the institutions of society, are root causes of the deeply embedded social and economic issues that confront many Aboriginal people. But it is also to say that a part of empowerment for Aboriginal people comes from within—from within their communities, their leadership and themselves. It means recognizing and learning from the mistakes of the past that everyone has made. In 1984, at a constitutional conference on Aboriginal rights, then prime minister Pierre Trudeau set out the challenge of empowerment in terms of the responsibility that Aboriginal people must accept:

> In the end your fate, and the fate of your children's children is in your own hands. You are the custodians of an ancient

spirituality. Your lives are rich in culture and tradition. Take advantage of all that a modern society can offer. But for your soul's health, stand on your own feet, on the sure foundation that spirituality, tradition and family have laid.[42]

There are many layers to the challenge—cultural, sociological, economic, constitutional and political. For Saskatchewan, as in Manitoba and to a lesser, but not insignificant, extent Alberta and British Columbia, the reality of life for more and more Aboriginal people is in an urban setting. Seeking jobs and opportunity, a majority of Aboriginal people in Saskatchewan now live off reserve, predominantly in the cities. The migration means there has been a blurring of the lines of responsibility between the federal and provincial governments. Where on reserve social and economic issues are clearly a federal responsibility, the same is not true off reserve.

A growing urban population of people of Aboriginal ancestry has long been perceived as a "problem" by provincial governments. For example, in its 1960 submission to a joint committee of the House and Senate, the Saskatchewan government warned "the day is not far distant when the burgeoning Indian population, now largely confined to reservations, will explode into the white communities and present a serious problem indeed."[43] These kinds of attitudes in non-Aboriginal society have not declined over time and present a layer of racism that greets Aboriginal people when they migrate to cities. At the same time there are serious questions about the quality of governance on many First Nations, at a time when self-government by First Nations is seen by most as the key to improving economic and social outcomes for Aboriginal people. But unless, and until, the governance issues are addressed credibly, self-government will lack the moral authority required to function effectively.

All of these issues converge in Saskatchewan, yet the public debate around the subject is weak and faint in comparison to the grim reality faced by many Aboriginal people. That is not to say there are not some people trying to focus public attention. One such voice belongs to John Richards, a Saskatchewan NDP MLA in the 1970s and now a professor at Simon Fraser University. Richards is passionate about the plight of urban Aboriginal society, sees it as the most pressing issue facing Saskatchewan, and argues that all governments must turn their attention to innovative solutions. Richards maintains that just as the federal government's 1969 White Paper on Aboriginal issues focussed too much on "an unquestioning faith in liberal individualism," the 1996 Royal Commission on Aboriginal Peoples put too much emphasis on the anthropological argument that Aboriginal peoples' sense of confidence is tied intimately to the strength of their nations. In a 2002 paper for the C.D. Howe Institute, Richards wrote:

> Few agendas are more important to contemporary Canada. But the problems exceed the reach of either the liberal political ideas of the 1960s or the current wisdom rooted in

cultural anthropology. I make the case here for applying a little economics to the issue.[44]

One idea posed by Richards, and a position also advocated by Jean Allard of Winnipeg, a member of Ed Schreyer's former Manitoba government, is to make more of the federal transfers go to individual First Nations people, regardless of whether they live on or off reserve. This location-neutral approach would empower individuals and impose greater accountability on band leaders. Allard argues that such a change would, in fact, be consistent with the Aboriginal customs of the 19th century:

> A chief did not order his people to follow his wishes. He advised them of his plans, and if people disagreed with him, they were free to make their own decisions about whether to follow him or join a different tribe. It was an effective check and balance on the power of leaders.[45]

Richards also argues for greater own-source taxation by First Nations as a means to get improved governance and improved outcomes:

> Governments often perform poorly when not constrained by taxpayers debating how and how much to tax themselves. This problem applies to both authoritarian governments that exercise arbitrary power to tax and to junior-level governments with no need to tax because their revenues derive from transfers made by a senior government.[46]

Clearly, there is no single remedy that will change in a positive way the reality of a life on the margins of society for many Aboriginal people in Saskatchewan. It is an exceedingly complex subject, with deep roots in history, conflicting cultural norms, economics, politics and racist attitudes. But complexity, the paucity of clear answers and the lack of a public consensus are not excuses for a lack of leadership from both non-Aboriginal and Aboriginal people on the issue. In fact, the opposite is true. Just as the fiscal crisis of the early 1990s forced the Saskatchewan government to mobilize public will behind restoring the province's financial stability, the underclass of a growing Aboriginal population in the early years of the 21st century confronts the province with the greatest test of its history.

The challenge presented by the subject, in terms the province's social stability and economic progress, is so great that the continuing failure to deal with it in a concerted and substantive way will make the Saskatchewan myth more illusory and distortive than ever.

Fifteen   Conclusion

"Doubling Saskatchewan's population is not impossible. It has happened before and will happen again. Whether it is to happen in our lifetimes is really up to us."

(Graham Parsons, economist, June 2003)

The myth endures. A century later, Saskatchewan still yearns for its greater destiny. What persists is a powerful conviction that the province can, must and will do better. That if only the right policies were in place, if only the right opportunities seized, if only the right attitudes developed, if only others understood the truth about Saskatchewan, the province would again become a magnet attracting people. If only.

The attitude is manifest in many ways, but is most clearly evident in the public discourse among elites in the province. As has been the case for the past century, the politics of Saskatchewan today is driven by the continuing pursuit of its myth. At its core is how to build a bigger, better, more robust Saskatchewan. How can the economy be diversified, deepened and broadened? How can a more just and equitable society be achieved? How can the decades-long out migration of people, particularly the young, be stopped and a growing economy be reflected in a steadily increasing population? How can the province regain its rightful place in Canada, so that instead of an afterthought, it's seen as a credible rival for investment dollars and an engine of growth? The objective is to shed the image many others in Canada have of the province as a place that doesn't warrant much attention because it doesn't offer much reason for interest.

In other words, the challenge is to export the Saskatchewan myth by getting others to believe in it. If the myth can be the fuel for expectations of a greater future for Saskatchewan people, then why not for others? If they can be made to believe in the myth, then they too will join in its pursuit. As in the days of the National Policy, when government propaganda helped to construct an image of Saskatchewan as a promised land, perception becomes reality.

It was in this context that the Saskatchewan government in 2002 launched a $4.3 million public relations campaign promoting the province built on the theme of "Our Future is Wide Open."[1] Initially, the strategy focussed on a Saskatchewan audience as part of an effort to build a more positive attitude among Saskatchewan people themselves. It was then broadened to a national audience, with sessions held across Canada where business people were told about the province's opportunities, and Saskatchewan expatriates living in other provinces were enlisted as ambassadors to help sell the Saskatchewan message.

The government also launched a newspaper advertising campaign extolling the merits of Saskatchewan's quality of life, natural resource wealth and innovative economy. A special section of the May 4, 2004 *Globe and Mail* included a special six-page advertising section, entitled "Opportunity Saskatchewan," that created an image of a diversified and dynamic Saskatchewan economy:

> Buoyed by its cost competitiveness, surging commodity exports and the province's strengths in sectors from mining, forestry, energy, manufacturing and agriculture to high-tech indicate the province is headed for growth.[2]

The next phase of the selling of Saskatchewan to others was an international advertising campaign in 2004. As a government news release explained:

> Through a combination of investment missions, articles in trade publications, promotions aimed at Canadian embassies and targeted business and trade media advertising, the campaign will continue the message that Saskatchewan is a good place in which to live, work and do business.[3]

In retrospect, it's difficult not to draw parallels, not to think back 100 years to the similar efforts the federal government engaged in as part of the National Policy to sell the prairie West and Saskatchewan to people in the rest of Canada, the US and Europe. The modern-day campaign to sell Saskatchewan might not have the grandiose context of nation building of a century ago, but its impetus comes from the original myth fashioned out of the National Policy.

This desire to turn Saskatchewan into something it isn't, but what myth tells us it might be, to make it an engine for greater growth and opportunity, was never more evident than at an Innovation Saskatchewan Conference in June 2003 at the University of Saskatchewan. The theme of the conference—"Double the Population"—was also the objective. The program introduction stated:

> It is an idea that people across the province can visualize in real terms. Imagine what the future would look like if every community generated enough business and services to double its population.

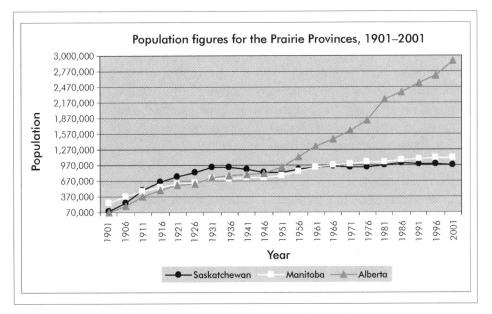

Saskatchewan's population compared to that of Alberta and Manitoba, 1901–2001

The organizers went to far as to compare the goal with the May 1961 declaration by then US president John Kennedy to put an American on the moon before the end of then decade:

> We must establish a tangible vision for the future of our province. It must be a BIG vision, which challenges and encourages us to capture the innovative and creative energy of Saskatchewan.

The goal of a province to have twice the population within 30 years reflects both the province's great strength and its weakness. Its strength is what is clearly a unique and enduring spirit. Saskatchewan is a province that is never deterred by its experience, or the odds it faces. Overcoming adversity has been a continuing current running through the province's history and, as a result, is deeply embedded in its psychology. Rising to the challenge and creating a better life on the prairies, by balancing communitarian values with the spirit of individual achievement, is the fuel of endless optimism. Out of shared adversity has come a powerful sense of collective identity. The modern Saskatchewan myth is very much about believing that a certain strength of character—a kind of personal resilience coupled with a commitment to a larger sense of community—comes with being from Saskatchewan. It's what makes Saskatchewan people unique.

Its weakness is a sense that Saskatchewan should be more than what it is, that somehow its true destiny is being denied. In and of itself, there is nothing wrong with that kind of attitude. Believing in, and working towards, a better future is what all communities need to animate the public discourse they share. In fact, the quest for a better life individually, for our families and for others, is the fuel of politics. But it must also be constrained by reality or else the quest itself helps feed a belief in unreal objectives.

The fact is, Saskatchewan is a success story. Often against enormous odds, it has built a unique society and economy and established a singular identity in Canada. People from Saskatchewan are deeply attached to each other and their roots because they understand what they share. They have experienced suffering and redemption. They know about the equal parts hardship, perseverance and courage that were central to the lives of their grandparents and great-grandparents. They understand the values of sharing and commitment that have been passed down from earlier generations of Saskatchewan people who needed both to survive. Those are incredibly important emotional and psychological anchors for the province and its people. They are products of the myth, the outcome of a century of hardship, of struggle and of achievement.

But for all those valuable qualities that are derived from the Saskatchewan myth, most particularly the sense of common purpose, shared values and belief in community, it also is distortive. The myth serves as a filter through which reality is perceived, expectations created and public policy choices made. In fact, believing in the myth becomes the single most important factor animating political discourse of the province and perceptions of its destiny. The belief in a much greater Saskatchewan—what began a century ago as the promised land of Saskatchewan—remains the motivating force that provides a clear objective, a destiny for politics to pursue.

Still, there is danger in adhering too firmly to our myths. Without the proper context, without understanding both the benefits and dangers of myth as part of the public consciousness of a community, it can become a debilitating barrier. Myth can become a shield that blocks out truth and reality, and with it, the understanding required to deal with the challenges facing the province. Consider, for a moment, a story that appeared in Montreal's *La Presse* newspaper late in 2005. It was entitled "Harlem sur la Saskatchewan."

The article was written by a journalist who was covering the federal election campaign and did a special feature on the economic divide, racial tensions and violence that plague west side Saskatoon:

> À l'Est, une population blanche, en majorité anglo-saxonne. À l'Ouest, les autochtones. La plupart des Blancs n'ont jamais mis les pieds à l'Ouest. Mais la frontière n'est pas seulement raciale, elle est aussi économique.[4]

The article recounted the stark reality of life for Aboriginal people on the west side of Saskatoon and how, as a city racially and economically divided east and west, the misery that Aboriginal people face is visible on the street. Perhaps it was due to the language barrier, but strangely the article, which painted such a stark and depressing picture of life in the city, received little to no attention in Saskatoon or the province. Yet it speaks directly to the most important public issue, the most crucial challenge that confronts the province at the dawn of its second century.

As was made clear at the outset, the role of myth is not unique to Saskatchewan, or its politics. Indeed, politics is by its nature aspirational. It is about believing in something better—in its most rudimentary form, a better life for all—and setting out to achieve it. The inspiration derived from pursuit of the myth can be, and is often, a positive force. It is the emotional fuel that drives change and unites people in common purpose to achieve a greater good for all. In that sense, myth is indispensable to social and economic progress. To not believe in the attainment of a better future—if there were no longing, individually and collectively, for a fairer, more just, prosperous and peaceful world—would empty our lives of purpose and meaning. Quite simply, myths are shared public dreams that shape societies and are essential elements of all cultures and societies.

But clearly, the mere existence of, and belief in, myth means unrealized expectations must also exist. One cannot be satisfied with reality and, at the same time, yearn for something better. Therefore, myth and reality co-exist, both in spite of each other and because of each other. They are opposites, one rooted in actual experience, the other in imagination. Thus, if one accepts that a Saskatchewan myth exists, then that can only lead to the conclusion that the reality of the province is that it has failed to live up to the expectations of its people.

The central question this raises is simple. Has myth played a positive or negative role in the history of Saskatchewan? It would be nice to be able to provide a "yes or no" answer. But history tells us that is not possible. The answer varies at different points in the life of the province.

As history has shown, the role myth played in the founding of the province was to distort reality and inflate perceptions of its future. It created an image and expectations in the minds of the thousands who flocked to settle in the province that was inconsistent with the reality they encountered. Not only was the rapid growth unsustainable, but so too was the society and economy that resulted from the waves of immigration. It is almost impossible to overstate the power of the vision expressed at that time about the potential of the province. Just consider the words of Walter Scott, the province's first premier:

> This province has as yet less than half a million souls and there is plenty room for at least 10 million. Just as sure as the sun shines there will be within the province alone some day a population running into the tens of millions.[5]

In that sense, the founding myth left a legacy that, throughout the last century, has proven to be a heavy burden for the province. Through every period, for each government and successive generations, the political and public policy debate has been shaped by the remnants of those early heady days. It has been about sustaining and realizing the dream of a much greater destiny for Saskatchewan than the reality that exists. In practical terms, modern day pursuit of the Saskatchewan myth is expressed most often in terms of how the province can escape the economic shadow of neighbouring Alberta.

But that should not lead to a kind of austere, deterministic conclusion that Saskatchewan's destiny is somehow beyond the control and aspirations of its people. It is not to say that believing in the Saskatchewan myth has not often been a force for progress. What it does say is that pursuit of the myth must also be tempered with reality and common sense. Because when myth, expressed in the political discourse as idealism, becomes so powerful that it impairs judgment, it moves from being a crucial source of motivation for advancement to a debilitating influence on social and economic progress.

It is finding the right balance, between myth as inspiration and reality as perspective, that is key. The challenge of politics, therefore, is clear. On one hand, it comes down to knowing how to use myth as a means to create a sense of collective identity and common purpose that can mobilize people to help change reality. On the other, it is recognizing that, if not restrained, myth can be a source of false expectations and political outcomes that lead to poor public policy choices.

In the broad sweep of Saskatchewan's history, the development of its political economy and the creation of its collective identity, myth has obviously played an important and ongoing role. It has been expressed in many ways. First, as part of the National Policy, Saskatchewan was portrayed as a promised land, which served as the psychological and economic foundation for the province. Then, with belief in Saskatchewan as a promised land shattered by the Great Depression and Dirty Thirties, the myth was reconstituted through the inspiration of the social gospel. It was then politically reinvigorated in the meaning of medicare and has been expressed in recent decades through the competing visions for economic development. Through all those eras, no matter what the tides of politics, there remained one constant. It was the singular, collective idea that Saskatchewan had unrealized potential.

The challenge for the public dialogue of Saskatchewan as the province enters its second century is to not replay the mistakes of the past. What Saskatchewan people must do is recognize the role that myth has played, and must continue to play, in the life of the province. But, at the same time, we must be able to differentiate it from reality, to understand the power of myth as a force for progress and its potential to create false expectations. For, once we come to terms with what we can reasonably hope for ourselves and what we already have, we might discover what my uncle Frank understood long ago—that the myth has become our reality.

Endnotes

Endnotes to Chapter 1

1. Karen Armstrong, *A Short History of Myth* (Toronto: Alfred A. Knopf Canada, 2005), 10.
2. Henry Murray, *Myths and Mythmaking* (New York: G. Braziller, 1960), 355.
3. W.O. Mitchell, *Who Has Seen The Wind* (Toronto: Macmillan, 1970), 1.
4. Wallace Stegner, *Wolf Willow* (New York: The Viking Press, 1967), 7–8.
5. Carlye King (ed.), *Saskatchewan Harvest* (Toronto: McClellan and Stewart, 1955), 87–88.
6. Sinclair Ross, *As For Me and My House* (Toronto: McClelland and Stewart, 1970).
7. Norman Henderson, *Rediscovering the Great Plains: Journeys by Dog, Canoe and Horse* (Baltimore: Johns Hopkins University Press, 2001), 7.
8. Benedict Anderson, *Imagined Communities* (London: Verso, 1994), 46.
9. W.T. Easterbrook and Hugh Aitken, *Canadian Economic History* (Toronto: Macmillan, 1956), 293.
10. Peter Rayment Sinclair, "Populism in Alberta and Saskatchewan: A Comparative Analysis of Social Credit and the Co-operative Commonwealth Federation" (PhD dissertation, University of Edinburgh, 1972), 53.
11. Vernon Fowke, "The National Policy Old and New, in Approaches to Canadian Economic History," in Easterbrook and Aitken (eds.), *Canadian Economic History*, 242.
12. Kenneth McNaught, *The History of Canada* (London: Heinemann Educational, 1970), 147.

Endnotes to Chapter 2

1. Dennis Gruending (ed.), *The Middle of Nowhere* (Saskatoon: Fifth House Publishing, 1996), 73.
2. Douglas Owram, *The Promise of Eden: The Canadian Expansionist Movement and the Idea of the West, 1856–1900* (Toronto: University of Toronto Press, 1980), 60.
3. Great Britain, House of Commons, *Report, Select Committee on the Hudson's Bay Company* (1857), app. 8, 399–400.
4. Owram, *The Promise of Eden*, 67.
5. Gerald Friesen, *The Canadian Prairies: A History* (Toronto: University of Toronto Press, 1987), 108.
6. Bill Waiser, *The Field Naturalist: John Macoun, the Geological Survey and Natural Science* (Toronto: University of Toronto Press, 1989), 34.
7. See John Macoun, *Autobiography of John Macoun, Canadian Explorer and Naturalist, 1831–1920* (Ottawa: Ottawa Field Naturalists' Club, 1979).
8. Waiser, *The Field Naturalist*, 16.
9. Owram, *The Promise of Eden*, 152.

10. Waiser, *The Field Naturalist*, 39.

11. John Macoun, *Manitoba and the Great North West* (Guelph, ON: World Publishing Co., 1882), 144.

12. Ibid.

13. Andrew Morton, *The History of Prairie Settlement* (Toronto: Macmillan and Co., 1938), 53.

14. Friesen, *The Canadian Prairies: A History*, 174.

15. W.A. Mackintosh, *Economic Problems of the Prairie Provinces* (Toronto: Macmillan and Company, 1935), 34.

16. Alexander Morris, *The Treaties of Canada With the Indians of Manitoba and the North-West Territories Including the Negotiations on Which They Were Based* (Saskatoon: Fifth House Publishers, 1991), 77.

17. Sarah Carter, *Aboriginal People and the Colonizers of Western Canada to 1900* (Toronto: University of Toronto Press, 1999), 117.

18. Quoted in Allan Cairns, *Citizens Plus: Aboriginal Peoples and the Canadian State* (Vancouver: University of British Columbia Press, 2000), 17

19. John L. Tobias, "Canada's Subjugation of the Plains Cree," in J.R. Miller (ed.), *Sweet Promises: A Reader on Indian-White Relations in Canada* (Toronto: University of Toronto Press, 1991).

20. Quoted in Cairns, *Citizens* Plus, 17.

21. Vernon Fowke, *The National Policy and the Wheat Economy* (Toronto: University of Toronto Press, 1973), 66.

22. Triadafilos Triadafilopoulos, "Building Walls, Bounding Nations: Migration and Exclusion in Canada and Germany, 1870–1939," *Journal of Historical Sociology* 17, no. 4 (December 2004): 394.

23. D.J. Hall, "Clifford Sifton: Immigration and Settlement Policy 1896–1905," in Howard Palmer (ed.), *The Settlement of the West* (Calgary: University of Calgary 1977), 64.

24. Ibid., 68.

25. Friesen, *The Canadian Prairies: A History*, 249–50.

26. Hall, "Clifford Sifton," 77.

27. National Archives of Canada (hereafter NA), Clifford Sifton papers, Vol. 255, 462–63.

28. Mabel Timlin, "Canada's Immigration Policy," *Canadian Journal of Economics and Political Science* (November 1960): 518.

29. Harold Troper, *Only Farmers Need Apply: Official Canadian Government Encouragement of Immigration from the U.S., 1896–1911* (Toronto: Griffin House, 1972), 81.

30. Klaus Peter Stich, "Canada's Century," *Prairie Forum* 1, no. 1 (April 1976).

31. Paul F. Sharp, *The Agrarian Revolt in Western Canada, A Survey Showing American Parallels* (St. Paul: University of Minnesota Press, 1948), 14–15.

32. PatrickDunae, "Making Good: The Canadian West in British Boys' Literature, 1890–1914," *Prairie Forum* 4, no. 2 (1979): 165.

33. Stich, "Canada's Century," 25.

34. James Gray, *Red Lights on the Prairies* (Saskatoon: Western Producers Prairie Books, 1986), 2.

35. Ibid., 26–27,

36. Owram, *The Promise of Eden*, 218.

Endnotes to Chapter 3

1. John Dales, *The Protective Tariff in Canada's Development* (Toronto: University of Toronto Press, 1966), 144.

2. Regina *Leader* (September 6, 1905), 4.
3. Simon McLean, *The Tariff History of Canada* (Toronto: Warwick Bros. and Rutter, 1895), 23–24.
4. Ibid., 22.
5. Government of Canada, *Royal Commission on Dominion Provincial Relations*, Book 1 (Ottawa: King's Printer, 1937), 19.
6. Thomas White, "The National Policy," Kelowna *Courier* (January 12, 1877).
7. Orville McDiarmid, *Commercial Policy in the Canadian Economy* (Cambridge: Harvard University Press, 1946), 207.
8. Fowke, *The National Policy and the Wheat Economy*, 67.
9. McDiarmid, *Commercial Policy in the Canadian Economy*, 208.
10. Edward Poritt, *Sixty Years of Protectionism in Canada, 1846–1912* (Winnipeg: The Grain Growers Guide, 1913), 422–23.
11. Dales, *The Protective Tariff in Canada's Development*, 109.
12. J. Lorne McDougall, *Canadian Pacific: A Brief History* (Montreal: McGill University Press, 1968), 29.
13. Canada, Royal Commission on Railways and Transportation, 1917.
14. Robert Chodos, *The CPR: A Century of Corporate Welfare* (Toronto: J. Lewis and Samuel, 1973), 156.
15. Ibid., 19.
16. John Eagle, *The CPR and the Development of Western Canada* (Montreal: McGill-Queen's, 1989), 15.
17. Charles F. Wilson, *Canadian Grain Marketing* (Winnipeg: Canagian International Grains Institute, 1979), 386.
18. J.F.C. Wright, *Saskatchewan: The History of a Province* (Toronto: McClelland and Stewart, 1955), 162.
19. Government of Canada, Dominion Bureau of Statistics, Ottawa, 1970.
20. Toronto *Globe* (August 2, 1910), 1.
21. Dales, *The Protective Tariff in Canada's Development*, 153.
22. Chester Martin, *Dominion Lands Policy* (Toronto: Macmillan and Company, 1938), 410.
23. Fowke, *The National Policy and the Wheat Economy*, 77.
24. Martin, *Dominion Lands Policy*, 324–25.

Endnotes to Chapter 4
1. Mackintosh, *Economic Problems of the Prairie Provinces*, 7.
2. Evelyn Eager, "The Government of Saskatchewan" (PhD dissertation, University of Toronto, 1957), 48–49.
3. Ibid., 69.
4. Quoted in David E. Smith, "A Comparison of Prairie Political Developments in Saskatcvhewan and Alberta," *Journal of Canadian Studies* 4, no. 1 (February 1969): 19.
5. See J. William Brennan, "The 'Autonomy Question' and the Creation of Alberta and Saskatchewan," in Howard Palmer and Donald Smith (eds.), *The New Provinces: Alberta and Saskatchewan 1905–1980* (Vancouver: Tantalus Research Ltd., 1980).
6. Saskatchewan Legislature, *Debates and Proceedings*, 1905, Vol. 2, p. 3157.
7. David Smith, *Building a Province: A History of Saskatchewan Documents* (Saskatoon: Fifth House Publishers, 1992), 67.
8. Brennan"The 'Autonomy Question'," 50.
9. Government of Canada, Dominion Bureau of Statistics, 1931 census.
10. Jim Wright, *Saskatchewan: The History of a Province* (Toronto: McClelland and Stewart, 1955), 128.

11. Martin, *Dominion Lands Policy*, 410.
12. Government of Canada, Dominion Bureau of Statistics, *Census of Canada, 1931*, Volume 8, *Agriculture* (Ottawa: King's Printer, 1931), 588–89.
13. John Archer, *Saskatchewan: A History* (Saskatoon: Western Producer Prairie Books, 1980), 147.
14. Wilfred Malenbaum, *The World Wheat Economy, 1885–1939* (Cambridge: Harvard University Press, 1953), 9, 175.
15. Ibid., 174.
16. Government of Canada. Historical Statistics of Canada, M109-118.
17. Mackintosh, *Economic Problems of the Prairie Provinces*, 4.
18. Government of Saskatchewan, Saskatchewan Agriculture Credit Commission (1913), 13.
19. Mackintosh, *Economic Problems of the Prairie Provinces*, 32
20. Archer, *Saskatchewan: A History*, 155.
21. Statutes of Saskatchewan, 1908.
22. Canada, *Royal Commission on Railways and Transportation 1931–32*, 81–82.
22. Statutes of Saskatchewan, 1912–13.
24. George Britnell, *The Wheat Economy* (Toronto: University of Toronto Press, 1939), 12.
25. Local Government Continuing Committee, *Local Government in Saskatchewan* (n.p.: March 1961), 8.
26. Ibid., 51.
27. Government of Saskatchewan, *Department of Education Report*, 1907, 12.
28. Government of Saskatchewan, *Department of Education Report*, 1916, 11.
29. Government of Saskatchewan, *Royal Commission of Agriculture and Rural Life*, 77.

Endnotes to Chapter 5

1. John Bennett and Seena Kohl, "Characterological, Strategic and Institutional Interpretation of Prairie Settlement" in Anthony W. Rasporich (ed.), *Western Canada Past and Present* (Toronto: McClelland and Stewart, 1975), 15.
2. Friesen, *The Canadian Prairies: A History*, 309.
3. W.L. Morton, *The Progressive Party in Canada* (Toronto: University of Toronto Press, 1971), 20.
4. W.L. Morton, "The Bias of Prairie Politics," in George Melnyk (ed.), *Riel to Reform* (Saskatoon: Fifth House Publishers, 1992), 14.
5. Mackintosh, *Economic Problems of the Prairie Provinces*, 20.
6. Government of Saskatchewan, *Elevator Commission Report* (1910), 17.
7. Paul Sharp, *The Agrarian Revolt in Western Canada, A Survey Showing American Parallels* (St. Paul: University of Minnesota Press, 1948), 20.
8. Barry Wilson, *Beyond The Harvest:Canadian Grain at the Crossroads* (Saskatoon: Western Producer Prairie Books, 1981), 241.
9. David Smith, "A Comparison of Prairie Political Developments in Saskatchewan and Alberta," *The Journal of Canadian Studies* 4. no. 1: 20.
10. Vernon Fowke, *Canadian Agriculture Policy: The Historical Pattern* (Toronto: University of Toronto Press, 1946), 244.
11. John Conway, *The West: The History of a Region in Confederation* (Toronto: J. Lorimer, 1983), 51.
12. Sharp, *The Agrarian Revolt in Western Canada*, 29–30.
13. Edward Porritt, *Sixty Years of Protection, 1846–1907* (London: Macmillan and Co., 1908), 439.
14. David Smith, *Prairie Liberalism: The Liberal Party in Saskatchewan 1905–71* (Toronto: University of Toronto Press, 1975), 68.

15. Duff Spafford, "The Elevator Issue, The Organized Farmers and the Government, 1908–11," *Saskatchewan History* 15 (Fall 1962): 83.
16. Government of Saskatchewan, *Elevator Commission Report* (1910), 95.
17. Statutes of Saskatchewan, 1910–11, Chapter 39.
18. Ibid., 1915, Chapter 33.
19. Ibid., 1917, Chapter 7.
20. Government of Saskatchewan, *Report of the Grain Markets Commission* (1914), 119.
21. Ibid., 11.
22. Ibid., 120.
23. Government of Saskatchewan, *Report of the Roral Commission on Agriculture Credit* (1913), 13.
24. Garry Fairbairn, *From Prairie Roots: The Remarkable Story of the Saskatchewan Wheat Pool* (Saskatoon: Western Producer Prairie Books, 1984), 6.
25. Ibid., 28.
26. Eager, "The Government of Saskatchewan," 359.
27. James M. Pitsula, "Muscular Saskatchewan: Provincial Self-Identity in the 1920s," *Saskatchewan History* 54, no. 2 (Fall 2002): 7.
28. Abraham Rotstein, "Innis: The Alchemy of Fur and Wheat," *Journal of Canadian Studies* 12, no. 5: 18.

Endnotes to Chapter 6

1. Ernest Renan, www.nationalismproject.org/what/renan
2. Sharon Butala, *The Gates of the Sun* (Saskatoon: Fifth House, 1985), 112.
3. Robert Collins, *Butter Down The Well: Reflections of a Canadian Childhood* (Saskatoon: Western Producers Prairie Books, 1980), 53.
4. E.F. Dyck (ed.), *Essays on Saskatchewan Writing* (Regina: Saskatchewan Writers Guild, 1986), 43.
5. Sinclair Ross, *As For Me and My House* (Toronto: McClellan and Stewart, 1970), 19.
6. Government of Canada, *Royal Commission on Dominion-Provincial Relations*, Book 1, 236
7. Government of Canada, *Report of Hearings, Saskatchewan*, Volume 1, 1202
8. Ibid., 1225.
9. Ibid., 223.
10. Ibid., 224.
11. See Sharp, *The Agrarian Revolt in Western Canada*.
12. Garry Fairbarin, *From Prairie Roots: The Remarkable Story of the Saskatchewan Wheat Pool* (Saskatoon: Western Producer Prairie Books, 1984), 99.
13. Government of Canada, *Royal Grain Inquiry Commission*, 1938, 34–35.
14. Mackintosh, *Economic Problems of the Prairie Provinces*, 52–53.
15. Quoted in Fairbairn, *From Prairie Roots*, 95.
16. Ibid., 102.
17. Mackintosh, *Economic Problems of the Prairie Provinces*, 54.
18. Paul Johnson, *Modern Times: The World From the Twenties to the Eighties* (New York: Harper and Row, 1983), 246.
19. Government of Canada, *Royal Commission on Dominion-Provincial Relations*, Book 1 (1940), 140.
20. Charles Kindleberger, *The World in Depression, 1929–1939* (Berkeley: University of California Press, 1986), 292.
21. Johnson, *Modern Times*, 139.
22. Government of Saskatchewan, *Department of Municipal Affairs Annual Report* (1937), 7, 11.

23. Ibid., 11.
24. Dominion Bureau of Statistics, *Handbook on Agriculture Statistics*, Part 2, Farm Income, 1926–65, Catalogue No. 21-511.
25. Government of Canada, *National Income*, 1939, Appendix 4, 55.
26. Government of Saskatchewan, *Brief to the Royal Commission on Dominion-Provincial Relations*, 39.
27. Ibid., 22.
28. ibid. 16.
29. Gordon Barnhart (ed.), *Saskatchewan Premiers of the Twentieth Century* (Regina: Canadian Plains Research Center, 2005), 129.
30. Government of Saskatchewan, *Royal Commission on Taxation*, 1936, 24.
31. Statutes of Saskatchewan, 1932, Chaper 2, 1934–35, Chapter 10; ibid., 1936, Chapter 10.
32. Government of Saskatchewan, *Brief to the Royal Commission on Dominion-Provincial Relations*, 26.
33. Ibid., 19.
34. Ibid., 38.
35. Ibid., 1245.

Endnotes to Chapter 7

1. George Melnyk, *Beyond Alienation: Political Essays on the West* (Calgary: Detselig Enterprises Ltd., 1993), 115.
2. JohnHutchinson and Anthony Smith (eds.), *Nationalism* (Oxford: Oxford University Press, 1994), 15.
3. Walter D. Young, *The Anatomy of a Party: The National CCF, 1932–61* (Toronto: University of Toronto Press, 1969), 40.
4. See Lorne Brown, "The Progressive Tradition in Saskatchewan," in Dimitrios Roussopoulos (ed.), *Canada and Radical Social Change* (Montreal: Black Rose Books, 1973).
5. Young, *The Anatomy of a Party*, 18.
6. Seymour Martin Lipset, "Rural Community and Political Leadership in Saskatchewan," *Canadian Journal of Economics and Political Science* (August 1947): 411.
7. Grace MacInnis, *J.S. Woodsworth: A Man To Remember* (Toronto: Macmillan of Canada, 1953), 265.
8. Ibid., 273.
9. F.R. Scott, "The CCF Convention," *Canadian Forum* (September 1933): 447.
10. Alan Whitehorn, *Canadian Socialism: Essays on the CCF-NDP* (Toronto: Oxford University Press, 1992), 39.
11. Ibid., 43.
12. Andrew Milnor, "Agrarian Protest in Saskatchewan 1929–1948: A Study in Ethnic Politics" (PhD dissertation, Duke University, 1962), 94.
13. Toronto *Globe* (July 20, 1933), 1.
14. Regina *Leader-Post* (July 22, 1933), 1.
15. Toronto *Globe* (July 21, 1933), 4.
16. Ibid. (July 24, 1933), 4.
17. James Gray, *Men Against the Desert* (Saskatoon: Western Producer Prairie Books, 1967). 53.
18. *Saturday Night* (April 11, 1931), 11.
19. Friesen, *The Canadian Prairies: A History*, 404.
20. David Smith and Norman Ward, *Jimmy Gardiner: Relentless Liberal* (Toronto: University of Toronto Press, 1990), 94.

21. Milnor, "Agrarian Protest in Saskatchewan: 1929–1948," 28.

22. Ibid., 85.

23. J.T. Morley, "Social Credit," in *The Canadian Encyclopedia* (Edmonton: Hurtig Publishers, 1988), 2024.

24. Seymour Martin Lipset, *Agrarian Socialism: The Cooperative Commonwealth Federation in Saskatchewan, A Study in Political Sociology* (Berkley: University of California Press, 1971), 145.

25. Argument often made by former Saskatchewan Progressive Conservative party leader Dick Collver, interview with author, 1986.

26. Lipset, *Agrarian Socialism*, 144.

27. Regina *Daily Star* (May 14, 1938), 9.

28. Lipset, *Agrarian Socialism*, 224.

29. George Grant, *Lament for a Nation: The Defeat of Canadian Nationalism* (Toronto: McClelland and Stewart, 1965), 59.

Endnotes to Chapter 8

1. See Thomas McLeod, "Public Enterprise in Saskatchewan" (PhD dissertation, Harvard University, 1959).

2. Two key figures in the U.S. social gospel movement were Charles Sheldon and Walter Rauschenbusch. Sheldon's book *In His Steps*, published in 1897, was one of the most popular and influential books in the movement. *Christianity and the Social Crisis* by Rauschenbusch in 1907 became an important work about the theories and purpose of the social gospel.

3. *Grain Growers' Guide* (January 12, 1969).

4. Regina *Leader* (February 22, 1919).

5. Richard Allen, "Social Gospel as the Religion of the Agrarian Revolt," in R. Douglas Francis and Howard Palmer (eds.), *The Prairie West: Historical Readings* (Edmonton: University of Alberta Press, 1985), 440.

6. Lipset, *Agrarian Socialism*, 170.

7. Albert Johnson, "Biography of a Government: Policy Formation in Saskatchewan 1944–61" (PhD dissertation, Harvard University, 1963), 97.

8. L.D. Lovick (ed.), *Tommy Douglas Speaks* (Lantzville, BC: Oolichan Books, 1979), 11.

9. *Farmer Labour News*, May–June, 1934.

10. Doris French Shackleton, *Tommy Douglas* (Toronto: McClellan and Stewart, 1975), 81.

11. The Reverend T.C. Douglas, "The Problems of the Subnormal Family" (MA thesis, McMaster University, 1933), 2.

12. Ibid., 26.

13. Thomas McLeod and Ian McLeod, *Tommy Douglas: The Road to Jerusalem* (Edmonton: Hurtig Publishers, 1987), 39.

14. Allan Chase, *The Legacy of Malthus* (New York: Alfred Knopf, 1977), 77–78.

15. Lewis Thomas, *The Making of a Socialist: Recollections of T.C. Douglas* (Edmonton: University of Alberta Press, 1982), 109.

16. McLeod and McLeod, *Tommy Douglas*, 73.

17. Campbell McConnell, Stanley Brue and Thomas Barbiero, *Macroeconomics* (Toronto: McGraw, Hill Ryerson, 1993), 264–70.

18. Charles Kindleberger, *The World in Depression 1929–39* (Berkeley: University of California Press, 1986), 201–02.

19. Robert Samuelson, *The Good Life and Its Discontents: The American Dream in the Age of Entitlements* (New York Times Books, 1995), 19.

20. K.J. Rea, *A Guide to Canadian Economic History* (Toronto: Canadian Scholars' Press, 1991), 166.
21. Ibid., 170.
22. Desmond Morton, *When Canada Won the War*, Booklet No. 54 (Ottawa: The Canadian Historical Associatioon), 4.
23. W.A. Mackintosh, *The White Paper on Employment and Income in Its 1945 Setting* (Ottawa: n.p., 1965), 18.
24. Michael Bliss, "Canada's Swell War," *Saturday Night Magazine* (May 1995).
25. Lovick, *Tommy Douglas Speaks*, 77.
26. Mitchell Sharp, *Which Reminds Me* (Toronto: University of Toronto Press, 1994), 21.
27. Archer, *Saskatchewan: A History*, 256.
28. Ibid., 256.
29. Ibid., 257.
30. Smith, *Prairie Liberalism*, 230.
31. Rea, *A Guide to Canadian Economic History*, 166.

Endnotes to Chapter 9

1. Ludwig von Mises, "Human Action—A Treatise on Economics," in Alvin Rubinstein and Gerald Thumm (eds.), *The Challenge of Politics: Ideas and Issues* (Englewood Cliffs, NJ: Prentice Hall, 1963), 143.
2. Archer, *Saskatchewan: A History*, 267.
3. Raymond Sherdahl, "The Saskatchewan General Election of 1944" (MA thesis, University of Saskatchewan, 1966), 22–23.
4. Government of Saskatchewan, Department of Natural Resources and Industrial Development 1944–45, *Annual Report*, 35.
5. Thomas, *The Making of a Socialist*, 179–80.
6. Toronto *Globe and Mail* (June 17, 1944).
7. Quoted in Sherdahl, "The Saskatchewan General Election of 1944," 93.
8. Moose Jaw *Times-Herald* (June 4, 1944), quoted in Sherdahl, "The Saskatchewan General Election of 1944," 96.
9. Ibid., 23.
10. Regina *Leader-Post* (June 12, 1944).
11. For an overview of early CCF government years see Johnson, "Biography of a Government: Policy Formation in Saskatchewan 1944–61," McLeod and McLeod, *Tommy Douglas: The Road to Jerusalem*, and Sherdahl, "The Saskatchewan General Election of 1944."
12. Government of Saskatchewan, "1945 Budget Speech," 15.
13. Ibid., 16.
14. Government of Saskatchewan, "1946 Budget Speech," 11–12.
15. Ibid., 19.
16. See McLeod and McLeod, *Tommy Douglas: The Road to Jerusalem*.
17. Saskatchewan Legislature, *Debates and Proceedings* (March 1, 1949), 489.
18. Saskatchewan Heath Services Survey Committee, 1944. 3.
19. Ibid., 6.
20. Ibid., 4-7.
21. Duane Mombourquette, "An Inalienable Right: The CCF and Rapid Health Care Reform, 1944–48," *Saskatchewan History* (Autumn 1991): 106.
22. Government of Saskatchewan, Department of Agriculture, *Annual Report, 1949–50*, 6.
23. Ibid., 55.
24. New Democratic Party of Saskatchewan, *The Commonwealth* (December 1995), 21, 23.

25. Jerry Granatstein, *Canada 1957–67: The Years of Uncertainty and Innovation* (Toronto: McClelland and Stewart, 1986), 170.

26. John Richard and Larry Pratt, *Prairie Capitalism: Power and Influence in the New West* (Toronto: McClelland and Stewart, 1979), 143.

27. Quoted in ibid., 116.

28. Quoted in Johnson, "Biography of a Government: Policy Formation in Saskatchewan, 1944–61," 134.

29. Richard and Pratt, *Prairie Capitalism*, 116.

30. Quoted in Thomas McLeod, "Public Enterprise in Saskatchewan" (PhD dissertation, Harvard University, 1959), 109.

31. Johnson, "Biography of a Government: Policy Formation in Saskatchewan, 1944–61," 100.

32. Robert I. McLaren, "George Woodall Cadbury: The Fabian Catalyst in Saskatchewan's Good Public Administration," *Canadian Public Administration* 38, no. 3 (Fall 1995): 477.

33. Jamesina Jamieson, "The Evolution of Executive Power in Saskatchewan, 1944–1982" (LLB thesis, University of Ottawa, 1989), 60.

34. Ibid., 96.

Endnotes to Chapter 10

1. Co-operative Commonwealth Federation, *The Commonwealth* (October 20, 1948), 1.

2. Bill Waiser, *Saskatchewan: A New History* (Calgary: Fifth House Ltd., 2005), 350.

3. Toronto *Globe and Mail* (June 26, 1948), 2.

4. Ibid. (June 25, 1948), 2.

5. Winnipeg *Free Press* (June 25, 1948), 13.

6. Archer, *Saskatchewan: A History*, 289.

7. Joan Champ, "Rural Electrification in Saskatchewan During the 1950s." Prepared for the Saskatchewan Western Development Museum's "Winning the Prairie Gamble 2005 Exhibit (December 4, 2001).

8. Clint White, *Power for a Province: A History of Saskatchewan Power* (Regina: Canadian Plains Research Center, 1976, 265.

9. Statistics Canada, *Historical Statistics of Canada*, 2nd edition, *Population and Migration*, 2nd ed. (Ottawa: Statistics Canada with Social Science Federation of Canada, 1983), A1-14.

10. Thomas, *The Making of a Socialist*, 299.

11. "Socialism Calls Upon Private Enterprise," *Western Business and Industry* 20, no. 12: 87.

12. Government of Saskatchewan, Economic Advisory and Planning Board, *Saskatchewan Economic Review*, 1, no. 1 (November 1951): 1.

13. Ibid., 8.

14. *Western Business and Industry* (September, 1957), 23.

15. Government of Saskatchewan, *Saskatchewan Economic Review* (1961), 7.

16. Stanford Research Institute, *A Study of Resources and Industrial Opportunities for the Province of Saskatchewan (1959)*, Table 8, Page 41, SRI Project No. 1-2665. Prepared for the Province of Saskatchewan Industrial Development Office. Economic Advisory and Planning Board, Regina, Saskatchewan.

17. Ibid., 24–25.

18. Ibid., 25.

19. Government of Saskatchewan, *Prospects for Economic Growth in Saskatchewan* (1955), 11.

20. Ibid., 111.

21. Charles Schwartz, *The Search for Stability* (Toronto: McClelland and Stewart, 1959), 20.
22. Archer, *Saskatchewan: A History*, 197.
23. Ibid., 360–61.
24. Government of Saskatchewan, *Prospects for Economic Growth in Saskatchewan* (1955), 112.
25. Paula Rein, "These Changing Conditions: A Study of the Saskatchewan Royal Commission on Agriculture and Rural Life" (MA Thesis, University of Regina, 1994), 6–7.
26. Ibid., 16–17.
27. Ibid., 22.
28. Government of Saskatchewan, Royal Commission on Agriculture and Rural Life, 1955–57, *Report 5, Land Tenure*, 38.
29. White, *Power for a Province*, 284–85.
30. Quoted in James M. Pitsula, "The Saskatchewan Government and Treaty Indians, 1944–64," *Canadian Historical Review* (March 1994), 23.
31. David M. Quiring, CCF *Colonialism in Northern Saskatchewan* (Vancouver: UBC Press, 2004), 38.
32. Ibid., 51.
33. F. Laurie Barron, *Walking in Indian Mocassins: The Native Policies of Tommy Douglas and the CCF* (Vancouver: UBC Press, 1997), 61.
34. Pitsula, "The Saskatchewan Government and Treaty Indians, 1944–64," 30.
35. "This Is Our Alabama," *Maclean's Magazine* (July 6, 1963), 20.

Endnotes to Chapter 11

1. Fiona Colligan-Yano and Mervyn Norton, *The Urban Age: Building a Place for Urban Government in Saskatchewan* (Regina: Century Archive Publishing, 1996), 37.
2. *The Medicare Crisis in Saskatchewan: A Bibliography* (Regina: Saskatchewan Legislature Library, 1963," 2.
3. J. Harvey Perry, *A Fiscal History of Canada—The Postwar Years* (Toronto: Canadian Tax Foundation, 1989), 625.
4. Quoted in Robin F. Badgley and Samuel Wolfe, *Doctors' Strike: Medical Care and Conflict in Saskatchewan* (Toronto: Macmillan of Canada, 1967), 14.
5. Allan Rock, speech to the Canadian Federation of Agriculture, Ottawa, February 26, 1998.
6. W.P. Thompson, *Medical Care, Programs and Issues* (Toronto: Clarke, Irwin and Co., 1964), 57.
7. Thomas, *The Making of a Socialist*, 225.
8. Ibid., 226.
9. Regina *Leader-Post* (April 2, 1964).
10. Steven A. Lyons, "Labor Pains: The 1962 Battle Over Canadian Health Care," *The Whole Earth Review* (Winter 1995): 76.
11. Ibid., 77.
12. See Daniel Atwell Zoll, *Reason and Rebellion: An Informal History of Political Ideas* (Englewood Cliffs, NJ: Prentice-Hall, 1963).
13. Dale Eisler, *Rumours of Glory: Saskatchewan and the Thatcher Years* (Edmonton: Hurtig Publishers, 1987), 102.
14. Legislature of Saskatchewan, *Debates and Proceedings*, Part 3, Second Session (1961), 39.
15. Ibid., 38.
16. Chief Electoral Officer, "Provincial Elections in Saskatchewan, 1905–1983."
17. Thompson, *Medical CAre, Programs and Issues*, 73.

18. Regina *Leader-Post* (July 3, 1962), 1.
19. "There's More Fury Than Sense in the Medical Care War," *Maclean's Magazine* (June 16, 1962), 66,
20. Regina *Leader-Post*, "The Canadian Press" (July 5, 1962), 19.
21. Regina *Leader-Post*, "Bitter Controversy Ended" (July 24, 1962).
22. Perry, *A Fiscal History of Canada—The Postwar Years*, 628–32.

Endnotes to Chapter 12

1. Ronald C. Murray, *Provincial Mineral Policies: Saskatchewan*, Working Paper No. 6 (Kingston: Queen's University, Centre for Resource Studies, September 1978), 6–7.
2. Ibid., 7.
3. Government of Saskatchewan, Department of Mineral Resources, *Annual Report* (1947–48), 36.
4. Statistics Canada, *Historical Statistics of Canada*, Catalogue No. 11-516-XIE, 1983, Series R98-108; 112-122; 123-133.
5. Government of Saskatchewan, *Provincial Economic Accounts*, Saskatchewan Bureau of Statistics (November 1988).
6. Walter Gordon, *A Political Memoir* (Toronto: McClelland and Stewart, 1977), 67.
7. Michael Howlett and M. Ramesh, *The Political Economy of Canada* (Toronto: McClelland and Stewart, 1992), 201–202.
8. Gordon, *A Political Memoir*, 150.
9. Government of Canada, *Foreign Ownership and the Structure of Canadian Industry* (Ottawa: Privy Council Office, 1968), 346.
10. Speech to The Potash Show. Saskatoon, October 25, 1965.
11. Legislature of Saskatchewan, *Debates and Proceedings*, Sixth Session, 14th Legislature (February 11, 1964), 51.
12. Archer, *Saskatchewan: A History*, 316.
13. Smith, *Prairie Liberalism*, 303.
14. Legislature of Saskatchewan, Budget Speech (February 19, 1965), 3–4.
15. Regina *Leader-Post* (September 17, 1964), 1.
16. Ibid. (September 18, 1964).
17. Legislature of Saskatchewan, Budget Speech (February 19, 1965), 9.
18. Nancy Olewiler, *The Potash Corporation of Saskatchewan: An Assessment* (n.p.: The Economic Council of Canada, 1986), 20.
19. Richards and Pratt, *Prairie Capitalism: Power and Influence in the New West*.
20. Government of Saskatchewan, Department of Natural Resources, *Annual Report* (1968–69), 6.
21. Eisler, *Rumours of Glory*, 254. See also Waiser, *Saskatchewan: A New History*, 396–97.
22. James M. Pitsula, "The Thatcher Government in Saskatchewan and Treaty Indians 1964–71: The Quiet Revolution," *Saskatchewan History* (Spring 1996): 9.
23. Ibid., 8.
24. Saskatchewan Bureau of Statistics, *Saskatchewan Provincial Economic Accounts* (November 1988).
25. Saskatchewan Bureau of Statistics, *Saskatchewan Provincial Economic Accounts* (May 2002).
26. *Saskatchewan Economic Review* (1972), 7.

Endnotes to Chapter 13

1. New Democratic Party of Saskatchewan, "New Deal For People" (February 1971).
2. See Gerard Ruggie, "Taking Embedded Liberalism Global," Miliband Public Lecture, London School of Economics, June 6, 2002.

3. Eleanor Glor, "The Government Tango: Communications and Coordination," *The Innovation Journal*, Chapter 6, www.innovation.cc/Book/chapter8.htm
4. Government of Saskatchewan, *Saskatchewan Public Accounts* (1970–71), 516–17.
5. Government of Saskatchewan. Department of Mineral Resources, *Annual Report* (1970–71).
6. Government of Saskatchewan, *Saskatchewan Public Accounts* (1970–71).
7. David Anderson, *The Role of Mineral Taxation in Industry/Government Conflict* (Kingston: Queen's University, Centre for Resource Studies, 1981), 3.
8. Quoted in Richards and Pratt, *Prairie Capitalism*, 258.
9. Olewiler, *The Potash Corporation of Saskatchewan*, 20.
10. Government of Saskatchewan, *Saskatchewan Public Accounts* (1973).
11. Anderson, *The Role of Mineral Taxation in Industry/Government Conflict*.
12. Olewiler, *The Potash Corporation of Saskatchewan*, 26.
13. Ibid., 27.
14. See Roy Romanow, "The Justification and Evolution of Crown Corporations in Saskatchewan," in Nigel Bankes and J. Owen Saunders (eds.), *Public Disposition of Natural Resources* (Calgary: Canadian Institute on Natural Reosurces Law, 1983).
15. Anderson, *The Role of Mineral Taxation in Industry/Government Conflict*, 77.
16. Government of Saskatchewan, Government Finance Office, *Annual Report* (1975), 1.
17. Speech to Saskatchewan NDP Annual Convention, 1995.
18. Romanow, "Justification and Evolution of Crown Corporations in Saskatchewan," 57.
19. Allan Blakeney and Sanford Borins, *Political Management in Canada* (Toronto: McGraw Hill Ryerson Ltd., 1992), 180.
20. See Dennis Gruending, *Promises To Keep: A Political Biography of Allan Blakeney* (Saskatoon: Western Producer Prairie Books, 1990), 142–46.
21. Government of Saskatchewan, Department of Mineral Resources, *Annual Report* (1977–78).
22. Government of Canada. Department of Finance, Ottawa, provided statistics, 2003.
23. Quote from appendix to Government of Saskatchewan, Department of Intergovernmental Affairs, "Resources, The Saskatchewan Position." First Ministers' Conference on Constitution, Ottawa, 1980.
24. See Gruending, *Promises to Keep*, and references to national media interest in Blakeney government.
25. Government of Saskatchewan, Potash Corporation of Saskatchewan, *Annual Report* (1981).
26. Government of Saskatchewan, Crown Investments Corporation, *Annual Report* (1981), 3.
27. Government of Saskatchewan, Department of Mineral Resources, *Annual Report* (1979–80).
28. Ibid. (1980–81)
29. Ibid. (1981–82).
20. Statistics supplied by Department of Finance, Ottawa.
31. Government of Saskatchewan, *Saskatchewan Public Accounts* (1972, 1982), and Statistics Canada, *Canadian Economic Observer* No. 11-201 (1994–95).
32. Statistics supplied by Department of Finance, Ottawa.
33. Government of Saskatchewan, Saskatchewan Bureau of Statistics, *Historical Economic Indicators* (May 2002)
34. James M. Pitsula and Ken Rasmussen, *Privatizing a Province: The New Right in Saskatchewan* (Vancouver: New Star Books, 1990), 30–33.
35. Government of Saskatchewan, Crown Investments Review Commission, *Report to the Government of Saskatchewan* (December 1982), 17.

36. Lesley Biggs and Mark Stobbe, *Devine Rule in Saskatchewan* (Saskatoon: Fifth House Publishers, 1991), 1.8

37. D.J. Hall, "Clifford Sifton: Immigration and Settlement Policy, 1896–1905," in Howard Palmer (ed.), *The Settlement of the West* (Calgary: Comprint Publishing, 1977), 81.

38. Pitsula and Rasmussen, *Privatizing a Province*, 65.

39. Ibid., 64–66.

40. See Government of Saskatchewan, Crown Investments Corporation, *Annual Reports*.

41. For a time, both Pirie and Letwin were active in Canada, advising and speaking about the merits of privatization. See Michael Walker (ed.), *Privatization: Tactics and Techniques* (Vancouver: The Fraser Institute, 1988).

42. Legislature of Saskatchewan, *Debates and Proceedings* (April 19, 1989), 896.

43. Ibid., 899–900.

44. Institute for Saskatchewan Enterprise, "The Potash Investment," June 1989.

45. Government of Saskatchewan, Saskatchewan Bureau of Statistics, *Historical Economic Indicators* (May 2002).

46. See Government of Saskatchewan, *Saskatchewan Public Accounts* (1981–92).

Endnotes to Chapter 14

1. Janice MacKinnon, *Minding the Public Purse: The Fiscal Crisis, Political Trade-offs and Canada's Future* (Montreal: McGill-Queen's, 2003): 101–02. The $14.8 billion represents total accumulated annual operating deficits, as well as Crown corporation debt and other liabilities from government loan guarantees, some of which were deemed to be non-recoverable.

2. Government of Saskatchewan, News Release, November 13, 1991.

3. Government of Saskatchewan, *Saskatchewan Financial Management Review Commission* (1992), 1.

4. Ibid., 2.

5. MacKinnon, *Minding the Public Purse*, 101.

6. Government of Saskatchewan, *Saskatchewan Public Accounts* (1991–92).

7. Government of Saskatchewan, Budget Speech (1992), 1, 6.

8. Author interview with Roy Romanow, December 20, 2005.

9. Government of Saskatchewan, Budget News Release, 93-127, March 18, 1993.

10. Canadian Institute for Health Information, Provincial/Territorial Government Health Expenditure.

11. Government of Saskatchewan, News Release, 92-502.

12. This point was often made by Romanow, Simard and others during the period of rationalization of the rural health care system in 1993–94.

13. Government of Saskatchewan, News Release, 93-132.

14. Government of Saskatchewan, News Release, 93-131.

15. Waiser, *Saskatchewan: A New History*, 471.

16. anadian Institute for Health Information, *Health Care in Canada* (2004).

17. Government of Saskatchewan. News Release, Finance, 95-398.

18. Notes for Remarks, Premier Roy Romanow, Canadian Club of New York, June, 29, 1994.

19. Government of Saskatchewan, Saskatchewan Economic Review (1998), 4–5.

20. Ibid., 4.

21. Government of Saskatchewan, "Preparing For a New Century" (February 18, 1996).

22. Peter Diamant and Amy Pike, *The Structure of Local Government and the Small Community* (Brandon, MB: Brandon University, Rural Development Institute, 1994), 21.

23. Jack C. Stabler and M. Rose Olfert, *The Changing Role of Rural Communities in an Urbanizing World: Saskatchewan—An Update to 1995* (Regina: Canadian Plains Research Center, 1996), 1.

24. M. Rose Olfert and Jack C. Stabler, "Saskatchewan's Communities in the 21st Century: From Places to Regions," vii. Report prepared for Saskatchewan Agriculture and Food, Economic and Co-operative Development.

25. Ibid., 120.

26. Author's conversation with official.

27. Michael Mendelson and Ken Battle, *Aboriginal People in Canada's Labour Market* (Ottawa: The Caledon Institute, 1999), 1.

28. Statistics Canada, *The Aboriginal Population in Saskatchewan* (May 2004), 6.

29. Robert Roach, *The State of the West* (Calgary: Canada West Foundation, 2003), 6.

30. Ibid., 39.

31. Statistics Canada, *The Aboriginal Population in Saskatchewan*, 11.

32. Federation of Saskatchewan Indian Nations, *Saskatchewan and Aboriginal Peoples in the 21st Century* (Regina: PrintWest, 1997), 40.

33. Ibid., 13.

34. Statistics Canada, "The Daily," June 13, 2005: http://www.statcan.ca

35. Ibid., 20.

36. Calvin Hanselmann, *Urban Aboriginal People in Western Canada: Realities and Policies* (Calgary: The Canada West Foundation, 2001), 7–8.

37. John Richards, *Creating Choices: Rethinking Aboriginal Policy*, Policy Study 43 (Toronto: C.D. Howe Institute, 2006), 57.

38. Statistics Canada, *The Aboriginal Population in Saskatchewan*, 14.

39. Quoted in Jeffrey Simpson, "The Fatal Flaw of Separate but Equal Native Schooling," Toronto *Globe and Mail* (December 11, 2005), A23.

40. See Government of Saskatchewan, *A Framework For Co-operation: Saskatchewan's Strategy for Metis and Off-Reserve First Nations People: A Status Report 2001–02, 2002–03* (Regina: n.p., 2003).

41. Janice Stokes, *Demographic Trends and Socio-Economic Sustainability in Saskatchewan: Some Policy Considerations* (Regina: Saskatchewan Institute for Public Policy, 2003), 1.

42. Pierre E. Trudeau, "Opening Statement by the Prime Minister of Canada The Right Honourable Pierre Elliott Trudeau to the Consitutional Conference of the First Ministers on the Rights of Aboriginal Peoples" (Ottawa, March 8, 1984), 19–20.

43. Evelyn Peter, "Aboriginal People in Urban Areas," in Caroline Andrew, Katherine Graham Susan Phillips (eds.), *Urban Affairs* (Montreal: McGill-Queen's University Press, 2003), 56.

44. John Richards, *A New Agenda for Strengthening Canada's Aboriginal Population* (Toronto: C.D. Howe Institute), 2002.

45. Ibid., 5.

46. Ibid., 6.

Endnotes to Chapter 15

1. Canadian Taxpayers' Foundation, "News Release" (December 9, 2003).

2. *Globe and Mail* (May 2004), E1.

3. Government of Saskatchewan, "Industry and Resources News Release, 04-249" (May 7, 2004).

4. Agnes Gruda, "Harlem sur la Saskatchewan," *La Presse*, Montreal (December 12, 2005), A2.

5. Barnhart (ed.), *Saskatchewan Premiers of the Twentieth Century*, 11–13.

Index

What People Are Saying

Dale Eisler has written an extremely thoughtful and provocative book about Saskatchewan's economic and social development as a possible guide to future public policy. It challenges the conventional wisdom of that province's growth and will attract opposing views. The bottom line is that Eisler's book deserves a careful study as Saskatchewan and other jurisdictions in Canada plan for the 21st century.
Roy Romanow, Premier of Saskatcewan 1991–2001

A book to read and remember. Eisler's argument is that to understand Saskatchewan, we must understand the strength and pervasiveness of the Saskatchewan myth, the sense of unlimited potential and the accompanying sense of unfulfilled destiny. The argument is brilliantly developed—using the understandings of history, literature, political economy, social psychology and Aboriginal studies. An exciting example of imaginative interdisciplinary scholarship that allows us to understand the past, in order to better meet the challenges of the future. A lesson not only for Saskatchewan, but for all of us.
Caroline Andrew, University of Ottawa

Dale Eisler's central theme is the role of myth—both its power to distort reality and its power to amplify what is important. Saskatchewan has many myths: the myth of the European settlers who turned grassland into wheat basket, the myth of the cooperative movement that overcame the ravages of the Great Depression, the myth of the risk-taking entrepreneurs who developed the province's mineral resources, the myth of renascent Aboriginal communities. Saskatchewan is an important piece of the Canadian tapestry, and Eisler has written a valuable account of why that is so.
John Richards, Simon Fraser University and the C.D. Howe Institute

It is sometimes said that Americans celebrate what they have become, whereas Canadians celebrate where they came from. Dale Eisler's insightful book on the Saskatchewan political mind and its mythologies comes at the character of that province's people from a rather more revealing angle. He lays bare the successive myths that have imbued people with the hope of a better life, but often at the price of misunderstanding their real circumstances and real choices. Eisler's plea for a healthier balance between aspiration and reality shows a better way forward for Saskatchewan's next generation.
Brian Lee Crowley, President of the Atlantic Institute for Market Studies in Halifax

Saskatchewan is an iconic province for many Canadians; it has a mythical character. However, being an icon is not the same as being understood. Dale Eisler advances this level of understanding tremendously by providing a rich body of history and insight for readers across the country. He reveals the power of myths, and how they both shape and distort our understanding.
Roger Gibbins, President and CEO, Canada West Foundation